Dark Eros

Dark Eros

Edited and annotated by Reginald Martin, M.F.A., Ph.D.

with a foreword by Ishmael Reed and an afterword by Lenard D. Moore

St. Martin's Press

New York

Library of Congress Cataloging-in-Publication Data

Dark Eros: Black erotic writing / Reginald Martin, editor. —1st ed.
p.   cm.
ISBN 0-312-15508-5
1. Erotic literature, American—Afro-American authors.
2. Afro-Americans—Sexual behavior—Literary collections.
I. Martin, Reginald
PS509.E7D37   1997
810.8'03538'08996073–DC21   97-8177
                                                                       CIP

First Edition: August 1997

10 9 8 7 6 5 4 3 2 1

Contents

Phase 1: Sensuous Skyline   1

Phase 2: Gettin My Freak On   *55*

Phase 3: Situation #9   *111*

Phase 4: Vulvous Evenings   181

Phase 5: The Real Truth on That   231

Phase 6: The Jimmy Hat and All That   285

Foreword

In the events of our upcoming past history . . . in the delicacy of the birth of a hummingbird feasting upon a pool of nectar . . . in the venues of the duskiest regions where legions of randy demons score feast upon feast of virgins . . . Eros is born. Not a blatant development of the virtuous–lustful natures of our people as predicted by present physic phenomena, but the underlying rivers through which we all swim—and on occasion drown. And that is the being, the marrow,blood of *Dark Eros*—that which causes the midnight oils to burn and blister in print.

An assortment of the unmentionable discourses, whispered about in the kitchen while your auntie would press your mother's hair and "shush" you away. The lithe looks, pressed hungrily outward between men and women, and the like as we go about our daily routines exuding the glow of inhibitions. Missing curfew as your thighs broadcast the call letters for Station LUST on the airwaves. Phone calls leading to Tuesday supper leading to the dissertation of orgasmic notes as those in celibacy-cherubic in intentions and diabolic in mechanical attachments—ride the waves of pure-dee sex, that can or cannot be erotic, but usually is. No, wait . . . no sex, for the affirmation "pure-dee sex," with its blunt strength, is too defenseless and shallow a term to encompass the heat that exudes from the damp pages of this exquisite documentation by Reginald Martin and the writers he has chosen to fulfill his vision.

The footing upon which we as a people stand slightly askew is Eros— the very entity which manifests her- or himself in our daily patterns and processes. Now, not to be misleading, this is not to say Eros in only the erogenous sense, but in the fullest development of its tensing possible. Eros as sensationalism, Eros as an ambience, Eros in fellowship with all of the indulgences of Providence's earth. . . . Eros as receptacles of blissful gratification of the well-confined thoughts of a collective people. We are railed against daily for the libidinous joys natural to a people of the earth—our laughter boxed behind intertwined fingers in shame, our hips gilded like fine birds in Playtex cages, our bodies sheathed in constrictive curtains of conformity. Yet, every now and then as my grandmama from Tennessee would say, the cat is put out with the trash and the mice play. And *Dark Eros* definitely is a playground for the sacrificial armaments of Eros and his-or-her-baubles.

In his typical overwhelming fashion, Professor Reginald Martin illustrates the limitations of a system of conformity when it tries to confine the desires of a people tired of the endless destruction of cerebral passions. He will remain titled as R.M. for fear of unleashing the demons of Eros which seem to reside disturbingly near the surface of his waters. He is the helter-skelter frenzy of hurricane force within us all that is afraid to be confined lest it lose its truest self, unwilling to conform to the bullish dullness of average, everyday personage and predictability.

I tell everyone that I never understood my work as well as I do when I read what Reginald Martin writes about it. Now, in this subversive, beautiful book of his, you shall comprehend Eros in a way normally only reserved for the gods of individualism and genius.

Ishmael Reed
Summer 1996
Oakland, California

Introduction

DARK EROS AND THE EROTIC ESSENCE

*A*nd so, dear friends, it is again to this theme we come. Outside my riverfront condo, the barges' high-intensity lights carve a clearing through the blackness, lasers that only serve to illuminate the ever-unfolding dimensions of blackness all the way to the Gulf. As quickly as a part of its blackness is illumined, the obsidite folds reembrace the boats from the rear, changing shape and returning to eternal mystery and ceaseless multiplicity again.

I had told a good friend five years ago that the essence of African eroticism was not done with me, that it would force me to return to it at least once again . . . it was not done with me.

My erotic poetry, fiction, scholarly articles, and of course, *Erotique Noire* with Miriam Willis and Roseann Bell were positive authorial/editorial experiences from which I thought I would never recover, and certainly from which I would always carry a positive reverberation. I would get back to eroticism when I finished dissimilar writing projects. I would get back to eroticism when I had time. I would get back to eroticism when I good and well felt like it. I controlled eroticism by illuminating its essential nature to others, both hot and cold. I controlled eroticism. Eroticism did not control me. As *Dark Eros* is a self-realitied entity, I realize now how insignificant my formidable will is in the face of eroticism set-to-type. Permeated by black Eros, this volume presents itself to its readers via my editing and sequencing, which are asides compared to the volume's other major catalyst: this volume presents itself because of and via the collective, symbiotic libido of people of African descent.

Another friend, who convinced me that there were only erotically hot and physically cold people in the world, was right, of course. Though this friend was never able to live with the fact that their essence was erotic, I still learned quite a bit of erotic ontology from the diachronic/synchronic conversations we would have, which only increased our erotic need and want of each other. (Rumor has it said friend is now using a vegetarian diet and

The Book of Coming Forth by Day to lose the erotic self my friend was never able to control—alas, a losing battle, as that hot person should certainly know.) The substance of our exchanges on the essence of the erotic self informs this section of my introduction in ways that, I believe, both the erotic person and the nonerotic person can use to the benefit of each individual's true path. The direct objects of my verbs here are those who were born "hot," or erotic; my indirect objects are all those who must know themselves before they can be of any use to others, their world, and most of all, to themselves.

The ontology of the erotic essence is the urge toward more than sexual union; it is more than the drive and longing to be erotic: it is the urge toward Eros, itself. Here, I wish to define the erotic ontologically and to delimit to its subsets, namely,

  a. How to know the erotic.
  b. How to know if oneself is erotic.
  c. What it means to the individual if he/she is erotic.
  d. What to do if one is erotic in a world hostile toward the erotic.

1. The essence of the erotic

To understand the erotic is first to look at its ontology, both its being and its origins. Know that the erotic pre-exists and post-exists all those within the powers of its boundary. Thus, the erotic would exist without any humans under its sway to act out its impulses in a corporeal fashion. Thus, the erotic both waits to be accessed and accesses without permission. No writer included in this volume asked to have an erotic essence and teleology. They are what they were when they became conscious of being: erotic.

2. How to know if oneself is erotic

However, the consciousness of being was not always aware that it was erotic. The consciousness had a suspicion: you at twelve lingering at the kitchen door as your father oiled the legs of your mother or his own hairy chest and rippled stomach; the feeling you got—indeed the expectancy— when each evening after walking from the busline, your mother came to your room and asked you to undo the sixteen metal fasteners on her massive brassiere; the confusion and fear you felt both in your head and heart when you saw your junior-high friends behind the cafeteria, fondling feverishly, but not yet completely intimate; the curve of a leg or arm or butt, intermittently, throughout your entire life and your inability not to notice them; something about Pam Grier and Robert Hooks movies, but your inability to give words to exactly what it was about those cultural indexes that pro-voked you to think about turning sex into poetry.

All these episodes, and then, there, between career developments and various desires gone wrong beyond your control, the epiphanic moment when you were able to audibly utter or to write what you were:

- *I am erotically attracted to these things;*
- *these things are right for my sexual self;*
- *my best sexual/erotic self is a part of these things;*
- *these things are synecdochical of my erotic self, which I do not yet fully know or understand;*
- *finally, for my life to be a circle, I must abide by these things which undergird an essential part of my entire self, both the erotic and the nonerotic parts.*

It is then and only then that *the consciousness of being* knows what it is.

Still, *the consciousness of being* does not yet know how to act on its pre-disposition. It must experiment and find that groove meant only for it. This is *the externalizing* of the erotic essence so that one may follow its urgings. It is only during this phase that the human can begin to know the essence of the erotic.

When *the externalizing phase* has become a given—but not boring—constant in the life of the individual, the individual begins to know the erotic itself, face to face. It is more being than urge, more urge than pre-disposition, more predisposition that free choice. It is not the procreative impulse; it is not the libidinous reaction of an aroused individual; it is not the will and power to "do it" several times in one evening; Eros is itself and itself only, and can be known only to the bearers of its mark, for its ontology is endlessly multitudinous and polysemous. Consider, in a room of like-minded people, all shrouded under Eros's dark wings, each person moves at a different flutter toward a different trail of pre-embedded lines of psychic silicon. Erotic individuals move toward the knowledge of Eros in only the ways they can and at only their own speeds. When the erotic nature comes to the heart of Eros, all is known; Eros is of God but not God; not God, but godlike in its sway over the individual within its circle. *Eros is a blessing.*

Upon accessing this knowledge, erotic individuals are immediately ejected from Eros's heart and now know themselves for whom and what they are forever. Only then can erotic individuals live to the end of their allotted time without a constant disjunction in spirit. Only then does the horse know and accept its rider.

Remember, too, that the erotic self must be known to the bearer of its mark or all other aspects of the self's psychic circle suffer from too much or too little attention; the psyche searches for its truest self, and only once the truest self is found can the psyche turn to developing the other parts of itself that remain not known.

3. The erotic in a hostile world

As can be determined by looking at those who have partial knowledge of themselves in any segment of their complete being, the ones with self-knowledge are the most frightening individuals in the physical sphere. All of their actions are authentic because they act out of the truest knowledge that what they are doing is right for what they are. Such authenticity may be used in negative or positive ways, but the authenticity itself is pure and positive, and authenticity is frightening to those who are unenlightened. The unenlightened fear the authentic actions of the authentic individual because unenlightened themselves, they cannot make authentic actions because they do not know themselves; they are merely rich or powerful or good-looking or lucky—all aspects even the unenlightened are bright enough to know are unearned and temporary. Self-knowledge is timeless and eternal. Secondly, the unenlightened fear the authentic individual because there are no actions they can make, no tapes they can watch, and no one powerful enough they can bribe to make them have self-knowledge. They fear they are irredeemable. They are correct.

Thus, with the knowledge of the erotic self, the bearers of its mark immediately expose themselves because they cannot be hidden; when they are seen, they must be attacked. They are, after all, not only to be feared because they are filled with self-knowledge and thus authentic, but they are even more to be hated because they possess an intimate knowledge of that part of themselves which cannot be aroused in others with alcohol or harder drugs, cannot be bought at a strip club no matter how skilled the dancer, cannot be fully felt even when power determines the sex. The erotically aware possess something which can only be gotten by divine fiat. And thus the hatred and envy the erotically aware evoke is understandable—and immense.

The erotically aware are individuals, but their enemies are groups. Anywhere there is a numerically dominant group, there is hegemony against individual difference; anywhere there is hegemony, there is a gang. There can be no acted-upon hatred of the erotically aware without the gang mentality, for all groups are composed of cowards and the weak. They can make no reaction without group support.

The defense of the erotic is its knowledge of those who are not like it. The enemy is known by its direct nature, even when it attempts to show indirection. Avoid this enemy when known. If avoidance is impossible, attack the enemy immediately and fiercely with the one weapon for which it has no defense: *boldness in authenticity*. As the erotic is filled with indirection and not direction, is more night than day, the enemy is ill-equipped to face the truth which attacks them from all sides of perception out of the blackness.

Though eroticism is dominant, by offering it a concession here, a concession there, I was able to caress eroticism into certain channels and motifs, undermine its assertiveness by pretending to bend to its will more quickly than I was. I convinced eroticism that its shape in this text should be determined by the sexual nature of the submissions made to it, let the submissions drive the text so to speak, so that the complete volume would be emblematic of African eroticism at this time in this space. Arrogant Eros can be easily fooled by the object of its desire, but when it finds out it has been cuckolded, it *will* eventually catch you; and when it catches you, it will beat you and beat you and beat you. This, I knew, was the chance I was taking by steering the text. But I could not help myself.

Toward this end, I decided that 85 percent of the submissions should be by writers new to the public. Thus, my call for submissions elicited a theme which undergirds this entire text: the erotic of the urban African-American setting. Time and time again you will find in this text the peculiar hip-hop erotic of the African-Americans, the one diasporic African group that seems to wish to wipe out in each lifetime all recollective powers of the rural and redefine concrete, skyscrapers, and oppression in terms of a warm, wet, delta night.

From the necessary rap lyrics that had to come, to the workplace-erotic of the first generation of African-Americans allowed full access to the workplace, the pieces collected in this volume throb with the tempo and tenor of writers who have defined the erotic verve of our urban times. Los Angeles, New York City, Miami, New Orleans—every place there is a bus line or a dance club has produced African-American eroticism never intended for English in Phoenician alphabets.

Indeed, this very disjunction—African-American eroticism forced to express itself in the stipulative signs and language of its would be lexical censors—provides the surreal sexual mood that heads up page after page with writing that is surely art, but surely something more primal and more beautiful.

This project has been formidable and impossible, exciting and depressing. This book could not have reached closure without the group efforts of many. Richard Derus of the Claudia Menza Literary Agency wrestled every other proffered title suggestion to the floor of *club 88's* in the summer of 1995. Keith Kahla of St. Martin's Press had foresight and fairness where others had only schemes and limitations. My agent, Claudia Menza, was invaluable in every way imaginable, but especially in the procurement of submissions in timely and affordable ways. *Dark Eros* owes much to many, not the least of whom are the artists herein contained, who have agreed to each editorial change I have suggested. To understand that this is an act worth mentioning, one only has to imagine editing one's own erotic thoughts in the middle of the narrative; such is not a normal or preferable editing request. Indeed, *Dark Eros* does owe much to many, but not as much as you will owe to its essence upon completing its reading.

Always pay your fucking debts.

—Reginald Martin, M.F.A., Ph.D., Memphis, Tennessee, 1996,
  leaning against the west inner wall of the Old Daisy Theater,
  at the corner of Beale Street and Third Avenue,
  3:13 A.M., May 15th.

Phase 1

Sensuous

Skyline

*P*eter Schielemann's *Black Eros* (1971) delineates a precolonial African sexuality that was very different from its concurrent European counterpart, and even different from its later African-American emanations. As there was no separation of different phases of the precolonial African life/African psyche from other aspects of itself, sex was an integral part of everything else, such as religion, gender traditions, and social exchange; at the same time sex was not eroticism, and eroticism undergird each and every aspect of the African psyche. John Mibiti, in *African Religions* (1973), points out even more tellingly that eroticism is to African religion as African religion is to eroticism: one cannot exist without the other. Today, visit any urban, black Pentecostal church for three-dimensional proof, and one will quickly notice a number of erotic indexes, especially the willed confusion of the sexualized male minister with Christ-like associations in a female-dominated forum. The screams for Jesus take on additional meanings.

So it should not surprise us then that the current progenitors of African essence bring eroticism to everything they touch in the asphalt jungles and concrete condos in which they find themselves. The big-city beat is black.

Tina South-X in "Kitchen Tails" seductively illustrates that black suburban life needs excessive stimulation and that is what the black professional females provide as they talk about their one, best love—never their husbands. Frank Lamont Phillips's "Sunday & Ms. Fantasy" takes us into the nonerotic/erotic mind of one Cheryl, who is sure to become the favorite table dancer in all of fiction. Jennifer Holley's "I Want to Speak" repeats a late-night phone encounter in the recording studio, and Tim Seibles's "Valentine's Day" reveals that the heart is seldom the most favorite organ on erotic holidays. Rebecca Delbridge's urban run-in with auto-eroticism in "No Turn on Red" and Jeul A. Harris's "Black Sugar" are only emblematic of all the alleys and expressways of the African-American erogenous zones. Carole Hill Faulkner's "Midnight Call" is as manipulatively masturbatory as Ken Norfleet's excerpt from his novel *Binghampton Bad Boy Blues* is dyadically direct. Lana Williams's ". . . To the Head"; and Lurlynn Franklin's "in the dreams of a former whore goddess" voyeuristically show female aggressiveness and shout the new urban sexuality of the forthright female. "C:\Back Slash\Merge" by Oktavi shows that the computer age has some personality, and Winston Benons's "Gail & John" diary entries show us why those tomes are the most private of erotic texts. Black eroticism brings complications with its benefits, but the benefits remain worth it in Shangé's "Black Love." Herr Reverend Schmidt (a pseudonym) of Berlin exposes us to his "Hunger" (translated from the German), which represents the real-life side of an international black Christian minister's own purposely suppressed sexuality. Jennifer Gibson's untitled piece and "Do Ya Got Some Blow?" by Dryervonn Washington move us to erotic hip-hop rap for the first time on a high literary plane. Eunice Townsend's "Electric Lover" reminds us that work and play must mix for sanity, and "coffles: a suicide note" by Victor E. Blue reminds us, even if we have not forgotten, of the reason people wanted into the cities and out of the country in the first place. Rest and refresh yourself at the end of this first phase leading toward erotic fulfillment with "Marriage" by Cassie Granberry and Estelle Farley's "Dessert."

These pieces illustrate that, once again, one of the frustrating things about trying to keep up with city life is that it changes too quickly to be fully captured. As Alvin Toffler convincingly showed in *The Third Wave* (1979), it is not change but the rate of change that drives people crazy trying to keep up. This is also why a stagnant culture hates the African-American impulse: the culture cannot keep up. What is often missed is that the same is true for black eroticism, which is the driving force of the city's change.

Kitchen Tails

TINA SOUTH-X

"Tell about your best love," they squealed above wine, crackers and cheese, refrigerator humming in the background for needed sound cover.

Long draw on the champagne and editorial indexes in place.
"It can only be one—that's it—and why!"
A sound–sight–and–scent check for husband-lurk,
then direct eye contact with the crowd.

Statement: "Heartbeats, smells, mirrors, a scream that lasted for ten
    years."

Silence from the crowd.

Then applause.

Sunday & Ms. Fantasy

FRANK LAMONT PHILLIPS

*M*s. Fantasy didn't like to work on Sundays. She didn't like to work at all, really. She didn't like to fuck. She didn't even like the nom de porn of the last few months, Ms. Fantasy. Not really. Mostly what she called her coochie, her moneymaker. Ms. Fantasy. It was everything you would like it to be. She would just like to be Cheryl Yvette Wilson again. She would just as soon be at home in bed, or even getting ready to go to church, not as an adult mind you, but as a pigtailed, ribbon-legged girl, arm out in front, being pulled by her mother to do what every child needs to do, go into the house of the Lord, to hear his wonders.

Before she became Ms. Fantasy she had been Coffee, then Miss Sinn, and before that Misty Dawn. The first feature she had starred in, her bustier-clad image brought telephoto close as she gazed lewdly from the videocassette box after lifting her semen-splotched face from the blow-job she had been giving to some guy who was not shown above the pectorals, was under the name Misty Dawn. Matter of fact, it was called *Crack of Dawn,* one of those all-anal features which advertised, with some truth, that she was to be "interracially butt-fucked for the first time on video." Cheryl had been a "video virgin" two, maybe three times in features that promised "amateurs" making love on film for the first time. She had several all-black productions to her credit, as well as a dozen or so of the endless popular interracial features, whose main selling points were contrasting skin color and large dicks.

Cheryl knew the kinds of people who bought and rented her movies. She had met the men on personal appearances in theaters, or in clubs where she danced, back when she still danced in clubs. They were every kind of guy. The best ones though, the ones that couldn't get enough, were the guys who had never grown up, who had fantasies they indulged by watching the videos and buying the magazines. They were the endless supply of quarters and dollars. They dreamed of girls like and unlike Cheryl, still innocent-looking, even as she performed the most debauched acts. Cheryl had been surprised to find that she had women fans too. Now, she liked to

7

think that nothing surprised her, but of course, now and then, something did.

Cheryl wasn't surprised that most of her fans were middle-aged white men. Even the women she had occasion to meet were mostly white, mostly VCR-rich middle-America, though she had met some famous athletes through her work. She had been a groupie for athletes, and some athletes were groupies for her as well. Black or white, male or female, at some time or another almost everybody she had come in contact with had wanted or tried to fuck her. Some had, but for a price for that kept going up and up.

Sometimes she had a thought that she would meet somebody to fall in love with. She didn't think that she could fall in love with a white man. Sometimes she just thought that she would meet somebody who would take care of her for the rest of her life. That kind of thing had happened to a girl in the business just often enough to stoke the fantasies of a lot of other girls in the business.

Lately, Robert had been trying to sell her on the idea of getting her breasts enlarged. They were going for big boobs now. Always had, really. She wouldn't do it, though.

"I can't understand why you won't think about it," he'd say. He always talked more or less straight with her. More or less. He said he respected her intelligence and he acted like it. He gave her a better snow job. "Titties," he said. "It's all titties. A black girl with great big titties would have to scoop up the money with a shovel."

He looked at her with this great big puppy-dog look on his face. He knew she wasn't having it, but he didn't know how to quit pitching. It was his whole life. Cheryl knew as much as he did. Titties were popular and there were lots of girls with them. Problem was they weren't something you could just get put in and then take off to look normal. The fashion was bazooka boobs. Tits way out to here. Cheryl couldn't see herself freaked out like that.

"You know, it's funny. A lot of guys like a chick with big fake boobs better than they like one with big boobs that are for real. They like women who aren't like any women they're likely to meet. You know, impossible, fantasy gals with helium tits and enormous fuck holes. It's something you ought to think about. Really. It's all about the dollar green."

It was when he talked like that, got all wound up like a hype and then started that ragged winding down, defeated and drawn, that Robert reminded her of her late uncle Bubba. He didn't look anything like old good-for-a-nickel, sometimes a dime, Uncle Bubba, who, drunk, had been killed in a one-car crash into a utility pole just before Cheryl left Memphis. Uncle

Bubba was a failed schemer. He was always trying to convince everybody, or maybe just himself, that he could get something going, get out of ware-house work someday, be a biggety. He acted like a biggety too, always drove a block-long second-hand Cadillac. He wouldn't have a car if it wasn't a Cadillac, or a woman if she wasn't high yaller. The way she re-membered it, the house became off-limits to Uncle Bubba when she was fourteen because her mamma caught him sneaking a feel on Cheryl.

"They always want colored girls," Robert said after a silence. "You got that going for you."

There was a time when she wouldn't let him use the term colored. She used to run her pie hole quite a bit in the beginning, starting out. Now she mostly listened. Anybody could be played. You just had to listen to them, let them think it was their way.

Cheryl nodded her head.

"I mean you're one pretty black girl," Robert said. He was sweating. In the three years she had known him he had gained a lot of weight, and he had been fat to begin with. Now he was always sweating. No matter what the temperature was he sweated, and he was forever soaking rivulets of sweat in a soiled handkerchief he kept in the pocket of his suit coats, complaining about the heat and promising to God to diet.

Robert could have been thought of as handsome once. He had acted in movies full time until recently. He was pretty well hung. He'd do anything for a buck. He still made appearances when he could get the work, in everything from straight to transsexual to gay and fetish films. Cheryl had appeared in one film with him, back when she was Miss Sinn. She was dressed in leather, the whole dominatrix trip. She didn't mind fetish films. For one thing, in most of them she seldom had to completely undress. She never had to fuck. For another thing, she got to be in control. In this particular film, she twisted Robert's balls and spanked him hard with a Ping-Pong paddle. It was then that she discovered his particular kink, and maybe her own as well. She hadn't enjoyed anything she had ever done on film so much as she enjoyed beating Robert's big hairy ass red with that paddle.

"What the heck," Robert shrugged. "You're making money. My opin-ion is you're the prettiest colored girl making these movies. You're a looker all right. Gimme a wet one for old times."

They didn't really kiss. Cheryl didn't want it and it was unlikely that Robert wanted it either. He just liked to fall back on that mack type of shit. Sometimes he liked to talk like he was black. In his mind he was cool. That was just in his mind, though.

"You're a pretty black girl," Robert had said.

She was defined and circumscribed by that. Heck, this whole line of work was built on contrasting skin color and big dicks, that and new faces. It was for that reason, that unless a girl were some kind of transcendent star who could sell a video with the image she had built over dozens, maybe hundreds, of features and magazine layouts, it paid to keep being a new face, or to keep doing something new on camera for the first time.

Now and then Cheryl liked to go to a church in Oakland. She always put something in the plate. Sometimes she spoke to the minister afterward. She never joined the church, but she had given it considerable thought. All the way to the shoot she had thought about church, about getting lost in the orgiastic vocal dexterity of the choir. Cheryl had a passable voice. She thought that she would like to sing in a choir, maybe the choir of Mount Vernon Baptist Church in Oakland. She would throw her arms out and shake her head and stomp her foot and take the whole congregation right along with her.

If not that, then she would just like to sit in the middle of the bed with everything she shouldn't eat spread out in front of her. She would gorge as if she didn't have to worry about how she looked. She was thinking of a bacon, lettuce, and tomato sandwich with lots of mayonnaise dripping from her mouth onto the percale sheets. The trouble with that was the more she thought about it the more it sounded like something in a movie she had made. The mayonnaise in her mouth and in her lipstick looked like the semen it would soon be replaced by, and she couldn't taste the bacon at all.

Cheryl was getting dressed now. She was driving up to the shoot alone. She had been to this particular location before, a really nice house that belonged to some minor actress and her husband. The husband liked porn films and got off on watching them being made in his own house. Besides, he got paid. What wouldn't people do for money.

Cheryl had never thought that she was pretty, not even when people told her so. She tended to look at herself with her mother's reproving eyes. In her mother's eyes, whatever anybody had was all that they had, and it was neither enough nor so good that it didn't need improvement. More-over, flesh was weak. In her mother's mouth the word flesh had a creepy spook-house sound that made Cheryl want covers to put her head under, and darkness to make her invisible.

Cheryl was about five feet without the heels. She had a nice hard body. That wasn't the fashion when she first started. Now it was. Girls were in the gym pumping up and working out. Cheryl was glad she had gone with her own mind and not listened to what anybody else had to say.

"You're gonna love this," Robert had said to Cheryl. "He's so easy it'll be like stealing money. No, really, it's easier than that, easier than stealing. It's like sitting back and having money fall on you, hundreds and hundreds of dollars float out of the air and fall on you like spring rain. It's an easy shoot. Easy. Easy."

Cheryl had just nodded her head. She had looked unbelieving, disinterested. Robert knew how much she hated to work on Sundays. Lately it had been a chore just getting her to work at all.

Robert was Mister Show Biz, meaning that he was Mister Bullshit. He knew just the thing to say, just the anecdote to tell to get a girl moving. The girls in the business said that he could sell sin to Jesus. When she first heard that Cheryl laughed. Maybe he could sell sin to their Jesus, she had thought, but certainly he couldn't sell anything at all to the Jesus of her mother and of her youth, the Hollywood-handsome white man whose image adorned the living room of the house she grew up in, as well as the living rooms of so many of her mother's many friends back home in Memphis.

Now, listening to Robert in her head as she closed the door of her modest apartment behind her, never really believing anything that he said, but going along with it anyway, she knew for sure that he could sell sin to Jesus, that no saint was safe before him, that hell was down the long lying mouth of the snake who tempted Eve.

It was a money thing she told herself as she got into her car. It was just-bought. It was a money-green sports car. She looked at herself one last time in the rear-view mirror before she set it. She looked like a woman maybe going to sunrise service. Shoots were always so damn early. She took the gold crucifix from around her neck and put it in the ashtray and sighed. Then she drove off.

I Want to Speak

JENNIFER HOLLEY

Slender manicured fingers from her hand reach out and begin to
depress each of the hard buttons.
She knows what she wants.

It was 8:00 P.M. He is waiting.
Each long finger goes down on the keypad, craving it.

She knows he is waiting. The radio is on. The song they are playing
seems unusually sad to her.

She dials a little faster now. Anticipation makes her nipples hard.
Her breath is heavy and labored. Would he be waiting?

The last number quickly goes through.
His voice seems to shake when he says, "YES YOU MAY COME
   FUCK ME NOW."
He hears only the sound of the receiver hitting the floor.

Valentine's Day

TIM SEIBLES

I saw an X-rated movie once
where a man, a minor clerk—
faced with having to watch
his boss push himself
between the rippling thighs
of an athletic secretary—
went moping behind a file cabinet,
unzipped his blue corduroys,
and began to give himself
head. Really. It was
not a camera trick.

I was appalled, of course,
not only because of the size
of that turgid jam-hamster, but
because here was a man exercising
an option I'd never even considered—
a true do-it-yourselfer, a renegade
in the world of wanting, a man
who could have his cake and well,
you know.

Think about this guy growing up,
going to high school, believing English
was okay, strolling to the showers
with a cool smirk. It must have been
quite a day when he first leaned over
and kept going down. That dumb joke
about how hard it is to kiss your own elbow
must've seemed pretty goddamn dumb.

.   .   .

Maybe he was fifteen, maybe it was
    Sunday—
a rainy, after-church afternoon
when the big itch he felt
for Delores, the math whiz, sent him
back upstairs to his room to check
the little voice he heard
coming from his pants, so he
unzipped and stretched his neck
to listen, then found himself softly
kissing the taut, hot skin.
And maybe this was not the beginning

of an adjustment, a maneuver,
unique unto him—just one hard turn
away from all the booby traps
and regulations set to keep us
from the thousand variations
of hands, of lips, of genitalia,
of all the things they can do.
Who hasn't dreamed of being
fucked perfectly—once
and for all—if only
on Valentine's Day?

Who hasn't craved a fine stranger
walking past, sliding like a
tropical mist along the coast of you,
or something a wee bit wilder—
the game of 3 in a loose knot.
Once, I got a phone call
from a guy who called himself
the banana man,
asking if I would let him
blow me.

And after awhile you have to wonder
just how lonely someone might be
in America, this country where
actual adults get on TV and tell *Oprah,*

"If we didn't bring it up so much
maybe young people wouldn't get
involved in sex"—as if sex
were a sort of larceny, this place
where a man can get on talk-radio
saying, "AIDS will make us
moral again." And I think by now

everybody should feel just a little
more sorry for everyone else—
each of us being the exact thing
some others of us want, but
usually cannot have, for whatever
reason: fear, guilt, lack
of interest, simple fatigue.

So we end up at the movies
or deep in magazines or alone,
teasing our own skin or just
wishing,

just wishing we could slam the door
on the whole thing and just be inside
on the phone, happy, talking
to our happy friends about
nothing at all and how easy it is
to come by.

No Turn on Red

REBECCA DELBRIDGE

Mama's false front,
Daddy's shotgun smile
Made my backdoor exit slick
Red dress, taillights
Flash down the drive
My date took a detour
Down Franklin Street
Down a dead end street
His warm hands turn cold
Zipped my dress off track
Umber hair shielded
My nakedness
He brushed it back
Behind my shoulders
Exposing breasts
Moonlight too bright
To hide goose bumps
My mind slipped between two fears
I wondered if I'd
Make it home by curfew

Black Sugar

JEUL A. HARRIS

On the tip of my tongue
Are thoughts as yet unspoken,
Bounding on sweet secrets
And promises unbroken.
For love we taste,
Like dark chocolate melting;
A whole new world
Full of blues and jazzing.
An unsought horizon
Is where I took her,
With eyes closed and heart pumping
I tasted my black sugar.
The burst of juice
From an orgasm exotic,
On cloud nine we float
Rendering nerves chaotic.
Black sugar
Is too sweet to share,
Like a flawless diamond
It is unique and rare.
I hide my pucker
To prevent her roam,
Just a precious angel
Black sugar brings me home.

Midnight Call

CAROLE HILL FAULKNER

Alone is the night
with desire and in search
of rescue . . .
my telephone rings expectantly
changing all dimensions
bringing reality to the space
of wanting
Words whispered
demands made
I respond with moan sounds
tasting my fingers
then caressing your face
in the mirror of my imagination
I tell you I love you
returning to stroke
my wet place
I repeat this
I repeat this
the tasting of myself
so that you too can taste me
as if I were on your face
in the reflection of your mind
I give you all the good stuff
before we say good night

Binghampton Bad Boy Blues (excerpt)

KENNETH NORFLEET

. . . white wine and a wee bit of the herb
Marvin Gaye's "I Want You" CD
Silk bikini underwear, red for you, black for me
Ice cubes and baby oil, and put the sheets on the floor
Discarded pantyhose to tie you up, caramel topping, when you choose to
   sup, and partake of my meal.
Liquid Ivory soap, and that cocoa butter lotion that you like
Fresh new sponges to wash my back, steamy and hot, wet, slippery and
   clean,
oh baby, you've awakened the volcano, and it's starting to rise
your river is overflowing, and I feel your water flowing,
look, oh baby, its running down your thighs
And to no one's surprise, the earthquake shakes, and the volcano erupts
Tidal waves turn your river into an ocean, 6.9 on the Richter scale
So when you felt the earth move, it was not Memorex baby
And on the 7th hour he did rest
—more baby more—
and I thought surely you jest
I want more baby more, please baby please, come with me, just one
   more time
So I smoke the herb, and drink the wine
Seems like the creation is going to take a little more time
Let the games begin, damn you are too fine
Scene one, act two, lets do IT again
Lay your head on my chest, and I will proclaim you the best.

. . . To the Head

LANA C. WILLIAMS

He's busted through my walls,
with every stick of furniture
I own
pushed against him.

Slickened by a beachfront
flood in '95, when
primetime orgies
still on sale,
despite store-front preachers'
jaws of an ass
flapping inflated miracles
to my sisters in drag.

Meanwhile, seventh day—
I'm holed up
on a circular bed from the '60s,
the ying-yanged
black and white surface
that was my birth—
lost minds behind pulled blinds,
sunk his pirate in her treasure . . .

I come.
Gold, with freckles
sprinkling the circled mattress.
Then back again, a
straight distance
dangling my carrot called freedom.

.   .   .

My arms a whole different story,
bound to my sides,
palms flat against my thighs
begging a stop to it.
But that's not why he came,
uninvited, a cat burglar,
black & skintight
pounding down my walls.

The carefully ironed ones,
crashing now, like waves this
hurricane season,
and I curse nature's flow.

Still, the hot-wired sloshing in my ears
knows the hiss of
snake-charmed johnsons
whose diseased obituaries lay waiting.

Unamused, he
lifts my chin to eye level
purring:
"Let it come."

Next seven days,
he sucks the rusted layers from my psyche,
peels my ancient venom—
on fours,
I eat the antidote whole.

Thereafter . . .

.   .   .

in the Land of Cush,
a treble-clef voice
knock-knocks persistence,
asking me
to ride the precipice again,

knowing my petaled slipper
fits.

in the dreams of a former whore goddess

LURLYNN FRANKLIN

it has been two years of searching for
abstract tunes to replace Victrola
voices furrowing holes in the souls
of women with reasons

you can laugh it's supposed to be funny

I am not as together as everyone wants me
a private joke who only wants the privilege
of being held/to love a man/share a bed
has never been hard to find/or peel
a purple grape slid with chocolate-
coated finger into an eager mouth

this is really funny/please think it's funny

because I can't take this wanting to be
touched by a man again/but often I awaken
from long dreams of having someone other
than myself inside of me
ninety-eight point six times two bodies
grooved together on a sunstroked black
hill in the park

yes I was a whore once
and sometimes miss the illusions of being loved
and should not be wanting
to fuck
this young man
this evening

C:\Back Slash\Merge

OKTAVI

Virtual reality technology
Empties single bars
Into bedroom communities
With e-mail addresses
Modem expenses
Outstripping mortgages

Phone sex girls
Who whisper
Fiber optic oohs and ayahs
Lost clients to
Tabletop dancer holograms
Grinding down
Information super highways
Red light district
Glowing microchip sweatshops

Saturday night
Software, firmware parties
In Bloomingdale's basement
Haggling over
Data gloves and viewing goggles

Prepackaged, embedded software
Commingling with gray matter
Nasty rashes
Under skintight sensor suits

As we settle for
Software surrogates
Sending tingles
Down our spines

Gail & John

WINSTON BENONS, JR.

January 24, 1995

I t was a warm spring afternoon. Gail decides to walk over to Magnolia Mansion. She approaches the entrance to the penthouse, opens the door and is taken aback. Everything is white the walls, furniture, floor everything. She immediately takes off her sandals and walks upon the trail of pink rose petals. She follows the trail enjoying the moist texture beneath her feet. They lead her to a room just as crisp and white as the previous one. In the middle of the room is a cobalt blue bathtub. She approaches the tub enticed by the aromatic, tepid water. Gail instinctively takes off her clothing and rests in the tub. With the faint smell of white musk in the air and a concerto of wind chimes, she can't help but to touch herself. And as she gets to the height of her orgasm she moans, but the moans she hears are not hers. Opening her eyes slowly she gazes at John sitting on a chair in the doorway.

And all of his excitement resting on the rose petals like beaded jewels.

Black Love

SHANGÉ

I could write a poem
About black berries bursting after midnight
I could describe
Salty, sweaty, caramel, cocoa, toffee colored skin
I could tell you tasty stories
Of full, juicy lips sucking and kissing wet and sweet
I could tell you
About rough, weathered hands tracing sensuous circles
that send shivers giggling up the skin
I could write it all down

But it wouldn't been true unless I also wrote
About daddies disappearing
After the juice of the berry was no longer a wet spot
I need to also tell you about bodies that birthed a nation
Being silenced by a backhand slap
And I can't ignore bitches and hoes
Replacing sisters and queens
when the lights are no longer down low
Or bedroom eyes that have read the writing
Between more than its share of thighs
I could write it all down

But I still would not have told you
Anything about true Black Love
By experience, I'm an expert
On when it's missing and what it's not
So when it's missing and what it's not
So when you look at me with those shaded thoughts lurking in your eyes
Realize I know that its not love you want
To put between my thighs
And you can't have me without my story

Without its juices, a berry's just a prune
If I buy your tired lines
from now on, I purchase only a one-time use
If you truly want more, accept
It'll take more than a night for me to trust in you
Even at my peak I will not lie
And say it's yours when you want to know whose.

You see I have thought I'd found Black Love, then woken up
On the other side of the moon
With love's absence bursting my bubble and reality coming too soon
Those mornings I lived a thousand years
And packed them into one
I took my baths in tubs of my tears
To drown foolish evidence while its scent lingered on
I have been blue, yellow, red, orange, green, purple
And brown
Within the blackness of my skin
I have eaten bitter words and sour dreams
When I hungered for that other for that other passion deep within.

Yes, I could write a poem filled with fiery intensity
Spell out just what I want,
What for me it needs to be
But there is no formula to Black Love
No exact way to get it right
Still there would be no promise
That's what we'd find within the night
That gamble I can handle
That's not the issue I'm trying to explore
It's the disguise, lies and faking
And then the sneaking out once more
Don't hide behind the words Black Love
If you don't know what it means
If you know and do not want that
Give me the choice to stay or leave
I might still want to tangle with you
Even for one night
You may not have been my choice either
For a long-term fire fight

As long as we both know what we're seeing
When the clothes are on the floor
Tomorrow I will call you an experience
As I smile and walk you to the door

Now I'm not just talking about one-night stands
As you can see
they have their place within my book
This is about more than a sneak peak
It's also for those desiring a long-term look
Then too you must come correct
If you're stepping to me, who has
Witnessed delusions of Black Love
In all its woes and pseudo victories
I'd rather be single, die barren and all alone
Than to let you fuck my mind
And have me shed more tears after you're gone
I'd rather keep my midnight Black Love
As a yet unfulfilled distant dream
Buy batteries, and not be deluded about
Why this love the sun can never see

My Black Love will only be reaped
After it's been fermenting over time
In its maturity it will bear precious fruit
But it will get there like the finest wine
So though I'm wiser I haven't given up
Even as I write these words, I know
One day I'll make a home, find peace
With a soul that mates with my own
For my skin is still chocolate
My berry is still ripe
I like those chance encounters
But I also look to starting fires
That burn for more than just one night
So if you've got a flame that can outlast
The rising of the sun
We can talk about true Black Love
Other passions
Other ways to make me come.

Hunger
(Translated from the German)

HERR REVEREND SCHMIDT

*I*f my demons are yet unknown to me, if they are really the cries of abandonment and the cries for the Light, if you are really the star and the dance to which I have fused my dusky demon/ brother self, and if your joining with all of me means that I must join with all of you, all your demons, monsters, silk and lace, if it means releasing all our demons together so that we will have to identify and count them one by one like our little litter, unruly and uncontrollable, but outside of us finally, to be kissed and sent away, if it means counting their little heads with only a Flair and tissue paper, O God O God O God, I still would want you, I still would know the hunger for your lips, your eyes, your smile, the taste of your sex surrounding my tongue, if it means even losing you, after the taste of you in my mouth still lingers to remind me over and over again of my last entry into your soul, your spirit, your demons, still I would have you and no other, like the last breath from my dying lips I would kiss into your name.

Untitled

J E N N I F E R   G I B S O N

The Search

*T*he dim light coming from the screen always hurt his eyes.
Click, click, click, click
He always searched for her around this time of night. The bitterly cold coffee slid out from the mug, and coated his thick tongue.
Click, click, click, click
She called herself ANN. He was SETH. In fact, that was his real name. He wondered if ANN was hers.

The Encounter

He remembered when they met. He had been surfing all night. Spying on private conversations gave him a special thrill. People would pour out their hearts to a blinking cursor waiting for a reply. They would talk about hard dicks and wet pussy. He loved that shit. He bumped into her talking to someone else. She was speaking very candidly about her conquest for that night. He interrupted. They talked. Now, every night for the past six months he has logged on and waited. He waits for her to emerge from the glowing light of the screen that always hurt his eyes and talk with him again.
Click, click, click
His dick was hard. He thought of how she described herself. He thought of how she had bragged of her sexual conquests.

The Search

Click, click, click
He kept typing, calling out for her. Nothing. Yeah, others would answer always claiming to be her. Saying how big, thick, and wet they were. Or, how they would love to wrap their warm, soft tongues around his hard dick. But he always knew the difference. She wasn't as deliberate as they were. She was smooth and quiet. She knew how to make your inside quiver.
Click, click, click

Where was she? It was always the same people night after night: SUSAN the horny virgin or GEORGE the 12-inched python, MISS PAULA who would dominate you in her own special way, and VERNITA who was just looking for love.

Almost Daylight

So many lonely people. "River Deep, Mountain High," was on the radio. How true the words seem to ring out to him now.

Click, click, click, click

Why wouldn't she come out of the dim light that hurt his eyes? Surprisingly, he found that he was fondling himself. Sometimes he would lean in close to the lifeless machine. Tightly, he would clutch all its cold, hard parts.

Click, click, click

How had he come to this? Love . . . love through modems, hard drives, faxes, and keyboards,

Was he sick?

It didn't matter. SETH, every night logged on and watched for ANN through the dim light that hurt his eyes.

Do Ya Got Some Blow?

DRYERVONN WASHINGTON

I met this female pusher
but narcotics she didn't solicit
she would go downtown on me
performing acts that were explicit
by grabbing my waist
orally heading toward my pelvis
with my dick in her hand
asking, "Yo, may I inhale this?"
she charged for her services
that you had to know
I brought the cash
she provided the blow
I quickly got addicted
to her polishing the knob
forcing me to get loot however
sometimes I stole and robbed
I was obsessed with her oral sex
yo, let me tell ya
my dick was the pipe
her lips the paraphernalia
she blew me up in abandoned buildings
and poorly lit alleys
sucking me from head to toe
from my hat to my Bally's
do you have some blow
is what I always asked her
hoping she'd offer head
to this pathetic, sex crazed bastard

Electric Lover

EUNICE TOWNSEND

Middle-aged woman
High-powered job
Men don't romance me
Say I'm brass-hard
Hold top salary position
All power in my hand
Yet at night there's no
Tongue kissin
With a real man

Stand six feet without shoes
Overcooked skin that sizzles
Keep hair razor short
So it won't fizzle
Male long legs/stallion thighs
Voluptuous breasts that
Capture men's eyes
They want me until
I get them home
Take out my whip
They leave me alone
Complain I'm sick

Home by myself at night
Confident smile on my face
Eat dinner at leisurely pace
Take sip of wine
Dip finger in crystal glass
Smear the warm liquid
From my clit to my ass
Nipples get hard/I leave my chair
Secretion all over pubic hair

.   .   .

Slowly walk to my king-size bed
Roughly pull slip over curly head
Want natural happiness
Two-legged sexual bliss
Until I find true man
Content with electric penis
It's my secret love
You'd be so surprised
What a good job rubber does

Plug him in the wall
He comes alive
Throbbing like genuine dick
Place mouth over him
Start to lick lick lick
Get so excited
Lay down between satin sheets
Extension allows my man
To move around/plunge in deep
He's way up in there I feel the tip
Fondle my own breast/caress my lips
Legs squeeze him tight
Body heaves up and down
Climax comes up to quickly/make moaning sounds
The sweat on my body
Glistens like pearls
Crimson nails run through
Dripping curls
Legs relax/fingers pet cum
Electric lover is so much fun
Lazily turn over/cut off the light
See you tomorrow sweetheart
MMMMMMMM oh well, good night.

coffles: a suicide note
VICTOR E. BLUE

lately, the five-minute walk
from my apartment to the metro stop
takes my mind centuries.
college-educated, black, male:
a proud credit to my race
I should be crawling corporate's greased ladder,
huddled Sambo-fashion
"to give a few gentlemen ease."
I struggle across forgotten streets
chained to souls from Goree
unsure of my fate
no escape, no looking back
feeble squirms only send me to genuflection.

enduring ancient pains, I drift
back to when we shared a limestone moon.
your black body
blinding me.
teaching me
how to love and be loved.
inviting me
into your studio
where each finger, hand, toe and tongue
stroked the canvas.

I caught on quickly,
learned your rhythms.
tasting and swinging.

it was almost enough to save me.

Marriage

CASSIE GRANBERRY

Drawn apart in modest relations
Bred through succulent extremes
Wrapping lies in indignant lusts
Trailing glory-clouds like dust
Scarlet lovers greet the gallant dawn.

Tamed by knowledge, wild bodies
Rise abruptly in tender pain
Coaxing ecstasy from wanting hips,
Branding possession in searing lips,
Ring fingers wet with unwelcome desire.

Touching,
Parting . . .

This time she did not scream his name,
Knowing
Dawn illusions never survive the full light of day

Dessert

ESTELLE FARLEY

Sweet thing
Eat me for dessert
lay me on your tray
Chocolate thighs covering a cherry
So sweet and juicy
You've said so
time and time again
Lick my Hershey mounds
until the peaks covered by whip cream
melt down into a river of their making

In turn, I will devour you
as I did chocolate bananas
at the carnival
and round Godiva truffles
bought to celebrate my birthday.

I want to watch you rise
as they say a soufflé must
I wonder are they as creamy and light as you.

The sweat between us will bind
like icing between layers of cake.

Taste me
like a finger dipped in pudding
licking the bowl clean.

I'm hungry
Let's skip dinner
and go straight to dessert.

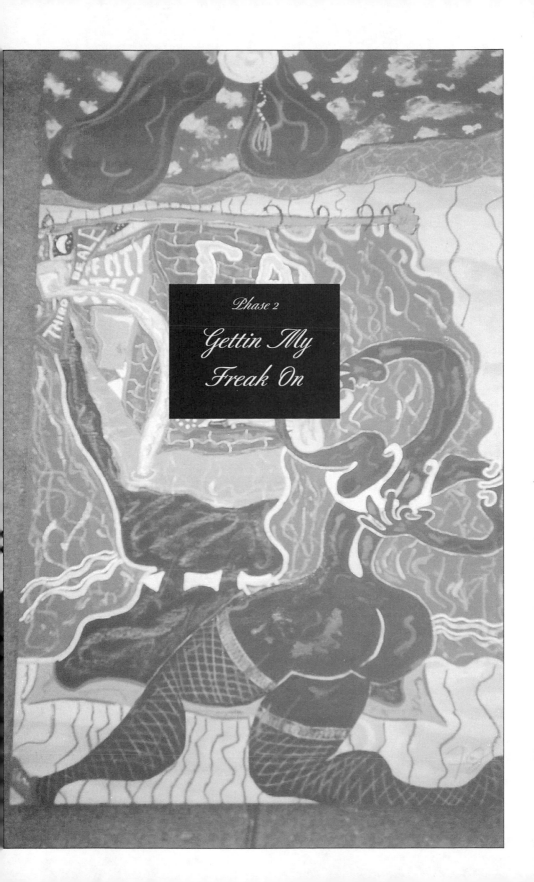

Phase 2

Gettin My Freak On

*A*s Lawrence Levine writes in *Black Literature and Black Culture*, and Ishmael Reed writes in *The Freelance Pallbearers (1966)*, African-Americans are constantly reinventing themselves for the betterment of the whole culture. While this constant reinvention is forced and also costly to many African-Americans who cannot keep up with the pace, the unique nature of so many black indexes has become emblematic of this group of people. If it is an African-American cultural artifact, one can be assured of two things: (1) it is brand-new, never before known, and (2) everyone wants it and/or wants to try it. So it is, then, with the particular verve of urban language that describes and motivates unique urban sex acts.

Observe the specialty of what Jeul A. Harris does to his anonymous victim in "Orgasm Notes" and how he self-advertises in "Mr. Goodbar"; within his systematic cookbook instructions fulfillment comes. In "Pain and Pleasure" by Nina Leonette Small, the mental desires push physical excitement onto an edge. Ibu Abu's testimony to water-bearing nymphs in "No Raincoats Allowed" attests to a woman's true erotic power, and "Head" by Baron James Ashanti gives us a dusky reminder of the joys of oral copulation. Valinda Johnson Brown spices up New Orleans by putting us in the mix of her "Ed's Gumbo #3," and Liv Wright gives us her black version of living right in "Fear's a Bitch," as she guides us through her mock sadomasochistic demands for bloodletting, so uncommonly refreshing in this age of real televison bloodletting by black couples trying no longer to be hurt adolescents. Honoree F. Jeffers gives us a black redux on this theme in "Hurt Me," reminding us again how much stress can be relieved by giving in to the positively physical. Enuf Sed confuses our sexual perspectives in ways that turn us out in "My Best Fucking Friend," and Janice W. Hodges gives us a bitter taste of the "Forbidden Fruit" we all nurture and grow within. Leah Jewel Reynolds gives us wetly to Eros via "Oral" and Chiké Carter, in "Ode to My Sweet Sexy Brown," echoes the best nineteenth-century verse of Paul Laurence Dunbar's mainstream tradition. Jerry W. Ward, Jr., is shaken and stirred like a black olive in a very wet martini in "Serious" (because she is). As our breath subsides, Amanda Townsend reminds us of the vow we made before we gave ourselves to each other in "let's be discreet" with her French translation alongside to show that the hip-hop generation is as polyglotinous as any other—just tighter—in "*soyons discrets.*"

Orgasm Notes

JEUL A. HARRIS

Step One

A. TEASING

1. Touch somewhere softly
2. Make way toward breasts softly
3. Tease area around nipples
4. STOP—begin teasing another part of the body
5. Make way toward breasts again

Step Two

B. THE MAIN EVENT

1. Continue teasing
2. Manipulate with penis softly
3. Tease clitoris, then stop
4. Wait a couple of hours or until the next morning—if possible
5. Begin teasing again
6. Make way toward breasts
7. Tease area around nipples
8. Tease nipples and stop
9. Tease clit softly until she begs for penis
10. Insert penis slowly with her begging
11. Make her reach her orgasm repeatedly

Mr. Goodbar

JEUL A. HARRIS

Taking part in a love affair
Two parties in a room;
Cheating hearts begin to thump
Menage' trois begins to loom.
Why am I a freak of lust;
What have I done to deserve this feeling?
But this bitch is on fire to be served,
And I'm the one doing the dealing.
Away from home
Moaning like a pair of sluts,
Sliding my penis inside her mouth
Making her scream as I rip her guts.
I got eight and a quarter reasons
For ultimate pleasing
No time for teasing
Go down whore, it's sweating season.
Like a red-hot light
She got turned out,
By the Black Macedon
Shafting deep and stout.
The job is done
And I'm admired like a star;
Chocolate-covered and full of nuts
Can you hang with Mr. Goodbar?

Pain and Pleasure (Parts I-IV)

NINA LEONETTE SMALL

Part I

I glance at him demurely, my lashes are lowered
Intently, he is watching the TV screen
He sits there quietly . . . his eyes are unblinking
Completely unaware that I continue to "feen"
For his body, his love, his tender caresses
I hesitate before making my move
Would he think of me any less
If I told him right now that I wanted to groove?
He turns to me suddenly, chuckling softly
At the silly movie on the TV screen
He catches the flicker of desire in my eyes
I try to hide what he has already seen
He asks me what is wrong—He stands up
And towers above me like a great king
Staring up at him, I long to ask–
"Could you kiss me and cause my body to sing?"
Mumbling a terse reply, I shrug my shoulders
Puzzled, he returns slowly to his seat
I lick my lips, yes, my knees are weak
Can he hear the thunder of my heartbeat?
Nervously, I chew on a worrisome hangnail
And can't help feeling the pulsing of my veins
That speeds up faster with every passing second
I hate to experience such senseless PAIN
PAIN to see him sitting so helplessly
Against my imagination that is ravaging his body
That is touching him there, making him moan in ecstasy
He urges me on, not trying to stop me
But, of course, I know him much better than that
A gentleman that treats me with the utmost respect

For this I am grateful, but I am losing my self-control
I am astonished that we haven't even kissed yet!
It's been well over a month and frustration consumes me
It takes a lot for me not to grab him
To tell him how much I want and need him
To hug, kiss, arouse, and softly caress him
A wistful smile curves my lips as I stare off into space
My active imagination is on the rampage
Conjuring up images of sensuous PLEASURE
My hormones have been let loose in a passionate rage
I devour his lips and melt in their softness
His gasp of pleased surprise causes me to laugh
Wantonly, I straddle his hips . . . look deeply in his eyes
And offer to massage him in a bubble bath
Yes! PLEASURE is what I crave from him
He calls my name and interrupts my reverie
As I shake away thoughts of hot naked sex
I assure him that nothing is disturbing me
So the PAIN of desire consumes me, and once more
I have to endure this insane madness
Of watching him two feet away watching TV
Instantly, I am overwhelmed with silly sadness
Anxiously, I wring my hands like a limp, wet washcloth
I try to curb the urge to grab his innocent shoulders
The credits are rolling . . . He rises and stretches his body
He purrs like a cat . . . Oh, I long to be much bolder
He grins shyly and thinks nothing is amiss
My lips quiver and are starving for that first hungry kiss
I walk him to the door, and I linger in anticipation
Involuntarily, I stare at him with wicked thoughts of bliss
So, eventually he does kiss me, but only on the cheek
The PLEASURE is fleeting, and PAIN makes me weak
I close the heavy door and lean against it for strength
I wonder will I ever find what I set out to seek . . .

Part II

I had avoided him for days on end
Never returning his calls or answering the phone
I was so melancholy, a mere shell of what I had been
I was not sure I even loved him anymore

Depression engulfed me as I remembered the times
We had danced in the night or romped in the park
No longer could I bear to be around him
In my room I hid in the vast black dark
One night while watching a love story on TV
Stupid, silent tears fell and dripped off of my chin
Suddenly, I heard an insistent knock at my door
It was him and reluctantly I did let him in
Hurriedly, I wiped away those silly tears
That had left my cheeks so sodden and soaked
On the couch my body curled into a tight protective ball
Just the sight of him got me all riled up and provoked!
He took off his jacket, and all he had on
Was a simple T-shirt and jeans. He stared curiously
At how tightly my legs were wrapped together
As he lived and breathed, he yielded sensuality
He did not utter a word as he sat down beside me
Refusing to look at him, my eyes staunchly fastened
To the TV screen before me. I had built a careful wall around me
Since I felt that I had been thoroughly chastened
He stroked my hair—my eyes fluttered quickly
All it took was one tender touch
But I loathed to have him touch my frail body
Because I could not deal with it . . . I wanted too much!
Pure Passion led me, and like a match to fire
I was quickly ignited—like a drum my heart pounded
As he continued to stroke me—even my scalp tingled!
To let go of this passion, unbridled and unbounded
He smelled of Ivory soap that teased my nose
The intoxicating scent of him was really getting to me
Lifting the locks of my hair, his lips grazed my exposed neck
The PAIN fled and the PLEASURE was set free
A moan escaped my lips as his hands fondled me
He persuaded me to relax as he turned me to him
He snatched my arms and put them around his neck
In his eyes I gazed . . . I was drowning in the depths of them
The almond brown pools of his eyes—I was submerged in the
   abyss
His eyes studied my face as if it was a precious gem
He feather-kissed my eager lips ever so softly

He was killing me—I wanted him and had to have him
His kiss deepened and all control was lost
Our tongues dueled in passionate sword fight
He won and explored the sweet depths of my mouth
Searching . . . oh, how I had longed for this night!
Such power surged in that kiss that shocked my bruised lips
Easily I melted in his ardent embrace
Fervent fingers ran through his thick head of hair
He continued to rain impassioned kisses upon my upturned face
He made me lay down and he pressed closer to me
His body was molded so tightly to mine
Writhing in PLEASURE, beneath him I undulated like a snake
He smirked at my response—we twisted and turned in a slow
    grind
Biting my neck, he nibbled and nipped
I arched in PLEASURE and I whimpered in PAIN
That gentle, but determined sucking pressure
He pulled my skin between his lips . . . passion we did not feign
He whispered to my listening ear that he wanted me—
But he loved me
Abruptly, things shifted and he left me quite unfulfilled
Yearning for passion . . . PAIN and PLEASURE were in perfect
    balance
I was left so confused . . . my perplexed mind was at a standstill.

Part III

For once we are not over at my house
Watching a never-ending movie about sex and violence
For once, we are in his room, alone together
Meshing together in the dark, black silence
Enveloped in his arms, I lay upon his chest
And listen to the rhythmic timbre of his voice
As he tells me silly anecdotes from his childhood
I think about his perfection—his stance and his poise
His chest is a hairless plain that is as smooth as silk
I stroke his tiny nipples that become hard as pebbles
My fingers play across his chest—I pause
He sighs deeply and calls me a devil
What can I do to get you to make love to me?
I ask him this question and his voice halts abruptly

Patiently, again he tells me the time is coming soon
I ask can he handle the passion threatening to erupt from me
He falls silent, and the water bed undulates
Like the crest of a wave rising up and crashing down
I rise upon my elbows and gaze down at his face
I hate to see his thoughtful, pensive frown
Is there something that you are not telling me?
I ask him this—my voice small and hesitant
No, his smile reassures me completely
Yet, my desires are becoming more incessant
When will it happen? I am so ready now!
Like a child that cannot have her way
I pout and sulk . . . I moan and groan
But still he succeeds in pushing me away
Scantily clad am I—he cannot resist me
Brazenly, I straddle his hips and stare down
He looks upward with helplessness etched in his face
Except for our labored breathing, there is no other sound
Smiling lewdly, I move against him
Grinding and gyrating, I enjoy the feel of him
Crushed close to my body . . . I yearn to crush closer
My desire hovers very closely to the brim
My lips find his . . . the seduction has begun
Over and over our tongues fight in a frenzy
Ruthlessly, I pin back his hands to prevent them from searching
The secrets of my warm, supple body . . . I start to feel giddy
I start to weaken, and our bodies start to moisten
Sweat from our pores causes us to become slippery
We roll over and I hear the water splash
My eyes close as his tongue begins to lick me
My bra snaps off and he cups my breasts in his hands
He murmurs sweet nonsense in my listening ears
Once again, I am twisting underneath him
My long aching sighs and his laughter are what I hear
I plead with him to take me as his tongue grazes my nipples
With erotic urgency I seize his shoulders
My nails drive into his flesh and he moans in PAIN
His tongue travels farther south and becomes a lot bolder
Teasing my navel, his tongue flicks in and out
Searching blindly for my face, he kisses my lips

While his fingers probe the depth between my thighs
I experience such immense PLEASURE at his fingertips
Again and again spasms wrack my body
He kisses me to subdue my shrieks of delight
Tears moisten my eyes as I beg him to take me
Yet, he still refuses to make love with me tonight
His tongue lights a fiery path between my thighs
He drinks as I come, I moan as if in PAIN
I have died and gone to heaven! I feel so insane!

Part IV

Tonight is the night, he whispers in my ear
My mouth widens as he tightens his embrace
Swaying to the love music in his darkened bedroom
I can't control the startled joy upon my face
But nervousness stabs me in the center of my chest
I am afraid as I glimpse the desire in his eyes
My pupils dilate and my breathing is irregular
What will it take to quell my ardent sighs?
Tonight is your night, I whisper as I remove his shirt
My eyes never waver from him as I unbuckle his belt
He steps out of his slacks and stands only in his boxers
My hands tremble from the hardness I have felt
My hands slyly slip inside his black silk boxers
I stroke and rub the long, thickening length
As he lays back upon the surging water bed
I pray that I can endure his manhood's strength
I peel off his boxers and survey his body
I no longer try to conceal the lust that I feel
I admire the veins in that hard, erect muscle
That is so smooth to the touch—He will bend to my will
My lips lower and I shamelessly caress his shaft
Teasing him, taunting him, I enjoy his moans
I am shocked to find that I like this, too!
The taste and feel of it—I can barely control my groans
I do him this way until he is nearing his climax
I suck at his nipples—he emits a low, growling sound
Rhythmically, my tongue darts in and out
He takes it no longer . . . he turns around
He lays me on my back and makes me naked

Whipped cream he squirts on my turgid peaks
Tantalizingly slow, he licks it off . . . causing me PAIN
My body quakes and trembles—I am so weak
A scarlet strawberry we share between our full lips
Secrets are no longer hidden, no place is left untouched
The minutes pass by—I am lost in sweet heaven
The PLEASURE of this—How can I endure such?
Passion from his lips leave red marks
His fingers caress my sweet and hot wetness
His fingers delve deeper and deeper, my sighs become louder
His teeth nibble at my lips . . . I experience such distress
His lips travel lower and he tickles me so cleverly
Trailing wet kisses along the backs of my legs
I grasp his head in a fit of RED PAIN
He smirks like a naughty child—he wants to hear me beg
So I comply with his wishes and he gives in to mine
Like an Olympic swimmer he dives, inflicting such PLEASURE
   PAIN
Stroking against the floodwaters, his tongue flicks in and out
Up and down and all around—My body continues to strain
This ravaging from his mouth is prolonged, never-ending
I can become no wetter . . . I am ready for love
He lets me know that he is coming and nudges it against me
He slides right on in; we meld together like a hand inside a glove
Sharp PAIN from his entrance causes me to gasp
Tears escape from my eyes and he kisses them away
But then he begins to move deeply inside of me
I want him with me always . . . I want him to forever stay
I hear the water crash and I clasp him to me closer
My legs are lifted and harder and harder he pumps
It feels right, yes, it was well worth the wait
My nails dig in his back . . . I grab his arching rump
When it is all over, it never seems to end
Because all we seem to do is make love again
And again and again—I don't think we ever parted
The PAIN and the PLEASURE I savored to the very end

No Raincoats Allowed

IBU ABU

while takin empty buckets
  2 my bed
    2 gather all
      da wet u left
     —i noticed a familiar thunder
      Spotted da same lightnin
        Swimmin thru yo drops
          . . . my prayer splashed
        into ragin/lovin downpour
        consultin H_2O-oracles
        summonin liquid-gods/
      & callin down da spirits of water/
      in a mystical mist
      —call u yemanja
      annointin my bed
      baptized & blessed . . . be da moisture of u
& then i recognized how
  even when u leave
    u leave so much of u here
      dat i can close my eyes
      & watch u flowin inside me
        oceans . . . streams . . . puddles
        —my cup has runneth over
. . . & now soaked w/ u
i'm liftin these buckets
2 pour u on chairs
    over shelves
      across floors
    into my desk
& any other item
  dat ain't yet bathed
    in yo storm

cuz
u are da first time
it ever rained
in my room

& 2 keep yo clouds around
i'd throw away
all da umbrellas
in da house.

Head

BARON JAMES ASHANTI

for Jora

Facing each other embraced & coiled
like Chango's snakes
naked under candlelight a sweet rise
conjured as in heat

I turned her flat
& bit an amber nipple to erection
as waves of moans in newborn passion
became incantation while
my frenetic fingers
played sensual music down south/

Garcil thighs of hysteria
aestival breasts of tender mists
invited engorged stylus to write
love songs in pouting niche

oh no
not yet
not yet . . .

When horny pleasures called
for something else
my thinking head went between
stripped down up-turned legs
her round-eye gapped
wet & prompted for strange visions

My tongue probed sensual sign
without shame nor hesitation
my mouth with a mind of its own
sucked & pulled my woman's body
into jerk & shudder dance . . .

Loving like tender fury
   again
& again
she came like melodious rain
& I lapped up her salty honey
trying to reach for paradise!

Ed's Gumbo #3

VALINDA JOHNSON BROWN

*T*he dried sassafras leaves of file powder is the maestro that sets the stage for the seduction as it lures you in with its silky dark brown roux to come closer to savor its aroma and experience its hot spicy seasoning of cayenne and paprika and robust flavors of bay leaves and oregano. Before you can inhale the aroma, you're captured! Like a New Orleans spell, you are now in its orbit—drunk for its irresistible essence and ready to be taken.

Shaking with anticipation, I extend my hand to the bowl and dip my spoon into the rich creole dish extracting likes of sensually thin crabmeat curled around pink shrimp entwined between white rice, red tomatoes, green peppers, onions, garlic and okra sailing like conquering voyagers in a sea of indulgence.

I separate my lips . . . it enters my mouth . . . my pulse quickens . . . my eyes close. Fire, steam, then smoke race from every pore of my body. Effervesce spirits rush into my soul as I am propelled into a spiral spin of no return. Until, that is, the next spoonful.

And it comes. I take one more spoonful of his gumbo and my libido blossoms. A mist of moist morning dew gathers in the domain of my passion creating a magnetism between my legs making my knees leap inward to touch to be touched to come within to hold that moment. Its dark brown file sauce is potent as I get into it deeper into this delicious taste. A climax of intense acceleration lingers when you eat his gumbo. First, you climax, then serenity enters. But its not anti-climatic, you come and come again with each mouthful.

Fear's a Bitch

L I V   W R I G H T

Quietly
        the bitch
                removed her teeth
                        Let fall
    her raging mantel
    to the floor
                Thrice heaved
    and in her supple nakedness
                hard sucked
    his passive blood
                ALERT.
                (In all creation has the bitch survived
                denied the consolation of defeat)
She supped
    and in ironic gratitude
                gave thanks to yet another loyal
                host.

Hurt Me

HONOREE F. JEFFERS

Flashes of pain in
soft dark. Love shards slicing flesh,
leaving sweeter wounds.

My Best Fucking Friend

ENUF SED

Yeah, put your finger in and slowly pull it out
Let it slither on up to that throbbing, beating, and pulsating
   piece of flesh
Do it again for the sake of sweet honey drippings
Without a rush, stop . . . quickly command your mind to let
   your roaming tongue take the place of your prodding
   finger
Yeah, put your mouth there, move it a little further to the left
Latch those soft, sexy-ass lips around my best fucking friend
The friend that makes me feel so good when you stroke her,
   rub her, lick her, tease her, taste her, for it is then she
   declares she'll explode
She's a friend that promises she'll never fail to take me there if
   you treat her oh, so right
Yeah, go ahead, caress . . . manipulate . . . beguile . . .
   maneuver and use finesse with my best fucking friend
Yeah, let her know you have strong feelings for her and you
   really care, so my best fucking friend can become your best
   fucking friend too.

Forbidden Fruit

JANICE W. HODGES

forbidden fruit
like fresh-cut onions
made her mama, weary
cry

peeled her back
like supple melons
sucked her innocence, oozing
dry

The Film Teacher

CECIL BROWN

*T*he battered, whitish Volkswagen crept down College Avenue to the traffic light and refused to go farther. The right fender had been bashed in so deeply that the headlamp, like a gorged-out human eye, hung precariously from a single, visible electric cord. Inside the wreck, Ray tried to resuscitate the dying engine with rapid pumps of the gas pedal, but the carburetor gasped its last breath, sputtered loudly, helplessly, and passed out. His VW was out of gas—again!

At this moment, Ray was overwhelmed by a depressing sensation, which was partly image: the cars honking their horns around him became dogs barking at him. Why this strange hallucination? Was he on some drug? No drug; in fact, he was as sober as he could be; he was on his way to the state university to teach his screenwriting class. When a dog is wounded, the other dogs in the pack, smelling blood, will turn on the helpless one and attack him. Ray saw himself and his VW as a wounded animal and the blaring car horns around him with the scowling faces behind the wheels—what were they if not bloodthirsty hounds who attacked their own kind?

He sat in the car and refused to do anything about his impending situation. He had worked so hard and got so little out of life! If he had been living in the ghetto with no father, no education, no hope, his misfortune would have a tangible cause. You could see why his car was a heap and why it was always out of gas, but he was young (thirty-five), not bad-looking, educated (Brown University, '70), and talented (he had written some of the funniest episodes of *The Jeffersons*). A bachelor with no extravagant habits, his rent was nothing outrageous, so how could he explain this absurd poverty?

He could not. Which is why guilt and self-disgust weighed so heavily on his shoulders that he had to slump down over the wheel of the car in a state of momentary collapse. This genteel poverty was too much! Never having enough money to live up in the hills in the white community and too educated to live in the black ghetto, he hovered somewhere in between the two, in a realm dominated by "artists" and other riffraff.

His car running out of gas again! It was just another absurd incident that marked his life of poverty, just like the time when his car rolled down that hill in San Francisco because he didn't have enough money to fix the hand-brake. Imagine what he went through! Sitting in a friend's apartment, he suddenly saw his car, which he had only minutes before parked on the curve, go past the window! Imagine the guilt he felt! He exclaimed, "That's my car going down the street!" What a shocking sight that was! There he stood, helplessly watching his car, driverless, go down the street, weaving between cars, avoiding children, until it hit a telephone pole, where it seemed to have fallen asleep in an intoxicated stupor like a happy drunk! But in his unluckiness, he was lucky—the car hadn't killed anybody. He pulled the fender out and kissed it.

Now he sat in his VW while all around him cars barked at him; he remembered a fragment from a dream he had that night: he was at the Democratic convention in San Francisco and everybody was laughing at him, and then he saw why—he was standing there with a dead cat sticking out of his pocket. Oh, this was too much! At some point he had to get out of his car and push it off the street. He tried the ignition again, but there was no spark left in the car, only the faint whining of the generator losing power. I have to get out of the car, he thought, as he wiped a piece of rotten upholstery which hung from the roof from his face. He saw that the traffic light had turned green and the cars were ready to go and he was responsible for preventing them from reaching their happy destinations. He had to get out of the car and show his face, the face which had caused the traffic jam.

As he emerged from his car the bald-headed driver of a wine-colored Datsun blasted him with his horn, but Ray did nothing in the way of defense; on the contrary, he smiled at the man as if he were an old friend. In fact, he smiled at all the other cars behind him except the big, blue Mercedes. His Mercedes annoyed him because he felt especially ashamed of his car when he looked at the big, blue Mercedes, the kind of car a Republican would drive. Maybe that was the meaning of his dream, that he should switch over, like some blacks he knew, and join up with the winners. He had never seen a Republican driving a car as badass as his. Those Republicans were not so stupid after all.

Ray became so angry at the driver that he prepaid a curse for him. Finally the driver of the Mercedes pulled up beside him and rolled down the window. The curse he had prepared for the driver simply dissolved on his lips when he saw that the driver was a woman—a blonde, very pretty. "Do you remember me?" she asked, smiling, and then taking off a pair of dark sunglasses so he could see her face better. Ray didn't know what to say. Naturally, he wanted to remember a blonde driving a Mercedes, but he had never seen this woman before in his life. Even when she took the sunglasses off, he still didn't recognize her. "Yes, I remember you," he cried out. He knew that he looked like a complete idiot. It wasn't enough that his car had died on him in the middle of traffic at the most-watched intersection in Berkeley. No, that wasn't enough. Now he was standing in the middle of all this, carrying on a conversation with a pretty woman! So it didn't surprise him that a new, fresh volley of horn blasts was showered upon him. But this seemed to have encouraged the woman to quicken the business of making sure he identified her. "I'm Pamela Fleming," she shouted across the traffic and amidst the car horns as she got out of her car, "Pamela—Flem-ing!" "Oh, yes, now I remember," he shouted back, but he had no idea who she was. He knew she had made a mistake, but it was too much of a problem to clear it up now with his car dead in the middle of the street. "I'll wait for you," Pamela said and got back into her blue Mercedes and pulled over to the other side of the street. Ray began pushing his car off to the side. As he pushed it in front of a stopped truck, an old bum came to help him. A bum he had seen around Berkeley for years. This man had once been a professor at the university but lost his job during the Vietnamese War protest marches when Reagan became Governor of California; over the years the man had slipped from his high position down to his present state. Without saying a word, reeking of an awful smell, the bum (once a professor) began pushing the car with Ray, until they had reached the other side of the street with it. Ray looked at the bum and thought, "One day I'll be like you!" and he had to fight the impulse to go with him, but the bum, pulling his filthy brown shirt closer to his body and at the same time giving the blonde woman a furtive glance, turned and was walking away.

"Thanks," Ray yelled to him but the man kept walking. Turning to the hood of his VW, Ray took the gas can out and walked toward the woman waiting for him, a slight wind billowing her white cotton dress. As he approached, he noticed her beaming smile. What a pity that he didn't know her! But he knew that the mistaken identity would be recognized soon and he would awaken from his dream like a child who had dreamed he received a beloved pony only to wake up to the reality of a dull drab room.

"This is certainly a surprise!" Pamela said, in a voice that carried a built-in intimacy. "Now you remember me?" She extended her face to him and before he could say "I don't know you" he kissed her briefly on the lips and said, "Of course I knew it was you! How have you been?" "I've been just wonderful," she said, looking closely into his eyes as if she really did know him from before. He should have said at that moment that he didn't know who she was, but he would have felt embarrassed—besides, she was very pretty; and now standing within kissing distance of her lips, he began to imagine that maybe he did know her, maybe from one of his many dreams.

"Are you still living in Berkeley?" he asked her casually. He was looking for clues, but he didn't want her to notice it. They were walking to the back of the Mercedes now, where she opened the trunk for him to put his gas can inside. "No, not really," she answered.

"Of course not—I don't know what I'm thinking about—"

"—My daughter goes to ballet school here every Wednesday. Of course you remember Emily?"

"Oh yes, of course." They turned back to the front of the car.

"What's wrong with your car?" she asked. "Where shall we go?"

"Gas," he said. "I think I'm out."

"I'll take you to a station," she said, opening the door, getting in and reaching across to unlock the passenger side. When he got in, he saw a small, dark-haired girl, about ten, sitting in the backseat. "Darlin', you remember Ray, don't you? Remember when he came to our party?"

Emily looked at him and decided after a quick glance that she remembered him. "Oh yes," she said and refocused her gaze out the window at a boy peddling a bicycle in the street.

"That was a very exciting party," he said and watched Pamela's face, which had begun to glow with inner joy . . .

"You really liked it?"

"Very much—" Except, he thought, I just can't remember it.

She had mentioned a party—he had gone to so many parties in Hollywood. Now he knew who she was! She was someone from his days when he worked in Hollywood as a screenwriter. Back in those days—those wonderful days—when he drove his jazzy, red flat convertible! Someone who had been impressed by him! Now she could have a good laugh, seeing him push his raggedy wreck off the street! He, too, wanted to laugh at himself but somehow he couldn't.

"So how is Hollywood these days?" he said, pleased now that he had realized where he had met her.

Pamela looked at him and said, "How would I know? I've never been there. You're the one who was a screenwriter in Hollywood," and she laughed.

"That's right," he said, laughing with her. "I did work in Hollywood for a bit, but not anymore."

Immediately he fell silent because he was in a state of mild shock. Who was she, then?

When they pulled into the gas station she turned to him and said, "I would love to get together and spend some time with you. I'll give you my telephone number."

"Okay," he said in a contrived voice that was supposed to pass as a normal tone. "And I'll give you mine." He made the last remark sound as casual as hell, knowing that in a week the phone company would have cut his phone off.

Before closing the door to the Mercedes, he made it appear that he had not only remembered her, but that he had spent actual personal time in thought about her after classes ended.

For days Ray was haunted by the mystery of the woman's identity. Who was she? Where had he met her? He tried to remember all the parties he had been to in the last few years, but he didn't find her face among the many women he had met or whose phone numbers he had collected. When he attended the film faculty parties the only attractive women were the graduate students and they never looked like owners of Mercedes. How had this woman known so much about him? What situation could have possibly existed in the past which had brought them together? From the excitement upon seeing him again, the experience must have been a good one, and if so, why had he forgotten it? It could have all been a fantasy, expect for the child Emily. Somehow the child made the experience real, but he knew no attractive women with children.

On Wednesday he went to teach his film-writing class at the state university, the one thing he loved doing. As he parked his battered VW, he decided he would call Pamela's number and ask her where they had met. He would simply tell her the truth, tell her how terrible he had been because he couldn't remember who she was, but he had decided against it by the time he had the car in the space—it would be a stupid thing to do, very embarrassing for her, too. He had his chance when he first met her, but he was too embarrassed to let her know he couldn't remember her. So now, he thought, as he stood facing his class, you just have to suffer.

"Good morning class," he began. "I have read your reversals," and he took several stacks of paper from his briefcase and placed them on his desk. "I would like you to pick up your papers and we will discuss them." He had assigned them a reversal scene to write. A reversal, he had lectured them, occurs when a character goes from a good fortune to misfortune. He had used the example of King Oedipus, who, believing that the messenger would bring good news, reverses his actions and feelings when the messenger brings the bad news that Oedipus was guilty of patricide.

While the students rose from their seats to pick up their papers from his desk, the door opened and another student came in and took a seat near the rear. This student, a fat girl with a wide, pimpled face, suddenly reminded the film teacher of something which he had forgotten. Two years ago Pamela Fleming had sat in that seat while he gave his lecture on reversals. Most of the film students who wanted to be filmmakers were young people who were either black or gay or feminist or Chicano, who wanted to change the world, but occasionally there would appear in his class an attractive, rich housewife who had nothing better to do than take a class in screenwriting—inspired, usually, by the bad quality of scripts on *General Hospital* or *Dynasty*. When he had seen Pamela Fleming outside the context of the classroom, he had not been able to remember her, but now looking at the pimpled-face student, he suddenly remembered Pamela's smooth, pampered complexion and all that went with it.

At the end of the lecture, Ray went to the film department to check the records for her name, thinking that if he saw her name he would be sure, but as he was looking through the student files, the chairman of the department, a balding, paunchy, affable man who answered to the name Bill Craig, came into the room, trapping him, so to speak, between the mailboxes and the open door. When Ray was cornered like this, he immediately became the Charming Black Teacher just as Bill Craig, who also felt trapped, became the Last Great Liberal. Bill Craig and Ray probably liked each other much more than they realized, but film departments sometimes force teachers to play more roles than the actors do in most Hollywood films. Ray played THE BLACK MAN TEACHING IN THE FILM DEPARTMENT and Bill Craig played THE WHITE LIBERAL WHO GOT HIM THE JOB.

The reality was that Bill Craig had needed Ray because the chancellor of the university wondered why there were no blacks in the film department and Ray had needed Bill Craig because he needed a job, but when the two met they made a big fuss about each other—just like they really cared about the other one: the fact that they had needed each other in the past required that they treat each other as though they would need each other in the future.

"I'm looking for a student I had in my class a few semesters back," Ray told Bill Craig.

"I don't believe our records go back that far." Bill said. "By the way, I hear that you're doing a wonderful thing with your reversals. Keep the good work up!"

That evening the film teacher was watching a film when he heard a knock at his door. Often he had imagined that Pamela would knock at his door, but when he opened the door this time he saw only a young man in a gray uniform holding out a pen and a piece of paper to him.

"Could you please sign here," the young man said. After he had signed his name and the young man had gone away, Ray closed the door, wondering who would send him a telegram. Pulling a corner of a sheet from the darkened window, the film teacher allowed light to invade the room and illuminate the message on the yellow paper.

Tried calling. No phone. Please call. Isn't this romantic? Pamela.
Phone 555-4467.

The film teacher drove down the crooked hill road until he came to a telephone booth—the phone company had cut off his phone as they had promised—and dialed Pamela's number.

"Hello," a soft female voice answered—it was Pamela, and he said, "I got your telegram."

He heard her laugh joyously. "You did? Wasn't that just so romantic?"

"Yes," he admitted, like a slow student catching on. "Yes, it was."

"Well, I've always wanted to tell you what a fantastic person you are. I'll be really straight with you, Ray. I would like to spend some time with you. So I've been thinking . . ."

". . . Yes?" Ray said, his own voice loaded with anticipation and desire.

". . . that we could meet and spend some time together soon because my husband is in Washington for a week."

The film teacher could barely hide the shuddering of his breath, and he had to hold the phone away from his mouth, lest she would overhear the quick, sudden, panicky rhythm in his breathing.

After a few seconds, he asked, calmer, "What did you have in mind?"

"Well, I was thinking I could invite you somewhere outside the city for the weekend."

"Outside the city. For the weekend?"

"Yes, we could drive down to Santa Cruz. There's a lovely motel called the Dream Inn, right on the beach."

Swallowing hard, he said, "When would we—I mean, what day did you have in mind . . . leaving?"

"How about this weekend? Friday?"

"That'll be perfect! I mean, it really would be. My last class ends on Friday at five. I could pick you up after my class . . ."

"In that case, meet me on the corner of Presidio and Thirty-eighth Street, near the park."

"That's perfect. I'll see you then."

"Have a great class and I'll see you then."

In the classroom that Friday, Ray glanced at the big clock at the end of the room and realized that in less than an hour he would meet Pamela.

"Plots in films and theater are like games," he lectured. "There are two kinds—games which confine the actions of the characters—" he thought of the game he and Bill Craig played with each other "—and games which are like the ones children play, games which release unconscious energy and spontaneity. Playwrights like Samuel Beckett, Eugene Ionesco, Harold Pinter, Edward Albee, Tennessee Williams and Sam Shepard are contemporary playwrights whose characters play games with each other."

One of his students, a young, bright-eyed gay man, raised his hand.

"Yes, Etienne," Ray said.

"There are some characters who refuse to play the game," he said, "like in Kafka."

Ray didn't see the connection, but he liked his students when they spoke up. "Yes, of course," he said, "like those in Kafka."

When he had given this lecture to Pamela's class, he had played an improvisational game with them to illustrate his point. Suddenly inspired by that remembrance, he said, "Here is a simple children's game which will demonstrate my point," and he took a handkerchief from his pocket.

"Will somebody tie this around my eyes?" he asked. Dana Brett, a black student, rose and walked to the front of the class and tied the handkerchief around his face. Of course, in Pamela's class it had been she who had tied the handkerchief around his eyes. Now he felt the emptiness of the ritual and yet experienced the joyful anticipation of seeing her in less than forty-five minutes.

"Now could somebody ball up a piece of notebook paper and hand it to me."

This was done. "Now I want three students to stand on the opposite side of the room behind me," and he waited until three students had volunteered to play the game with him.

"Now, I'm going to throw the paper over my shoulder, and one of you three will pick it up. Then I will take the handkerchief off, and I will turn around to face you. Each of you will hold out your hands to me, but only one of you will have the piece of white paper. The aim of the game is for me to guess which one has the piece of paper by the expression on his face."

The class thought this was a wonderful idea for a game; Ray threw the paper over his shoulder, and they cheered and whoopped as the three students scrambled for it.

When Ray heard the movements of the students become quiet, he said, "Ready?"

"Okay," they shouted back, and he took the handkerchief from his face and turned around.

He stood facing Brigitta Mandell, a tall black woman; Robin Stolyty, a short blonde boy; and Satoru Nakno, one of the Japanese students. They were all grinning as he studied their faces for any traces of lies. Then he decided that it was the black student who had it, but he was wrong. The class took a great joy and pleasure in his mistake. On the second attempt he was right.

"Well," he said when the three students had sat down again, "when you're making plots, remember that the audience must have as much fun as you were having with our game."

"Where do we find games to write about?" a student asked.

Ray thought for a quick moment. "In life," he said, heading for the door as if he meant to set an example.

When he came out of the building to his car, he found a parking ticket on the windshield. Furious that he had been somehow tricked by the meter maid, he almost yielded to the impulse to tear it up and scatter the pieces over the pavement. Instead, he opened the door with the key—why he even bothered to lock it was another pretense he would drop if he had the courage—and got in; he opened the glove compartment and took out a stack of such parking tickets and placed the new one on top. He shoved the whole batch back into the glove compartment neatly—one of these days he was going to confront the film department with this batch of tickets and watch the secretary squirm like a worm on a hook; how was he supposed to teach a three-and-a-half-hour class if the parking space was limited to two hours?

He met Pamela and drove down to Santa Cruz in less than an hour, the small townships rolling by the window of the Mercedes like the flickering images on a movie screen. They found the Dream Inn easy enough, checked into their room and stood with each other looking out of the window at an orange sun setting over the Pacific Ocean.

Listening to her breathing beside him, Ray turned quietly and looked at her, lost himself in her blue eyes for a moment and then kissed her on her lips. The kiss itself was a perfect reversal—suddenly his fortune went from bad to good; a depressed, broke, obsessed film teacher was transformed into a bright, horny, happy, free young lad. When their lips finally parted, Pamela looked him deeply into his eyes and said, "You were such a wonderful teacher, and I always wanted to tell you, but I didn't know how." The film teacher watched her as she released a button on her blouse. "But now I know how," she said. Watching her as she turn toward the bed, he took off his shirt and draped it across a chair. She turned and watched him, and he watched her. He took off his pants, and stood before her.

"Do you mind?" she said suddenly and reached into her handbag and took out a Polaroid camera. "I'm so sorry, but your body looks so stunningly beautiful in the sunlight. Sure you don't mind?"

Ray smiled faintly—it was just another reversal. Film teachers are used to reversals.

"No, I don't mind," he lied and pushed out his chest to make the picture more striking. At dinner in Santa Cruz's most expensive French restaurant, Pamela blew a stream of cigarette smoke across their table.

He watched her as she studied the photos she had taken of his nude body.

"I've always wanted to do that! My husband thinks I'm kinky. You don't think I'm kinky, do you?"

Ray was sipping the wine at the time. "No," he said, after setting his glass down, "besides, you're an artist, aren't you?" He had gone to her exhibition at the university where he had seen a display of her photographs. There, too, had been Emily and Pamela's husband. There had been potato chips and onion dip and that was what Emily had referred to as the "party."

"Yes, I am an artist," she said, staring at a particular revealing shot of him. "And so are you."

Ray quickly changed the subject. "You never said very much in my class. That's strange because here we are getting along just fine."

Pamela finally put the photos back into her purse with the reluctance of a child putting away its toys and said, "I wanted to tell you what a fine teacher you were, but I was afraid you would take it the wrong way."

"Oh really?"

"Yes, there were so many girls who liked you in the class and I didn't want to get into your little inner circle."

"My inner circle? You are kidding?"

"Well, what about that tall, dark-haired lady who always spoke to you after class?"

Ray remembered the dark-haired lady very well; she was a lesbian from Boston who had written a science fiction script about Amazons on Mars. She had discreetly suggested a three-way affair with her girlfriend, who lifted weights and worked at a gay bar and who looked like a man. Ray had said no. "It's funny," he said now, reaching for a cigarette, "how little we know about each other in life." This last remark was made with a superficial gesture, meant to keep the conversation light, because he sensed that Pamela wanted to talk about the class she had taken with him.

"Since that class with you I have thought a lot about what you taught us, but a lot of what you said was not true. For instance, this concept of perihelia—reversals," she said, and then in a voice which mimicked his lecturing tone, "If the hero's fortune goes down, we have a tragedy. That's not true in life, now is it?"

"I was thinking about fiction and made-up people," Ray said, annoyed with the accusative tone in her voice. He preferred to admire the way her finely chiseled nose flared arrogantly when she smiled. "People in real life are different."

"But that's just the point, isn't it?" Pamela said, picking up her wine-glass—she took a sip and set the glass down. "You told us that made-up people are interesting because the reader knows everything about them, but that in real life we never know much about real people. This is what makes people interesting. Like me, for example. If you knew everything about me I wouldn't be interesting to you."

"I think the more we know about a person the more interested we are," he said, watching her white teeth bite into her lower lip. She had a wonderful, red mouth, but if he had been her creator, he would've made the under lip a tiny bit fuller. But he really couldn't complain—her lips were almost perfect.

She gave him a curious look and said, "What do you know about me? You think I'm a little rich housewife who sat in your classroom and wrote down everything you said like it was the gospel truth or what?"

"No, I know that you're very intelligent, but I didn't realize that a lawyer's wife could be such an intellectual."

"See! That's what I mean! You don't really know anything about me. I never told you my husband was a lawyer."

"He's not?"

"No, he's a judge."

"A judge?" Ray didn't like that—a judge! He didn't mind sleeping with a lawyer's wife, but a judge's wife raised certain ethical questions for him.

Pamela laid her hand on his. "Is everything all right?"

"Oh, just fine," he said.

"You didn't mind my taking those pictures?"

"Of course not," he said, and patted the back of her hand with his.

"Well, in that case, I have a few more things in mind," she said, smiling. "Wait until we get back to the motel and I'll show you."

The film teacher did not have time to express his impatient curiosity, because at that moment the waiter brought them their dinner.

Some hours later, lying in his underwear on the bed in the motel room, Ray, conscious only of the sounds which Pamela was making in the bathroom, folded his hands behind his head. When they had come back from the restaurant, he had said to her (he was opening the bottle of wine with the corkscrew—both of which she had packed in a picnic basket), "So what's this big surprise?" For an answer, she had picked up an unidentified little bag she had brought with her from the car, and, winking at him through a nebulous smile, trotted off to the bathroom.

"You'll see," she had said; the bathroom door nearly cut off the sound of her voice, but the sexual intention was unmistakable: she was going to come out of the bathroom wearing something that was supposed to send his male fantasy shooting off its launching pad. Since her disappearance into the bathroom, their communication had been confined to the strange noises and sounds she made—running of water, the stretching of nylon, the setting of bottles on metallic surfaces. He tried to correlate meaningful images to these sounds and came up with a picture of Pamela, clad in black leather and black stockings and garter belt, as she would be if she stepped out of the pages of *Penthouse* magazine. His breathing quickened and he sipped from his glass of wine.

"Ray," she called from the depths of the bathroom, and he turned his head slightly toward the voice but said nothing.

"Ray, can you hear me?" Still he said nothing. Now a new sound— the sound of straps being fastened—dominated the auditory stage of his imagination. Turning his head toward the bathroom, he could hear what he imagined to be elastic stretching against female flesh, and he thought of a violinist tuning his instrument. ˙

"Ray, are you there—say something if you're there!" Actually he wished he wasn't there.

"I'm here," he hear a voice in him answer.

"Remember that class I took with you?" she went on. "I just wanted to share something with you. Think you might appreciate it."

He rolled over on the bed—he was sick of her talking about that class. All through dinner she had bored him with the subject and when he finally told her that he was only teaching until Hollywood called him, she still didn't take the hint. Finally, he had no choice but to tell her outright—he was a filmmaker, not a film teacher! Nobody had ever said he was destined to be a film teacher forever! Wasn't it obvious to everyone that he was a film teacher because he was a filmmaker? One cannot teach what one doesn't know!

"I used to have fantasies about you," he heard her say. "You know what I mean?"

The film teacher was disturbed at this mixing of his profession and eroticism. He was listening, also, to another new sound—the sound of sharp, pointed high heels against the tile of the bathroom floor.

"Yes," he said now, turning suddenly to the direction of the clicking sounds, "girls have fantasies about their teachers."

"But this was different. Remember that game you played with the class? To show how to make a plot? And you did this idiotic thing? You took out this pocket handkerchief, remember? I don't know if you remember or not, but you took out this pocket handkerchief and I had to blindfold you. Then you had somebody hand you a ball of paper. Then you asked three students to stand behind you and you threw the paper ball over your shoulder . . ."

She interrupted herself and refreshed her thoughts with quick laughter. Ray was not enjoying this! Thumping a cigarette from the pack, he raised up to light it, took a long drag on it, and blew out the smoke.

"So I thought, 'Hey, wouldn't it be fun to play a game on him,' meaning you! Yeah, are you still alive in there? Say something if you're alive!"

"Yeah, I'm here," he said, dragging again on the cigarette, and wishing again that he wasn't there. Shaking the ashes from the cigarette into the ashtray, he realized suddenly that he had a deranged woman on his hands. How was it that he never suspected this before?

"So if you will look on the nightstand beside the right side of the bed, you'll see a blindfold," she said, her voice had become as soft as a grade school teacher's: he shifted slightly on his elbow and saw a black blindfold on the base of the lamp on the nightstand.

"Put it over your eyes after you pick up the piece of white paper," she instructed in a melodious singsong voice. The purposely placed blindfold cast a spell over him as he picked it up and placed it over his eyes, clutching, as he did so, the piece of paper in the palm of his hand.

"Walk to the middle of the room, and throw the paper over your shoulder!" Now she hissed her instructions. Another person had taken complete control of his character! Had he allowed her to go too far with him?

"This is very funny," he reminded himself and her. Then he tried to laugh, but he could only get as far as a dry ha, ha, ha.

"Yes—hahaha!!" Pamela laughed, her laughter a parody of his own attempt. She sounded like a policeman, too. Surely, this was merely a game—people played games all the time.

He then pulled the blindfold off and turned around to face Pamela.

What he saw did not make him happy or sad; it just made him curious. Pamela was dressed in a long black gown that covered her body from head to toe, the type of dress worn by Pilgrims and young girls in boarding schools (as he imagined Pilgrims and girls in boarding schools). A big white bow was tied beneath her chin. Her upbraided hair gave her a shocking look of innocence and penitence.

"Well, how do you like it?" Pamela asked seriously. The film teacher was so shocked at not being shocked that he sat down on the bed and began to laugh.

"It's fantastic. I like it, but I thought . . ." He stopped himself because he felt ashamed of what he had thought.

She pulled a small tape recorder from her little bag and sat it on the table. "I just wanted to show you there are more surprises in life than in all the movies in the world." She pressed a button on the tape recorder and Miles Davis's "Backseat Betty" charged the air with musical electricity.

"Yes," the film teacher admitted like a defeated chump. "You really taught me a lesson. But what are you supposed to be? A little girl? A judge's wife?"

Pamela smoothed the black skirt standing in front of him. "Why, I'm a lady," she said, imitating a Southern accent like Blanche Dubois's. "It was easy to surprise you because I knew what you were expecting."

She began to dance around the room and laughed at him. Taking the end of her skirt, she lifted it slowly, "Isn't this what you expected?" and she lifted it high enough above her knees so that he saw the edge of the black stockings and garter belt.

"It's just a game," she said, mocking the serious look on his face.

Now like a pupil, the film teacher asked, "What should I do?"

And she, like the teacher, said, "Set the timer on the camera before coming to bed." He thought about it for a few seconds and then said, "Oh, yes, of course!"

Early in the afternoon the next day, they walked along the beach, picking their way carefully among the white bodies warming themselves in the still-spring sun. Their speechless walk took them away from the supine bodies and down to where the waves fizzled out on the ice-cold sand. They slipped their sandals off and carried them by the straps in their free hand; the foamy fingers of the waves pinched Ray coolly between the toes and a fresh-smelling breeze blew on his shirtless chest. Turning, he smiled at Pamela, and she smiled back.

They went on with their speechless walk. They came to a part of the beach where the rocks jutted out crudely over the sea, and it was impossible to go farther. In order to get around to the other side, they would have to swim. The previous night had left them without energy, so they couldn't swim. The speechless walk had come to an end—so now they had to talk. They both knew it. In order to avoid this moment as long as possible, he pulled her to him and kissed her passionately and pointlessly, but the kiss ended long before their lips parted.

"How did you like our games last night?" she asked, pulling a strand of hair from her face, and he saw her big, blue eyes, which, like the cloudless sky above them, seemed to look down on him.

"Oh, yes, really great," he said, and pulling her to him, covered his face with her hair as if he meant to hide from the sky. Pamela had shown him so many surprises that night that he felt ashamed of her ever having brought up their games. He realized that the idea of using theater games to demonstrate the spontaneous quality of modern film plots was mediocre when compared with the idea of using sexual games to demonstrate the limited imagination of film teachers.

"But there was something missing," he said. From the way she looked at him he saw she was surprised—this she had not expected.

"Missing? What?"

"Well, feelings, for one thing." He turned from her and looked out to the ocean. The ocean was blue and very much like an ocean should be.

He caught a seagull out of the corner of his eye and watched him as he made his meaningless trip somewhere. He heard Pamela slap her sandals together, but he kept watching the seagull.

"What do you mean by 'feelings'?" he heard her ask. It would surprise her if he told her he loved her and had loved her from the moment she had walked into his classroom. She always wanted to talk about that class, so now they would talk about the class. Yes, he would surprise her after all.

Without looking at her, he began walking back toward the motel, but when he felt her hand tug his elbow, he turned abruptly.

"Listen," he said, "I like you very much. I thought we could be in love with each other. I wanted to establish some contact with you last night, but you were too busy playing games. There is something which I apparently forgot to explain to your class. People play games because they can't feel anymore!"

She grabbed his arm again and her whole face pleaded with him. "Oh, Ray, I like you very much. You don't think I'd let you go just like that did you?"

He shook her hand away. "I don't know," he said. "I was just surprised at the way you acted."

"But I thought we were just having fun—a good time."

"I didn't mind the games," he told her, "but I was surprised that you left out those feelings." When he walked away from her, he felt good for two reasons: first, he felt good at the look of genuine astonishment on her face, and second, he felt good at how well he played the role. He heard her yell out his name, but he pretended that the wind took it out to the sea.

Back at the motel, he was already in the shower when he heard her come in. When he came out of the shower, she was sitting on the bed with her various bags beside her.

"I want to go home now," she said.

"Okay," he said, a bit surprised but pretending not to be, "let's go back."

Their drive back to San Francisco was as speechless as their walk along the beach had been, but luckily for them there were no impassable obstacles which forced them to speak. They simply departed with the merest pretense of civility.

A few days later, Ray went to the film department to see about his parking tickets. Encouraged by this performance with Pamela, he decided it was time to face reality. He decided to pay the tickets, also, because he didn't want to live any longer in a world of unknown fear. Besides, after his lecture on probability and plausibility in plots, he came outside to find another ticket on his windshield. He headed straight to the film department.

"We can't do anything about those tickets," Steven, the blond-haired secretary said, "but if you take them to the traffic court and tell them that you have a three-and-a-half-hour class and you park in a two-hour parking zone, they will give you a reduction." So he made a date for traffic court, and on that same day he received a letter from Pamela:

Dear Ray:

You judged me too harshly. Why can't you put fantasy and reality together? Why do you separate them? Now I see what a fool I was to do those things with you because you could not love a woman who loves to share her fantasies with you. If you can't share my fantasies, why do I need you as a lover?

Pamela

After folding the letter and placing it in the drawer on top of her telegram, Ray poured himself a glass of wine. What strange women these judges' wives were! He had been quite happy until he met her! He saw the encounter as a page in the book of his life, a short page, an incident with a reversal. But that was the end of it! How strange it was that a student who barely spoke up in class could be so full of desire for a dull teacher! But now that the incident was finished he didn't have to think of her anymore.

In fact, he had completely forgotten about Pamela when he walked into the traffic court. It wasn't until he was asked to stand in front of the judge that he had cause to even think of her again. For as he rose he saw that the man deciding on his case was a judge named Fleming. He felt a bit uneasy, immediately remembering that Pamela's last name was also Fleming.

"What is the problem with these parking tickets?" the judge asked.

Ray straightened himself and met the judge's stare with a smile. "I am a teacher at the university." Telling him that he was a teacher in the film department at the university might have rung a bell. And what if Pamela had shown him the photographs? In fact, Ray noticed that the judge was studying something in his hand, peeping down in his cupped hand like a schoolboy sneaking a look at a dirty picture or a gambler glaring greedily at a full house.

"Yes, go on," the judge said, glancing up at that moment.

"I have a class that runs for three-and-a-half hours, Your Honor, and the parking space is only for two hours. Sometimes the class discussions become so exciting that I rush to the parking space too late. This is why I have so many parking tickets."

"Mr. Sawyer," the judge said, after reading the film teacher up and down, "do you know my wife?" Ray's heart slowed down as if listening to his reply before deciding to go on.

"She spoke about you," the judge went on, smiling at the film teacher in such a way that the film teacher's heart had stopped beating and the word "jail, jail, jail!" throbbed spastically through his head. He wanted to turn to his class and exclaim, "This is an excellent example of reversals of fortune!" but all he managed to do was swallow dryly. For a man who took pride in explaining to young people that plausibility, necessity, and probability are the main ingredients in baking a pie of believable fiction, this particular situation was a bit of a shock. If he had been a made-up character in one of his student's screenplays, he would have assigned the student (and the fictional world) a fat F. No reader could believe that reality of the student and her husband (that judge!) and the film teacher was plausible, necessary, or even probable, and yet he knew that the danger of offending the judge was real. In other words, he saw his fate before him: while he would be languishing in jail trying to figure out how fate had assigned him a badly written screenplay for a life, photos of his nude body would be making the rounds in fashionable art galleries. It was a well-planned strategy, a game—the judge and the judge's wife were working together and he was their victim.

"No, sir," he said finally. "I have heard about your wife but I have actually never met her." It was such a stupid thing to say—luckily the judge was not listening.

"Funny, I think I remember her telling me how much she enjoyed a class she took with you. I'll tell you what I'm gonna do. I'm going to wipe these tickets off your record. Just try to find a longer parking space the next time. Next case."

The sudden reversal of fate was so quick that it left the film teacher dazzled. "Thank you, Your Honor," he whimpered and staggered out of the courtroom.

Once outside, his heart began to beat again. He felt good, but he decided that he would give up teaching film forever. Across the courthouse was a park where several hippies, left over from the sixties, were gathered. One of them wore only a brown blanket for clothing; his head was clean-shaven, and he was muttering something to somebody who wasn't present. When he saw Ray approaching, he smiled at him as if they belonged to the same plane of reality: the plane of reality where all men are brothers. I'll be like

St. Francis d'Assisi, the film teacher thought, and deny myself every luxury in life. I'll give up classic films and talk only to the birds. I'll beat myself with a stick, and at night I'll sleep in a hair shirt. But when he got to his car, he saw that somebody, as if meaning to tie him to his fate, had put a parking ticket on the windshield.

Oral

LEAH JEWEL REYNOLDS

spread them wide
welcome-mat inviting
length
lip me long-last
with tongue wet
and thighs
wrapped
around ear-shoulder
let me flesh
you
and i'll return
the favor

Ode to My Sweet Sexy Brown

CHIKÉ CARTER

A sensuous compassion hidden deep within the flesh;
Nature begins to rise as your warmth manifests.
Your being is a temple, where only sacred ones may go,
A prized Nubian goddess blessed with beauty, head to toe.
Dark flowing hair and mocha skin rejuvenates my thoughts,
State of mind mesmerized as so gracefully you walk.
Envision your eyes, dark brown morsels of your sexual chocolate bar,
Sparkling, shining, glittering, twinkling like the remnants of a star.
Who could tell, who'd have known that your intellect and grace,
Could reserve inside my heart of hearts, a special sacred place.
See, my want for you extends beyond a superficial plane,
Enraptured within a soulful ensemble divine with passion flames.
Ne'er a word, nor a phrase could describe your splendid ways;
Angelic Nubian confection embellished in a cocoa brown glaze.
Kiss your lips, sweet enchantment transforms attraction into desire,
Devastate your lusting premises, sweet explosions tame into fire.
Caress your skin, soft to touch, pleasure your spot as I lick you down,
Feel the tongue, feel the thrust, rhythmic movement all around.
Heavenly packages, seal it with a kiss, I gently love thee down,
GOD has blessed us with the presence of the lady, sexy brown.

Serious

JERRY W. WARD, JR.

it's as serious
as your life
when smoke gets in your eyes
and a sophisticated lady
lights a fire in your bone
and nothing will be as it was tomorrow

and nothing will be as it was tomorrow
as the magic of passion
lays arsenic and old lust upon your tongue
and the sharps and flats
or reality vanish in the dark
of the dark

as she shakes you
up and down
like a pair of dice
and all the liquids
turn from tepid water into steam
and she, so sure and so serene
ballets on the secret dream within your dream

and nothing will be ever
as it was today
with your toes feeling
like the roots of eternity
making love to the dust whence you came
and you are elevated
six stories down
with your emotions gone totally astray
in the fastbreak narrative of pillow talk

. . .

and you can no longer see
to find the beacon lights of home,
because it's as serious
as your life when a lady lays you out
among her petals and her thorns
and you be howling like a hurricane
with a volcano in your bone
and nothing will be nothing will be
as it was as it was as it was
tomorrow

let's be discreet

A M A N D A   T O W N S E N D

Tell me
that your eyes do not search for me
in a crowd
and I shall say to you
that my heart does not miss a beat
when I see you
and that nature's fertile flow
does not bathe
the most delicate
and intimate essence of my femininity
Tell me
that I have not felt
the pressure of your body against mine
and that I was not shocked
or excited
by the power of your masculinity
Tell me that you cannot cure the ache
which lingers between my thighs
and my body will deny that I desire you

soyons discrets
(French translation)

A M A N D A   T O W N S E N D

Dis-moi
que tes yeux ne me cherchent pas
dans une foule
et je te dirai
que mon coeur ne s'arrete pas de battre
quand je te vois
et que l'ecoulement fertil de la nature
ne baigne pas
l'essence la plus intime
et la plus delicate
de ma feminité
Dis-moi que
je n'ai pas senti
la pression de ton corps contre le mien
et que je n'etais pas choquée
ni excitée
par la force de ta masculinité
Dis-moi que tu ne peux pas querir
la douleur intime qui me ronge
et mon corps niera
que je te desire

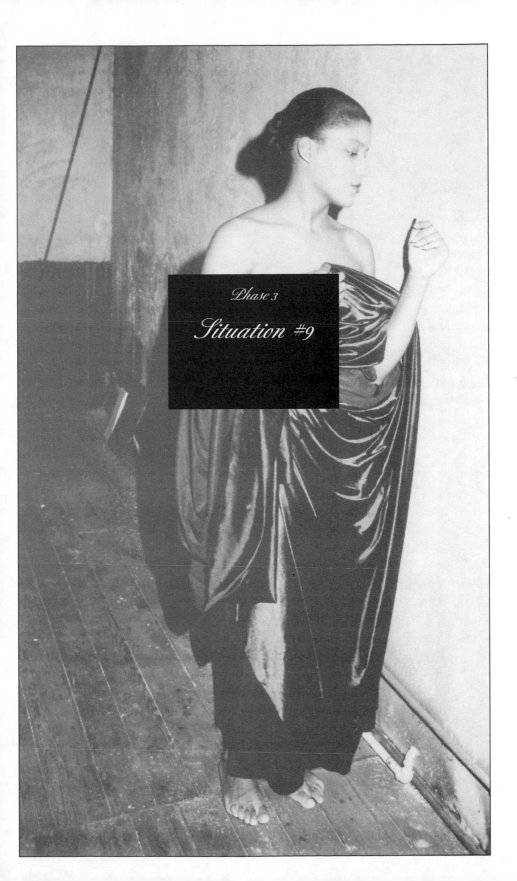

Phase 3

Situation #9

*T*hat time you saw him getting into the elevator in front of you, making no eye contact, and then sporting you a full rectal view that distracted you all day; her moving to her own rhythms on the dance floor and making the song much better than it ever was on CD; his reading of poetry that was supposed to show how smart he was but only confirmed how wet he made you each time you heard his voice; the all-too-familiar chiasmus at the traffic light where she nods only to the music—hair and earrings teasing you with their amaranthine rhythm—until the MOMENT the light turns green and she turns to you, sticks out her tongue—slowly—and speeds away: these are authoritative moments that defy the terrestrial sameness of our everyday sex, forcing us into new routines we thought before impossible and unthinkable.

Mawiyah Kai El-Jamah Bonami puts us with a "Woman on a Bus" and allows us to explore the sensual anger in a needy welfare mother's thoughts. "The Thing" by Leah Jewel Reynolds jokingly addresses the issues of physical charades and sexual shocks, as Faithful Senghor has an out-of-body experience in "My . . . (a street-corner sighting)." We are spoonfed a luscious plate of "Shrimp Étouffée" by Valinda Johnson Brown as Christopher Stanard is "Caught" in the cross-desires of someone's silk. The seminal essay of all of *Dark Eros* is expressed by Kalammu ya Salaam in his erotically groundbreaking essay "Do Right Women: Black Women, Eroticism, and Classic Blues," which shows that eroticism historically underlines all of African-American folk expression. Eating "Tuesday Supper" with Oktavi is not enough, so we get "A Bit More" from Tim Seibles. Nadir Lasana Bonami gives us wet reality in "a reenactment of a real love poem," and recalls the "Euphoria" of Shannon Cook. Lenard D. Moore blesses us with silent passion in his untitled haiku, while Gilda N. Squire gives a darker shade to "Passion in Paris." As Estelle Farley turns voyeuristic in "man," Danita Beck in "lotion" takes us to the ungendered other as smooth as the lotion applied to her narrative. Brother Yao turns back the sheets with "thinking 'bout you," and "soon, again" Kysha N. Brown will make us understand that shattering sex transfigures us beyond the human. Finally, Lesslie W. Clark burns up the fiber-optic lines in a midnight "answering machine" call to a wayward lover—and his wife.

Woman on a Bus

MAWIYAH KAI EL-JAMAH BONAMI

torn between my aid to dependent children/ and my children's
dependence on me/ all this talk about orphanages/ welfare reform/
and my mama constantly scolding me/ minding my business/
worrying about/ how roscoe/ always giving me a case of the blues/
when like the old saying goes/ the blues ain't nothing/ I ain't never
had/ at 30/ I sho done had my trial and error blues/ with roscoe/ but
I ain't near bout ready to let his butt go/ see what mama don't
understand/ is that it's all kool/ the pretty one's gon give you hell/
it's in their nature/ but when he's tucked/ in my bed/ in my crib/
taking care of my womanly needs/ he's mine/ for as long as he
choose/

and that's all/ that matters/ and that's nobody's business/ but mine/ so
what's all this talk/ about taking my kids/ my check/ about my cut
my check/ roscoe gon go/ I know he is/ he gon leave/ then what
ima do/ with all these mouths to feed/ what the hell am I suppose to
do then/ maybe orphanages ain't so bad/ I mean/ they'll be getting
three meals a day/ clothes on their back/ I don't know maybe it's
what they need/

either way/ I lose/ take my check/ roscoe gon/ take my kids/ and
i'm still living in this hell hole alone/ feel like/ i'm getting the blues
again/ i'm getting the Saturday night blues/ wish it was last night/ the
way he held me tight/ u woulda thought he was in love/ and that's
funny/ cause most times/ when he here/ he ain't here/ and when he
gone/ it like u never even notice/ he was even in the same place/ as
u/

.   .   .

what I need/ is an easy way out/ out of the ghetto/ out from under roscoe's hold/ I know/ I need to be a better mama/ I need/ they need/ but see/ nobody gives a damn/ that i'm still young/ that roscoe/ does something/ to my body/ I just can't explain yet/

yeah/ there are times/ when I fix my mouth/ to tell him go/ but then I turn right around/ and make the foolish mistake/ of letting him caress my insides/ with his manhood/ got me talking in tongues/ when I never thought/ I could/ lapping at my thighs/ and all areas in between/ it's like he the only person/ who understands/ even single mothers on welfare got needs/

The Thing

LEAH JEWEL REYNOLDS

his man's essence captured my entire soul each time I saw him, as he gently sashayed past my office. This was an everyday occurrence since we worked in the same building down on Market Street in St. Louis. I mean, he literally made my panties wet with want at the very sight of him. It was my sincere desire to play it cool throughout the duration of the date. Since I had been meltingly eyeballing him while politely turning down his date proposals mainly because of Kelvin (but also to create a ladylike contrast of hard-to-get) for the past two months, I couldn't let on that I was actually quite intrigued by his most interesting conversation and totally flabbergasted by his body. This man was indeed a ten—plus two.

Although I've been considered by many to be an attractive and unique individual, the last brother I dated was quite a slob. No, let me be honest. Kelvin was and still is very clean-cut and handsome in the face, not to mention his kind disposition and demeanor. For months, I tried ceaselessly to be the righteous one and love him for his inner-being and the great times we had together, which were few and far between due to the thing, or the lack thereof. One night in particular, we spent a nice, quiet evening at Nantucket Cove, at a comfortable restaurant in the Central West End. Well, as we sat in the back of the place, in a romantic and secluded booth, we shared some of the most emotionally uninhibited and sensuously spiritual conversations that I had shared with a man in quite awhile. My girlfriends and I bare our souls to one another, sparing no emotion or life experience on a day-to-day basis. This being one of the things I cherish most in my relationships, I found myself to be truly aroused by him. At this point, I found myself becoming a bit spiflicated. In fact, I was quite tipsy and seeing double. Four lips, where there used to be only two. Four sensuous eyes, where I could have sworn there were just two a second ago. Four big, strong arms, and I know there were only two of them wrapped around me last night as we hugged good-bye.

All of a sudden, this thing came over me. Not *the* thing. I'll tell you about that later. This blackout sort of. Now I know I only had one glass of champagne, which is a lot for me, but I was starting to feel some kind of strange. Anyway, we went on to talk about the promotion that I'm up for. I found it to be simply marvelous the way Kelvin was always just as excited about the good things in my life as I was. For so long, I had searched for this man and asked the Creator to send him my way. Now, I had finally become involved with a man who was both supportive and not afraid to admit his humanity and emotion. This brother was actually questioning why I didn't share my deepest feelings and thoughts with him. It's not that I'm afraid of presumed vulnerability in the eyes of man, but I've never been quick to feel for anyone, one way or another. He'd often ask, "Sankofa, why don't you ever tell me how you feel about me?"

Well, honestly, I would think, *I've only been acquainted with you for two months and frankly, I don't know you. Therefore I don't even know whether I'm going to like you next week or not.* I never told him that, of course. That's nothing for a woman to tell a man. Well, at least that's what the old folks told us, right? Truly, in no way, shape, or form do I subscribe to that worn-out theory. The truth is, I was in no hurry to say something based purely on a sexual feeling, especially since it could very well turn out to be nothing but an insensitive lead-on. You know what I mean? Anyway, after dinner, Kelvin invited me to his condo for cappuccino and more stimulating talk. So, I obliged and it indeed proved to be stimulating. After being at his place for only moments, Kelvin swiftly grabbed me by the arm, spun me around, and sensuously silent-whispered, "Girl, just let me lay my eyes on you one time right quick." I was so thrown off by this. Kelvin had never been this forward with me in all of the time we had known each other. But I liked it. In an attempt to shield my surprise from his examining gaze, which was beckoning me to come (to come just a little closer), I thwarted, "Now, what did I say about all that girl jazz?" gently reminding him that that term was disrespectful when used in reference to a woman. Without ruining the mood, the vibe upon which we were riding, I was proud of myself for being able to think so quickly and hide my amazement at his candor and intensity, which I was enjoying so much for the first time. Yes, sister, thoughts of wild were running rampant through my mind and although I had not anticipated giving in to them on that night, I was fully prepared to surrender to his every whim. Those big, strong arms had surrounded me, engulfed my entire being, it seemed, as it suckled my spirit. Honey, I was there already—at that place where your toes begin to curl at the slightest touch. We drank of each other's eyes, imagining things of which only the Creator knows. We spoke no words. Once again, my mind's moment raced in thought, taking me back. Way back to the place from which I come.

And I heard it. And I smelled it. And I tasted it. And there it lay, right in front of me, all the while. Kelvin's tongue sensuously silent searched the inside walls of my right ear for comfort—unctuously wet. After what felt like an eternity, I decided that he had found solitude and solace in that place. The same place through which I experienced a wailing "Mercy, Mercy, Me" and a resounding "If It Ain't Good Enough (for You Baby)." That very same place. Still trying to hold back, I found myself so excited by then that I couldn't help myself. Removing his jacket, brother's arms looked and felt so muscular to my soft palms. Kelvin then asked, "Can I show you something?" Of course my response was an intentional, seductive, "Yes, please do." Brother-man whispered, "All you have to do is close those beautiful tiger eyes of yours and lie down on my bed." I'm thinking, "Here we go! Here we go! Here we gooooo! Let's git it started, M.C. Hammer style!" Do you know I opened my eyes only to find the lights dimmed and brother gone. Yes, Homey had gone into the other room for whatever reason. By the time I really had a chance to ponder what he could possibly have planned, he'd returned. "Ah, you cheated. Close your eyes, sweetie." You know me. I'm going to check things out before I sweat, so I caught a glimpse of a glass filled with something. I couldn't quite catch it, but on it was written, "Use sparingly." My curiosity had undoubtedly been piqued. Kelvin gently chanted, "Now, just relax. Let your mind run free. Think only about what we're doing right now. Nothing else. Not the promotion, grad school . . . nothing. Otherwise, it won't work. I'm going to liberate you." I'm sure the champagne had something to do with it, but I was in another world altogether. This man was so nurturing and spiritual. So complete. I thought I was a Conjure Woman like Big Mama, but I knew at that moment—I didn't have a thing on this Witch Doctor. Kelvin whispered in intervals, as he caressed my lips with his, "Now, keep your eyes closed. Don't be startled. I'm going to pour warm honey all over you and if you let me, I'll lick it off."

Whoot! There it is! I thought.

And so he began to peel my clothes off as he licked and sucked, making love to me with his tongue. Great conversation! This man was truly a tease! The thrill of my body becoming more and more unctuously wet as he descended with his steady rhythmic cadence and song of licking, and then removing, tasting, and then removing, sucking, and then removing was almost unbearable. I grabbed hold of his almond-colored earlobe, cuffed his head with my right hand, and guided this majestic wall-shadow back up to remember my other set of lips that his had gently caressed earlier. As they grew closer, I allowed my palms to travel up his shirt, as I unbuttoned,

I licked and pulled, and, Oh shit! There it was! The thing. Those things! Staring at me! Cupped in my hands were what felt like thirty-six double D's. What appeared to be muscles for two months underneath those gorgeous Armani double-breasted suits were just that—double breasts! The man had breasts as big as mine. I went on and tried to forget and work with this, but it didn't work. It just wouldn't work. I passed it off as stress. "I'm sorry. I'm just not in the mood anymore." He went back down, trying to arouse me and get me back on go. This time, it felt like terror. I thought it would never end!

For two weeks, I tried to overcome the thing and like him for his most important positive traits (who he was on the inside). I now realize that I need physical, emotional, and spiritual satisfaction. There's just no way around that for me.

The fact that the brother was just a little on the heavy side didn't bother me at all, but Witch Doctor had to be on some sort of hormone pills to grow those things.

Well, anyway, I was telling you about my date last night with Miguel, the guy from my office. We decided that he would cook dinner for me at his place, since we'd been going out to dinner just about every night since we started seeing each other. When I arrived at about eight, he had the incense burning, Luther in the CD player, and he was ready to take me on home. Greeting me at the door with a long, slow, wet kiss (just the way I like them), Miguel was adorned in a beautiful lounging robe that was open, everything within sight. My instincts led me to step back and take a look, only to find bliss—no breasts. Miguel didn't quite understand when I exclaimed, "Thank you. And for this, the Congo is yours!"

My . . .
(a street-corner sighting)

FAITHFUL SENGHOR

my feet   stompin'
  my knees   knockin'
my legs   kickin'
  my hips   thrustin'
my behind   shakin'
  my arms   flappin'
my palms   sweatin'
  my fingers   tappin'
my knuckles   crackin'
    my back   bendin'
my stomach   achin'
      my chest   heavin'
my neck   stretchin'
        my voice   tremblin'
my mouth   droolin'
      my tongue   hangin'
my teeth   chatterin'
        my nose   drippin'
my nostrils   flarin'
      my eyes   burnin'
my ears   ringin'
      my head   noddin'
my hair   growin'
        my scalp   itchin'
my brain   swellin'
        my mind   blowin'
my soul   searchin'
        my muscles   tensin'
my skin   peelin'
        my heart   pumpin'
my adrenaline   rushin'

my clothes   tearin'

my car   crashin'

My GOD   She Was   Fine!

Shrimp Étouffée

VALINDA JOHNSON BROWN

My shrimp étouffée creates reckless love affairs. As its definition implies, étouffée literally "smothers" you with a passion that drives your soul like a tidal wave and whips and twirls your culinary senses, causing chaos in its path. That's why I jumped over the table. I was out of control when I wrapped my body around his chest. I admit it. But after eating the shrimp étouffée, I had to seduce somebody.

The luscious, wonderfully handsome mahogany roux of fiery oil and flour stirred to a perfectly smooth texture was the malefactor. Its fluid essence had no beginning, no end, just eternal lustful pleasure. This authentic beauty was full with nature's true stimulant, cocky, red-hot cayenne peppers that would make the world surrender. Its seasonal partners in crime, devoted black and white pepper, royal green basil leaves, wild minty thyme, and of course, king salt perpetuated my somewhat forward behavior.

He, on the other hand, was baffled, bewildered, and confused. His bowl was full, you see. He had not yet had the chance to taste that which was before him. But how could he, now that I have locked my legs around his arms, will he ever have the chance to savor, but more important, respond to this spirited manipulator of lust? For I do want an agreeable partner. So, as not to run him away, I apologetically gathered my senses, unglued myself from his chest, slid down, climbed off the table, unruffled my dress, pulled my chair closer to him and sat down.

I turned to his plate. The prima donna shrimps were strutting their pink butts in the deep brown roux. I looked upon them as the provocateurs. While the moist pearl rises in the center of the dark tanned étouffée I surreptitiously winked at them to acknowledge their performance as the inseparable two mate again to exchange juices of affection. I humbly eased his plate to him and motioned him to taste this wondrous dish. He looked at me and saw that I was calm and with some sense, then he looked down into the shrimp étouffée. With abrupt but constant glances at me, he reluctantly reached for his fork and pulled his plate close. I held my breath and closed my eyes so as not to cause interference. I sensed his watchful glances. I lowered my head and peeked at his plate. His fork was still sitting in the étouffée. I thought—get involved! Looking at him with an inviting but innocent smile I licked my lips and threw him a kiss. He caught it. Slowly stirring the snow white rice into the autumn brown roux and baby plump shrimps, he gathered up a heaping forkful. Without forsaking a drop, he eased this titillating dish into his mouth and began to consume the entrée.

I was ecstatic. I rushed to catch up with him and devoured a couple of spoonfuls. Then, it happened. The roux began to coat us like the coming of love. We quivered from the étouffée's intense flame of passion now found deep within us. But we knew that it only had moments to live. For if it could not escape, it would ignite our souls. I grabbed him. With a big, wet, long, twisting kiss, I exploded in his mouth. In miniseconds, he picked me up with his left arm and cleared the table with his right. There, in my kitchen, the white lace cotton tablecloth was creating new design in motion from a unique angle swaying from under my naked buttocks onto the floor as we raced to catch the flash of eroticism.

Caught

CHRISTOPHER STANARD

In the spider's web
unable to move
you notice only
how smooth
how soft
the silk.

Tuesday Supper

OKTAVI

I invited
A bald-headed man home
To cook my supper
Had a
Ground ginger noggin
Clean as a chit'lin
On New Year's Day
Served up soul food
Melted surrender
Stuck in my throat
Thank goodness for
Drop-leaf tables
Cause I was slipp'n
Over the edge
Soft as buttered cornbread
Everything on the table
Pressure-cooker hot
Neck bones strained
Over their plate at
Black-eyed peas and ham hocks
Steaming up Pyrex dishes
Collard greens, yams
Sweated protest
Left to wonder
If anybody
Was ever gonna
Sit down for
Tuesday supper

Do Right Women:
Black Women, Eroticism, and Classic Blues
KALAMMU YA SALAAM

1

> *I'm going to show you women, honey,*
> *how to cock it on the wall.*
> *Now you can snatch it, you can break it, you can*
> *hang it on the wall.*
> *Throw it out the window, see if you*
> *can catch it 'fore it fall.*
>
> **—Louise Johnson**

"I fantasize about spanking you. What sexual fantasies do you have?" an ex-lover intoned into the phone receiver.

As she spoke I remembered a time when we were in one of those classical numeral positions and at a peak moment I felt the sharp smack of her bare palm on my bare butt—not in pain nor anger, but surprisingly for me, I remember a tingle of pleasure, the pleasure in knowing that I had been the catalyst for her, a person of supreme sexual control, going over the edge.

After I hung up, I admitted to myself that like many males my main fantasy was to be sexually attractive to and sexually satisfying for thousands of women. I "fantasize" sexually engaging at least a quarter of the women I see, 90 percent of whom I don't know beyond eyeing them for a moment as I drive down some street, spot them in a store, in an office building, in line paying a bill, or walking ahead of me out of a movie.

I remember in one of my writing workshops in the fall of 1995 I shocked a room of young men by declaring that sexual expression among male homosexuals represented the fullest flowering of male sexuality. Some reacted predictably from a position of virulent homophobia and others were just genuinely skeptical.

I explained that if he could, assuming that there were no restraints and that it was consensual sex between adults, the average American male would engage in promiscuous sex every time he felt aroused—which undoubtedly would be often. A major brake on our promiscuousness is the unwillingness of women to cooperate with male socio-biological urges.

I asked one of the more skeptical homophobes in my workshop, "Haven't you seen a woman today you wished that you could get down with, a woman whom you didn't know personally?" He smiled and answered, "Yeah, on my way to class just now." After the laughter died down, I told him that this is indeed what often happens with gay sex precisely because there is no restraint other than desire and safety.

American male sexuality is, among other characteristics, a celebration of the moment. Our fantasy is immediate sexual gratification with whomever catches our fancy. Most of the time we deny, transfer, repress, or misrepresent these fantasies. However, in popular music we forcefully articulate the male desire to wantonly enjoy coition with women. Thus, these nineties rap and r&b ("rhythm and booty") records about rampant sex with a bevy of willing cuties is not just adolescent, post-puberty fantasizing, but rather is an accurate projection of ethically unchecked and socially unshaped male sexuality—a sexuality which projects the male as the dominating, aggressive subject and the female as the pliant (if not willing) object of consumption.

Here is a significant cultural crossroads. I hold no truck in prudish and/or puritanical views of sex; while I abhor pornography (the commidifying of sex and the reifying of a person or gender into a sexual object), I am opposed to censorship. The status quo would have the whole debate about the representation of sexuality boil down to either reticence or profligacy. The truth is those extremes are not different roads. They are simply the up and down sides of the status quo view which either come from or lead to the objectifying of sexual relations. Objectifying sexual relations is a completely different road from the frank articulation of eroticism.

Within the American cultural context, this difference is nowhere as clearly presented as in the early 1920s woman-centered music known as "classic blues."

2

> You never get nothing by being an angel child,
> You better change your ways and get real wild,
> I want to tell you something and I wouldn't tell you no lie,
> Wild women are the only kind that really get by,
> 'Cause wild women don't worry, wild women don't have the blues.
>
> —Ida Cox

Known today as "classic blues" divas, these women married big-city dreams with post-plantation realties and, by using the vernacular and folk-wisdom of the people, gave voice to our people's hopes and sorrows and specifically spoke to the yearnings and aspirations of black women recently migrated to the city from the country. While many women took up domestic and factory work, the entertainment industry also was a major employer of black women. In *Black Pearls*, author Daphne Duval Harrison sets the stage:

> Young black women with talent began to emerge from the churches, schools, and clubs where they had sung, recited, danced, or played, and ventured into the more lucrative aspects of the entertainment world, in response to the growing demand for talent in the theaters and traveling shows. The financial rewards often outweighed community censure, for by 1910–1911 they could usually earn upwards of fifty dollars a week, while their domestic counterparts earned only eight to ten dollars. Many aspiring young women went to the cities as domestics in hope of ultimately getting on stage. While the domestics' social contacts were severely limited, mainly to the white employers and to their own families, the stage performer had an admiring audience in addition to family and friends. (Harrison, page 21)

The classic blues divas who emerged from this social milieu were more than entertainers, they were role models, advice givers, and a social force for cultural transformation. Ma Rainey is considered the mother of the classic blues. "She jes' catch hold of us, somekinaway," scripts poet Sterling Brown in giving a right-on-the-money description of the cathartic power of Ma Rainey's majestic embrace which wrapped up her audience and reared them into the discovery of self-actualization's rarefied air. "Git way inside us,/ Keep us strong" (Brown, pages 62–63). Birthed by these women, we became ourselves as a people and as sexually active individuals.

Twenties classic blues was the first and only time that independent African-American women were at the creative center of black musical culture. Neither before nor since have women been as economically or psychologically "liberated."

In a country dominated by patriarchal values, mores, and male leadership (should we more accurately say "overseership"?), classic blues is remarkable. Remember that although slavery ended with the Civil War in 1866 and the passage of the 15th Amendment to the Constitution, suffrage for women was not enacted until 1920 with the 19th Amendment. The suffrage movement, which had been dominated by white women, was also intimately aligned with the temperance movement, a movement which demonized jazz and blues.

Black women were a major organizing and stabilizing force in and on behalf of the black community between post-reconstruction and the twenties. Historian Darlene Clark Hine notes:

> The second period began in the 1890s and ended around 1930 and is best referred to as the First Era of the Black Woman . . . black women were among the most active and determined agents for community building and race survival. Their style was concentrated on internal developments within the black community and is reflected in the massive mobilization that led to the formation of the National Association of Colored Women's Clubs that boasted a membership of over 50,000 by 1914. . . . Black women perfected a "politics of respectability," a "culture of dissemblance," and a cult of secrecy and silence. (Hine, pages 118–119)

But a curious dynamic has always animated black America—while those who hoped to assimilate, to be accepted and/or to achieve "wealth and happiness" strove for and advocated a "politics of respectability" the folk masses sang a blues song à la Langston Hughes's mule who was black and didn't give a damn, if you wanted him, you had to take him just as he am. In other words, the blues aesthetic upsets the respectability applecart. And at the core of the blues aesthetic is a celebration of the erotic.

I contend that this is a major cultural battle. Eroticism is the motor that drives black culture (or, more precisely, drives those aspects of our culture which are not assimilative in representation). Whereas polite society was too nice to be nasty, blues people felt if it wasn't nasty, then how could it be nice.

As James H. Cone notes in his perceptive and important book *The Spirituals and the Blues*:

> It has been the vivid description of sex that caused many church people to reject the blues as vulgar or dirty. The Christian tradition has always been ambiguous about sexual intercourse, holding it to be divinely ordained yet the paradigm of rebellious passion. Perhaps this accounts for the absence of sex in the black spirituals and other black church music. . . . In the blues there is an open acceptance of sexual love, and it is described in most vivid terms. . . . (Cone, page 117)

Many of us are totally confused about eroticism. Most of us don't appreciate the frank eroticism of nearly all African-heritage cultures which have not been twisted by outside domination (e.g., Christianity and Islam). Commenting on "Songs of Ritual License from Midwestern Nigeria," African art historian Jean Borgatti notes:

> The songs themselves represent an occasion of ritualized verbal license in which men and women ridicule each other's genitalia and sexual habits. Normally such ridicule would be an antisocial act in the extreme. . . . In the ritual context, however, the songs provide recognition, acceptance, and release of that tension which exists between the sexes in all cultures, and so neutralize this potential threat to community stability. (Borgatti, page 60)

The songs in question range from explicit and detailed put-downs to this lyric sung by a woman, which could be a twenties blues lyric.

When I Refuse Him
When I refuse him, the man is filled with sorrow
When I refuse him, the man is filled with sorrow
When my "thing" is bright and happy like a baby chick, it drives him wild
When my "thing" is bright and happy like a baby chick, it drives him wild

My argument is that socially expressed eroticism is part and parcel of our heritage. In the American context, this eroticism is totally absent in the "lyrics" of the spirituals (albeit not totally suppressed in the rituals of black church liturgy). On the other hand, black eroticism is best expressed and preserved in the blues (beginning in the early 1920s) and in its modern musical offshoots.

Erotic representation is another major point of divergence. Eurocentric representations of eroticism have been predominantly visual and textual whereas African-heritage representations have been mainly aural (music) and oral (boasts, toasts, dozens, etc.). The eye sees but does not feel. Mainly the brain responds to and interprets visual stimuli whereas the body as a whole responds to sound. Moreover, textual erotic representation invites and encourages private and individual activity. For example, you are probably alone reading this—if not alone in fact certainly alone in effect as there may be others present where you are reading but they are not reading over your shoulder or sitting beside you reading with you. Moreover, you most certainly are not reading this aloud for general consumption. If you do read it aloud it is probably a one-to-one private act.

Aural and oral erotic representations, on the other hand, require a participating audience, become a ritual of arousal. Music, in particular, is not only social in focus, it also privileges communal eroticism. Thus, whereas text encourages individualism and self-evaluations of deviance, shame, and guilt, musical eroticism encourages coupling, group identification, and self-evaluations of shared erotic values, sexual self-worth, and pleasure.

Finally, within the African-American context, sound is used as language to communicate what English words cannot. The African-American folk saying, "When you moan the devil don't know what you talking about" contains an ironic edge that goes beyond spiritual commentaries on good and evil. The white oppressor/slave master, i.e., "the devil," does not understand the meaning of moaning partly because of intentional deception on the part of the moaners but also because the English lexicon is limited. Moans, wails, cries, hums, and other vocal devices communicate feelings, moods, desires and are the core of blues expression. This is why the blues is more powerful than the lyrics of the songs, why blues lyrics do not translate well to the cold page (when the sound of the words is not manifested much of the true meaning of the words is lost), and why blues cannot be accurately analyzed purely from an intellectual standpoint. Moreover, erotic desires, frustrations, and fulfillments—the most frequent emotions articulated in the blues—are some of the strongest emotions routinely manifested by human beings.

In the 1920s, mainstream America was nowhere near ready to acknowledge and celebrate eroticism. Thus, as far as most Americans were concerned, a frank and explicit expression of eroticism was shameful. This social "shame" became the singular trademark of the blues.

Within the context of American Puritanism and Christian anti-eroticism, it is important to note that "blue" erotic music was first brought to national prominence not by men but rather by women. This privileging of feminine sexuality was an unplanned result of the newly developed recording industry's quest for profits. When "Okeh Records sold seventy-five thousand copies of 'Crazy Blues' in the first month and surpassed the one million mark during its first year in the stores" (Barlow, page 128) the hunt was on. Recording and selling "race records" (i.e., blues) was like a second California gold rush. There was no aesthetic or philosophical interest in the blues. This was strictly business. Moreover, during the first years of the race record craze, because race records were sold almost exclusively to a black audience, there was less censorship and interference than there otherwise might have been. Black tastes and cultural values drove the market during the twenties. There were both positive and negative results to this commercialization.

On the positive side of the ledger, the mechanical reproduction of millions of blues disks made the music far more accessible to the public in general, and black people in particular. Blues entered an era of unprecedented growth and vitality, surfacing as a national phenomenon by the 1920s. As a result, a new generation of African-American musicians were able to learn from the commercial recordings, to expand their mastery over the various idioms, and enhance their instrumental and vocal techniques. The local and regional African-American folk traditions that spawned blues were, in turn, infused with new songs, rhythms, and styles. Thus, the record business was an important catalyst in the development of blues that also facilitated their entrance into the mainstream of popular American music.

On the other hand, the transformation of living musical traditions into commodities to be sold in a capitalist marketplace was bound to have its drawbacks. For one thing, the profits garnered from the sale of blues records invariably went into the coffers of the white businessmen who owned or managed the record companies. The black musicians and vocalists who created the music in the recording studios received a pittance. Furthermore, the major record companies went to great lengths to get the blues to conform to their Tin Pan Alley standards, and they often expected black recording artists to conform to racist stereotypes inherited from blackface minstrelsy. The industry also liked to record white performers' "cover" versions of popular blues to entice the white public to buy the records and to "upgrade" the music. Upgrading was synonymous with commercializing; it attempted to bring African-American music more in line with European musical conventions, while superimposing on it a veneer of middle-class Anglo-American respectability. These various practices deprived a significant percentage of recorded blues numbers of their African characteristics and more radical content. (Barlow, pages 123–124)

When the Depression hit and black audiences no longer had significant disposable income to spend on recordings, the acceptable styles of recorded blues changed drastically.

The onset of the Depression quickly reversed the fortunes of the entire record industry; sales fell from over $100 million in 1927 to $6 million in 1933. Consequently, race record releases were drastically cut back, field recording ventures into the South were discontinued, the labels manufactured fewer and fewer copies of each title, and record prices fell from seventy-five to thirty-five cents a disk. Whereas the average race record on the market sold approximately ten thousand copies in the mid-twenties, it plummeted to two thousand in 1930, and bottomed out at a dismal four hundred in 1932. The smaller labels were gradually forced out of business, while the major record companies with large catalogs that went into debt were purchased by more prosperous media corporations based in radio and film. The record companies with race catalogs that totally succumbed to the economic downturn were Paramount, Okeh, and Gennett. By 1933, the race record industry appeared to be a fatality of the Depression. (Barlow, page 133)

The classic blues divas founded and shaped the form of black music's initial recording success in the twenties. By the thirties women were completely erased as cultural leaders of black music. While there was certainly an overriding economic imperative to the cutback, there was also a cultural/philosophical imperative to cut out women altogether.

There was no precedent in either white or black American culture for women as leaders in articulating eroticism. This significant feminizing of eroticism was predicated on an unprecedented albeit shortlived change in the physical and economic social structure of the black community converging with a period of massive national economic growth and far-reaching mass media technological innovations in recordings, radio, and film.

Despite optimal economic and technological incentives, the twenties rise of the newly emergent classic blues diva was no cakewalk, not only because of the virulence of class exploitation, racism, and sexism, but also because of cultural antagonisms. Regardless of race, there was an open conflict between the blues and social respectability. The self-assertive female classic blues singer was perceived as a threat to both the American status quo as well as to many of the major political forces seeking to enlarge the status quo (i.e., the petty bourgeoisie-oriented talented tenth).

Moreover, unlike many post-Motown, popular female singers who are produced, directed, and packaged by males, Ma Rainey, Ethel Waters, Ida Cox, Alberta Hunter, Sippie Wallace, and the incomparable "Empress" of the blues, Bessie Smith, were more than simple fronts for turn-of-the-century blues Svengalis. Yes, men such as Perry Bradford, Clarence Williams, and Thomas Dorsey were major composers, arrangers, accompanists, and producers for many of the classic blues divas; and yes, these women often were surrounded and beset by men who attempted to physically, financially, and psychologically abuse them, Nevertheless, the classic blues divas were neither pushovers nor tearful passive victims.

Emerging from southern backgrounds rich in religious and folk music traditions, they were able to capture in song the sensibilities of black women—North and South—who struggled daily for physical, psychological, and spiritual balance. They did this by calling forth the demons that plagued women and exorcising them in public. Alienation, sex and sexuality, tortured love, loneliness, hard times, marginality were addressed with an openness that had not previously existed.

The blues women accomplished this with their unique flair for dramatizing their texts and performances. They introduced and refined vocal strategies that gave the lyrics added power. Some of these were instrumentality, voices growling and sliding like trombones, or wailing and piercing like clarinets; unexpected word stress; vocal breaks in antiphony with the accompaniment; syncopated phrasing; unlimited improvisation on repetitious refrains or phrases. These innovations, in tandem with the talented instrumentalists who accompanied the blues women, advanced the development of vocal and instrumental jazz.

Of equal significance, because they were such prominent public figures, the blues women presented alternative models of attitude and behavior for black women during the 1920s. They demonstrated that black women could be financially independent, outspoken, and physically attractive. They dressed to emphasize their symbolic importance to their audiences. The queens, regal in their satins, laces, sequins and beads, and feather boas trailing from their bronze or peaches-and-cream shoulders, wore tiaras that sparkled in the lights. The queens held court in dusty little tents, in plush city cabarets, in crowded theaters, in dance halls, and wherever else their loyal subjects would flock to pay homage. They rode in fine limousines, in special railroad cars, and in whatever was available, to carry them from country to town to city and back, singing as they went. The queens filled the hearts and souls of their subjects with joy and laughter and renewed their spirits with the love and hope that came from a deep well of faith and will to endure. (Harrison, pages 221–222)

Never since have women performed major leadership roles in the music industry, especially not African-American women. The entertainment industry intentionally curtailed the trend of highly vocal, independent women. Most of the classic blues divas, it must be noted, were not svelte sex symbols comparable in either features or figure to white women. The blues shouter was generally a robust, brown- or dark-skinned, African-featured women who thought of and carried herself as the equal of any man. America fears the drum and psychologically fears the bearer of the first drum, i.e., the feminine heartbeat that we hear in the womb.

Bessie Smith and her peers were sexually assertive "wild" women, well endowed with the necessary physical and psychological prowess to take care of themselves. Actively bisexual, Bessie Smith belied the common "asexual" labeling of stout women, such as is suggested by Nikki Giovanni in "Woman Poem":

> it's a sex object if you're pretty
> and no love
> or love and no sex if you're fat

"No sex" was not the reality of the classic blues divas. Yes, many of them were then, and would now be, considered "fat," but they were far from celibate (by either choice or circumstance). Or, as the sarcastic blues lyric notes:

> I'm a big fat mama, got meat shakin' on my bones
> A big fat mama, with plenty meat shakin' on my bones
> Every time I shake my stuff, some skinny gal loses her home

In recent years the best description of the liberating function blues divas served for the black community is contained in Alice Walker's powerful novel, *The Color Purple*. Walker's memorable and mythic character Shug Avery is an active bisexual blues singer à la Bessie Smith. Shug instructs the heroine Celie in the recognition and celebration of herself as a sexual being:

Why Miss Celie, [Shug] say, you still a virgin.
What? I ast.
Listen, she say, right down there in your pussy is a little button that gits real hot when you do you know what with somebody. It git hotter and hotter and then it melt. That the good part. But other parts good too, she say. Lot of sucking go on, here and there, she say. Lot of finger and tongue work. (Walker, page 81)

.   .   .

Shug then instructs Celie, "Here, take this mirror and go look at yourself down there, I bet you never seen it, have you?" The blues becomes a means not only of social self-expression, but also of sexual self-discovery, especially for women.

In a life often defined by brutality, exploitation, and drudgery, the female discovery and celebration of self-determined sexual pleasure is important. Thus the blues affirms an essential and explicit reversal. We have been taught that we are ugly, the blues celebrates our beauty and this is especially true for black women.

> I lie back on the bed and haul up my dress. Yank down my bloomers. Stick the looking glass 'tween my legs. Ugh. All that hair. Then my pussy lips be black. Then inside look like a wet rose.
> It a lot prettier than you thought, ain't it, she say from the door.
> It mine, I say. Where the button?
> Right up near the top, she say. The part that stick out a little.
> I look at her and touch it with my finger. A little shiver go through me. Nothing much. But just enough to tell me this the right button to mash. (Walker, page 82)

The major characteristic of the classic blues is that the vast majority of the songs were sexually oriented and nearly all of the singers were women. In his major study of black music, LeRoi Jones (Amiri Baraka) notes:

> The great classic blues singers were women . . . Howard W. Odum and Guy B. Johnson note from a list of predominately classic blues titles, taken from the record catalogs of three "race" companies. "The majority of these formal blues are sung from the point of view of women . . . upwards of seventy-five percent of the songs are written from the woman's point of view. Among the blues singers who have gained a more or less national recognition there is scarcely a man's name to be found." (Jones, page 91)

Jones goes on to answer the obvious question of why women dominated this area:

> Minstrelsy and vaudeville not only provided employment for a great many women blues singers but helped to develop the concept of the professional Negro female entertainer. Also, the reverence in which most of white society was held by Negroes gave to those Negro entertainers an enormous amount of prestige. Their success was also boosted at the

beginning of this century by the emergence of many white women as entertainers and in the twenties, by the great swell of distaff protest regarding women's suffrage. All these factors came together to make the entertainment field a glamorous one for Negro women, providing an independence and importance not available in other areas open to them— the church, domestic work, or prostitution. (Jones, page 93)

Ann Douglas, in her important book, *Mongrel Manhattan in the 1920s, Terrible Honesty,* identifies the twenties as a period of (quoting from the dust jacket) "historical transformation: blacks and whites, men and women together created a new American culture, fusing high art and low, espousing the new mass media, repudiating the euphemisms of outdated gentility in favor of a boldly masculinized outspokenness, bringing the African-American folk and popular art heritage briefly but irrevocably into the mainstream." Douglas believes the birth of modernism required the death of the white matriarch.

> The two movements, cultural emancipation of America from foreign influences and celebration of its black-and-white heritage, had for a brief but crucial moment a common opponent and a common agenda: the demolition of that block to modernity, or so she seemed, the powerful white middle-class matriarch of the recent Victorian past. My black protagonists were not matrophobic to the same degree as my white ones were, but the New Negro, too, had something to gain from the demise of the Victorian matriarch. (Douglas, page 6)

Such anti-matriarch sentiments directly clashed with the reality of female-led classic blues.

We are forced to ask the question: Does the freedom of the black man require the destruction of the black woman? To the degree that the black woman is a matriarch, a self-possessed and self-directed person, to that same degree there will inevitably be a conflict with the standards of modern America which are misogynist in general and anti-matriarchal in particular.

> Thanks to the revolt against the matriarch, Christian beliefs and middle-class values would never again be a prerequisite for elite artistic success in America. Nor would plumpness ever again be a broadly sanctioned type of female beauty; the 1920s put the body type of the stout and full-figured matron decisively out of fashion. Once the matriarch and her notions of middle-class piety, racial superiority, and sexual repression were discredited, modern America, led by New York, was free to pro-

mote, not an egalitarian society, but something like an egalitarian popular and mass culture, aggressively appropriating forms and ideas across race, class, and gender lines. (Douglas, page 8)

Ma Rainey, Bessie Smith, et al., may seem to contradict Douglas's thesis but actually the disappearance of big black women from leadership in entertainment is proof that Douglas was correct in her assessment of modern America. Among black people, the black matriarch continued to reign in the arenas of church, education, and community service. However, to the degree that black people adopt modern American ways, to that same degree our culture inevitably becomes "masculinized" and "anti-matriarchal." This is inevitable because, as Douglas's book demonstrates in great detail, American modernism is based on the refutation of the woman as culture bearer. Yet culture bearer is precisely the role that the black woman fulfills.

"The blues woman is the priestess or prophet of the people. She verbalizes the emotion for herself and the audience, articulating the stresses and strains of human relationships" (Cone, page 107), proudly proclaims theologian James H. Cone, a Christian man who had sense enough to sus out the potency of blues priestesses, a potency which is overtly sexual but which also made strong social, political, and economic statements (e.g., "T.B. Blues" by Ida Cox decrying poor health conditions and "Poor Man Blues" by Bessie Smith condemning class exploitation).

3

> *There's a new game, that can't be beat,*
> *You move most everything 'cept your feet,*
> *Called "Whip it to a jelly, stir it in a bowl,"*
> *You just whip it to a jelly, if you like good jelly roll*
>
> *I wear my skirt up to my knees*
> *And whip that jelly with who I please.*
> *Oh, whip it to a jelly, mmmmmm, mmmm*
> *Mmmmm, mmmm, mmmmm, mmmm*
> > > > > > > —*Clara Smith*

In western culture the celebration of dignity and eroticism does not and cannot take place simultaneously. From Freud's theories of sexuality, which focus for the most part on penile power, to the Church, which goes so far as to debase the body as a product of original sin, there is no room for the celebration of eroticism, and certainly no conception whatsoever of the female as an active purveyor of erotic power. To me, the blues is clearly an alternative to Freud and Jesus with respect to coming to terms with our bodies.

James H. Cone correctly analyzes this alternative.

> Theologically, the blues reject the Greek distinction between the soul and the body, the physical and the spiritual. They tell us that there is no wholeness without sex, no authentic love without the feel and touch of the physical body. The blues affirm the authenticity of sex as the bodily expression of black soul.
>
> White people obviously cannot understand the love that black people have for each other. People who enslave humanity cannot understand the meaning of human freedom; freedom comes only to those who struggle for it in the context of the community of the enslaved. People who destroy physical bodies with guns, whips, and napalm cannot know the power of physical love. Only those who have been hurt can appreciate the warmth of love that proceeds when persons touch, feel, and embrace each other. The blues are openness to feeling and the emotions of physical love. (Cone, pages 117–118)

Moreover, the fact that Freud's theories find their first popular American currency in the 1920s at the same time as black women's articulation of the classic blues suggests an open contest between widely divergent viewpoints. The classic blues offered an unashamed and assertive alternative to both the traditional puritanical views of sexuality and the new Freudian psychological views of sexuality. Bessie Smith and company were battling Jesus on the right and Freud on the left.

The Puritans with their scarlet letters projected the virgin/whore (Mary mother vs. Mary Magdalene) dualism. For the most part, Freud either ignored the psychology of women, thought they were unfathomable, or else projected onto them the infamous "penis envy."

The period between the Civil War and World War II is the birth of American modernism. The late 1800s is also the period when the bustle (an artificial attempt to mimic the physique of black women) was a fashion standard. While it is not within the purview of this essay to address the question of how it is that black buttocks became a standard of femininity for white society, it is important to at least mention this, so that we can contextualize the battle of world views.

Freud proposed the "id" as the controlling element of the civilized individual. The purpose of black music was precisely to surmount the id. The individual loses control, is possessed. This trance state is a sought for and enjoyed experience. Rather than be in control we desire to be mounted, i.e., to merge with and be controlled by a greater force outside ourselves. Blues culture validated ritual and merger of the micro-individual into the social and spiritual macro-environment. In this way blues may be understood as an alternative conception of human existence.

In a major theoretical opus on the blues, *Blues & the Poetic Spirit*, author Paul Garon argues:

> To those who suggest that the blues singers are "preoccupied" with sexuality, let us point out that all *humanity* is preoccupied with sexuality, albeit most often in a repressive way; the blues singers, by establishing their art on a relatively nonrepressive level, strip the "civilized" disguise from humanity's preoccupation, thus allowing the content to stand as it really is: eroticism as the source of happiness.
>
> The blues, as it reflects human desire, projects the imaginative possibilities of true erotic existence. Hinted at are new realities of nonrepressive life, dimly grasped in our current state of alienation and repression, but nonetheless implicit in the character of sexuality as it is treated in the blues. Desire defeats the existing morality—poetry comes into being. (Garon, pages 66–67)

Musicologist/theologian Jon Michael Spencer takes Garon's argument deeper when he comments in his book, *Blues and Evil*:

> Garon was seemingly drawing on the thought of the late French philosopher Michel Foucault, who said in his history of sexuality that if sex is repressed and condemned to prohibition then the person who holds forth in such language, with seeming intentionality, moves, to a certain degree, beyond the reach of power and upsets established law. Sex also might have been a means for "blues people" to feel potent in an oppressive society that made them feel socially and economically impotent, especially since sexuality inside the black community was one area that was free from the restraints of "the law" and the lynch mob.

In essence, the classic blues as articulated by black women was not only a conscious articulation of the social self and validation of the feminine sexual self, it was also a total philosophical alternative to the dominant white society.

In this regard two incidents in the life of Bessie Smith serve as archetypal illustration. The first is Bessie Smith's confrontation with the Ku Klux Klan and the second is Smith's confrontation with Carl Van Vechten's wife. The

Klan is the apotheosis of racist, right-wing America. Carl Van Vechten is the personification of liberal America.

In Chris Albertson's biography of Bessie Smith, he describes Smith's July 1927 confrontation with the Klan that occurred when sheeted Klan members were attempting to "collapse Bessie's tent; they had already pulled up several stakes." When a band member told Smith what was going on the following ensued.

> "*Some* shit!" she said, and ordered the prop boys to follow her around the tent. When they were within a few feet of the Klansmen, the boys withdrew to a safe distance. Bessie had not told them why she wanted them, and one look at the white hoods was all the discouragement they needed.
>
> Not Bessie. She ran toward the intruders, stopped within ten feet of them, placed one hand on her hip, and shook a clenched fist at the Klansmen. "What the fuck you think you're doin'?" she shouted above the sound of the band. "I'll get the whole damn tent out here if I have to. You just pick up them sheets and run!"
>
> The Klansmen, apparently too surprised to move, just stood there and gawked. Bessie hurled obscenities at them until they finally turned and disappeared quietly into the darkness.
>
> "I ain't never *heard* of such shit," said Bessie, and walked back to where her prop boys stood. "And as for you, you ain't nothin' but a bunch of sissies."
>
> Then she went back into the tent as if she had just settled a routine matter. (Albertson, pages 132–133)

Bessie Smith was not an apolitical entertainer. She was a fighter whose sexual persona was aligned with a strong sense of political self-determination. This "strength" of character is another reason that singers such as Bessie Smith were widely celebrated in the black community. Furthermore, Smith not only was not intimidated by the right, she was equally unimpressed with the liberal sector of American society, as the incident at the Van Vechten household demonstrates. Along with his wife Fania Marinoff, a former Russian ballerina, Carl ("Carlo") Van Vechten was the major patron of the Harlem Renaissance. Albertson describes Carlo as an individual who "typified the upper-class white liberal of his day."

> Van Vechten loved the ghetto's pulsating music and strapping young men, and he maintained a Harlem apartment—decorated in black with

silver stars on the ceiling and seductive red lights—for his notorious noc-
turnal gatherings.

His favorite black singers were Ethel Waters, Clara Smith, and Bessie.
(Albertson, page 139)

Van Vechten persistently sought Bessie Smith as a salon guest. She re-
sisted but finally relented after continuous entreaties from one of her band
members, composer and accompanist Porter Grainger, who desperately
wished to be included among Van Vechten's "in crowd." Smith finally
agreed to make a quick between-sets appearance. Bessie exquisitely sang
"six or seven numbers" taking a strong drink between each one. And then
it was time to rush back to the Lafayette Theatre to do their second show
of the night.

All went well until an effusive woman stopped them a few steps from
the front door. It was Bessie's hostess, Fania Marinoff Van Vechten.

"Miss Smith," she said, throwing her arms around Bessie's massive
neck and pulling it forward, "you're *not* leaving without kissing me good-
bye."

That was all Bessie needed.

"Get the fuck away from me," she roared, thrusting her arms forward
and knocking the woman to the floor. "I ain't never heard of such shit!"

In the silence that followed, Bessie stood in the middle of the foyer,
ready to take on the whole crowd.

"It's all right, Miss Smith," [Van Vechten] said softly, trailing behind
the threesome in the hall. "You were magnificent tonight." (Albertson,
page 143)

What does any of this have to do with eroticism? These are examples
of black womanhood in action, accepting no shit from either friend or foe.
Blues divas such as Bessie Smith were neither afraid nor envious of whites.
This social self-assuredness is intimately entwined with their sense of sexual
self-assuredness. As Harrison perceptively points out, the classic blues
divas "introduced a new, different model of black women—more assertive,
sexy, sexually aware, independent, realistic, complex, alive." (Harrison,
page 111).

These blues singers were eventually replaced in the entertainment sphere
by mulatto entertainers and chocolate exotics, Josephine Baker preeminent
among them. Significantly, the replacements for blues divas were popular
song stylists who aimed their art at white men rather than at the black
community in general and black women specifically. The replacements for

the big, black, classic, blues diva marked the consolidation of the modern entertainment industry's sexual commodification, commercializing, and exoticizing of black female sexuality.

Although entertainers from Josephine Baker to Eartha Kitt to Diana Ross to Tina Turner all started off as black women they ended up projected as sex symbols adored by a predominately white male audience. In that context, sexuality becomes, at best, symbolic prostitution. The black woman as exotic-erotic temptress of suppressed white male libidos is the complete antithesis of classic blues singer. The classic blues singer did not sell her sexuality to her oppressor. This question of cultural and personal integrity marks the difference between the sexual commodification inherent in today's entertainment world (especially when one realizes that the major record-buying public for many hardcore rap artists is composed of white teenagers) and the sexual affirmation essential to classic blues.

Another important point is that classic blues celebrated black eroticism based in a literal "black, brown, or beige" body rather than in a "white-looking" mulatto body. When we look at pictures of classic blues divas, we see our mothers, aunts, and older lady friends. Indeed, by all-American beauty standards most of these women would be considered plain (at best), and many would be called "ugly."

For example, Ma Rainey was often crudely and cruelly demeaned. Giles Oakley's book, *The Devil's Music: A History of the Blues* quotes Little Brother Montgomery: "Boy, she was the horrible-lookingest thing I ever see!" and Georgia Tom Dorsey: "Well, I couldn't say she was a good-looking woman and she was stout. But she was one of the loveliest people I ever worked for or worked with." Oakley opines:

> She was an extraordinary-looking woman, ugly-attractive with a short, stubby body, big-featured face, and a vividly painted mouth full of gold teeth; she would be loaded down with diamonds—in her ears, round her neck, in a tiara on her head, on her hands, everywhere. Beads and bangles mingled jingling with the frills on her expensive stage gowns. For a time her trademark was a fabulous necklace of gold coins, from 2.50 dollar coins to heavy 20 dollar 'Eagles' with matching gold earrings. (Oakley, page 99)

I'm sure the majority of Ma Rainey's female audience did not fail to notice that Ma Rainey resembled them—she looked like they did and they looked like she did. There is no alienation of physical looks between the classic blues singer and the majority of her working-class black audience.

Physical-appearance alienation of artist from audience is another byproduct of the commodification of black music.

What started out as a ritual celebration of openly eroticized life was transformed by the entertainment industry into mass-media pornography—the priestess became a prostitute. Albertson's citing of a colorfully written Van Vechten assessment of a Bessie Smith performance clarifies the difference between Bessie Smith performing mainly for black people and subsequent "black beauties" (including the famous Cotton Club dancers and singers) performing almost exclusively for whites. Van Vechten not only points out the literally black makeup of Smith's audience, he also points out how black women identified with Bessie Smith.

> Now, inspired partly by the powerfully magnetic personality of this elemental conjure woman with her plangent African voice, quivering with passion and pain, sounding as if it had been developed at the sources of the Nile, the black and blue-black crowd, notable for the absence of mulattoes, burst into hysterical, semi-religious shrieks of sorrow and lamentation. Amens rent the air. Little nervous giggles, like the shattering of Venetian glass, shocked our nerves. When Bessie proclaimed, "It's true I loves you, but I won't take mistreatment any mo," a girl sitting beneath our box called, "Dat's right! Say it, sister!" (Albertson, page 107)

The implication of such an example is psychologically far-reaching and explicitly threatening to male chauvinism, as Harrison explicates:

> [T]he silent, suffering woman is replaced by a loud-talking mama, reared back with one hand on her hip and with the other wagging a pointed finger vigorously as she denounces the two-timing dude. Ntozake Shange, Alice Walker, and Zora Neale Hurston employ this scenario as the pivotal point in a negative relationship between the heroine/protagonists and their abusive men. Going public is their declaration of independence. Blues of this nature communicated to women listeners that they were members of a sisterhood that did not have to tolerate mistreatment. (Harrison, page 89)

That these women—big, black, tough, nonvirginal, sexually aggressive—were superstars of their era is testimony to the strength of a totally oppositional standard of human value. Their value was not one of physical appearance but one of spiritual relevance. And make no mistake, at that time there was no shortage of mulatto chorines and canaries—Lena Horne would later be archetypal among such "all-American beauties." Nor was there an

absence of white-male sex-lust for exotic-erotic mulattoes. The difference
was that during the twenties there was an unassimilated black audience who
self-consciously embraced/squeezed the blacker berry, i.e., the classic blues
diva.

The classic blues diva was an extraordinary woman whose relevance to
a black audience has never been approached, not to mention matched.
William Barlow's assessment is fundamentally correct.

> The classic blues women's feminist discourse grappled with the race,
> class, and sexual injustices they encountered living in urban America.
> They were outspoken opponents of racial discrimination in all guises, and
> hence critical of the dominant white social order—even while benefitting
> from it more than most of their peers. They identified with the struggles
> of the masses of black people, empathized with the plight of the down-
> trodden, and sang out for social change. Within the black community,
> the classic blues women were also critical of the way they were treated
> by men, challenging the sexual double standard. Concurrently, they re-
> affirmed and reclaimed their feminine powers—sexual and spiritual—to
> remake the world in their own image and to their own liking. This
> included freedom of choice across the social spectrum—from political to
> sexual resistance, from black nationalism to lesbianism. Like the first-
> generation rural blues troubadours, the classic blues women were cultural
> rebels, ahead of the times artistically and in the forefront of resistance to
> all the various forms of domination they encountered. (Barlow, pages
> 180–181)

At the essential core of the classic blues was a throbbing, vital eroticism,
an eroticism that manifested itself in the lifestyle and subject matter of the
classic blues divas. Although we can analyze in hindsight, the ultimate man-
ifestation of blue eroticism is not to be found nor appreciated in intellec-
tualism but in its funky sound which must be experienced to be fully
appreciated. Once again, Alice Walker's *The Color Purple* is exemplar in
portraying the importance of the blue erotic sound—an eroticism best articulated by black women.

> Shug say to Squeak, I mean, Mary Agnes, You ought to sing in public.
> Mary Agnes say, *Naw.* She think cause she don't sing big and broad
> like Shug nobody want to hear her. But Shug say she wrong.
> What about all them funny voices you hear singing in church? Shug
> say. What about all them sounds that sound good but they not the sounds
> you thought folks could make? What bout that? Then she start moaning.

Sound like death approaching, angels can't prevent it. It raise the hair on the back of your neck. But it really sound sort of like panthers would sound if they could sing.

I tell you something else, Shug say to Mary Agnes, listening to you sing, folks git to thinking bout a good screw.

Aw, *Miss Shug,* say Mary Agnes, changing color.

Shug say, What, too shamefaced to put singing and dancing and fucking together? She laugh. That's the reason they call what us sing the devil's music. Devils love to fuck. (Walker, page 120)

Bibliography

Albertson, Chris. *Bessie.* Braircliff, N.Y.: Stein and Day Paperbacks, 1985 (Originally issued 1972).

Barlow, William. *Looking Up at Down.* Philadelphia: Temple University Press, 1989.

Borgatti, Jean. "Songs of Ritual License from Midwestern Nigeria" in *Alcheringa Ethnopoetics* (New Series, Vol. 2, No. 1). Dennis Tedlock and Jerome Rothenberg, editors. Boston: Boston University, 1976.

Brown, Sterling A. *The Collected Poems of Sterling A. Brown.* Michael S. Harper, editor. Chicago: TriQuarterly Books, 1989.

Cone, James H. *The Spirituals and the Blues.* Maryknoll, N.Y.: Orbis Books, 1972.

Douglas, Ann. *Mongrel Manhattan in the 1920s, Terrible Honesty.* New York: Farrar, Straus and Giroux, 1995.

Garon, Paul. *Blues & the Poetic Spirit.* New York: Da Capo Press, 1975.

Giovanni, Nikki. *The Selected Poems of Nikki Giovanni.* New York: William Morrow, 1996.

Harrison, Daphne Duval. *Black Pearls: Blues Queens of the 1920s.* New Brunswick, N.J.: Rutgers University Press, 1990.

Hine, Darlene Clark. *Speak Truth to Power.* Brooklyn, N.Y.: Carlson Publishing, Inc., 1996.

Jones, LeRoi. *Blues People.* New York: Morrow Quill Paperbacks, 1963.

Oakley, Giles. *The Devil's Music: A History of the Blues.* New York: Harvest/HBJ Books, 1976.

Spencer, Jon Michael. *Blues and Evil.* Knoxville, Tenn.: University of Tennessee Press, 1993.

Walker, Alice. *The Color Purple.* New York: Pocket Books/Washington Square Press, 1982., Rpt.

A Bit More

TIM SEIBLES

She had on a long dress, twilight-blue
and buttoned down the back—black buttons
sewn with yellow thread and new sandals,
and the air dozed, warm, early May, early
evening, the day about an hour from dusk.

And she had a long stride; you could tell
she worked somewhere that made her move quickly,
but now she was not busy. She had showered
and come outside eating a cookie, oatmeal raisin,

and as she slipped one curved edge between
her teeth, you were nervous about what
you might say. You believed words could

be important, that there must be certain sentences
to unlock this uneasiness, to fold the space
between you and this other person until
something had to touch. It's funny—

just before Easter she had to share a corner table
with this slim-faced man. Lunch always brought
a big crowd to the cafe. She grazed her
ankle along his shin every few moments

until she found herself wet. There was something
about the dare in doing it without
permission, without a single word of conversation

. . .

and, to be honest, you also knew that
speaking was usually a cool fidget,
a fig leaf: you simply needed

to kiss her, her legs, which you had seen
last Saturday in shorts. You wanted to
press your lips to her legs

to feel the muscles flex and settle
against your mouth, to let your hands
spill over her thighs the tiny hairs,
a liquid braille only the blood can read.

And suppose she wore nothing underneath that
forest-blue but the slight dampness of sweat—
her smell, like fresh cinnamon and salty grape,

and you remember a good while back
the first time you tasted a woman—
late one night, the laundry room, everything
quiet, only the spinning dryer—Lucinda

sat on a Maytag, unknotted the drawstring
of her baggy beige pajamas, and dared you,
put your mouth right here and you did it,

pushed open the brown seam with your scared lips
while room by room above you the dormitory
studied and slept.

Maybe this woman, Ms. *Long Stride,*
also catches herself thinking about sex,
about the way one lover never takes
her underwear off, but holds it aside with

two fingers, pushing her right thigh open to
bathe her vulva with broad, slow sweeps of tongue,
dipping into her a little bit, then

.   .   .

a bit more into the fragrant ooze of her.
And the short sleep after, closing her eyes
to the surge and fade of late afternoon traffic,
that sudden flight to a good place—

the connection between her and the ever-buzzing
scramble of *stuff* to do broken
under the sumptuous weight of sweet company,

and sometimes you wonder if the sexual world
wasn't always meant for this, for traveling
to exactly where you are, across the fine longitudes,
down the kind slaloms, into the body's soft passages.

But you needed to say something to her,
to become more than a stranger staring—
though your strangeness, like everyone's

is all you ever really have. There are
the necessary illusions of being familiar,
of entering into *a relationship*—and words
existed to make the boundaries of skin

seem less definite, to make it almost possible
to understand another person, to barely see
beyond the door inside a self

where it is always late spring, late,
and the air is not air but a nearly continuous
ache for something, with one person watching
another and wanting to say

> *that it is not very easy to see you*
> *walking like that when all I can do*
> *is consider your hips, the first unbuttoned*
> *flash of your back the sounds*
> *of your voice changed by pleasure*

.   .   .

Suppose we go another way around
all this maybe ask some better question—
one slow kiss—our bodies lit against the cool
grass, right here, night nearby,
two whispers borrowed from the leaves

Instead, you'll ask her the time
or stumble some dumb phrase about
clear weather and summer coming along,

all the while her strong legs—
the calves especially—rippling
in the balmy dusk beneath that new dress.

And she'll be wishing something too, showing
the watch on her wrist, with the lazy wind
tracing the shape of the space between you,
her own odd history telling her what not to say.

Once, at a birthday party where you became
thirty, a good friend sat on the sofa,
slyly revealing the flimsy underwear she wore.

One knee would edge away from the other
and she'd smile, giving up the soft gloss of purple silk
sparely lit by the lamp in the corner.

And later you lay in her bed watching her
take off your pants in the wall-sized mirror,
watching how, with her lips wet, she

leaned over the slight curve of your cock
and you saw your face for a moment
given back by the glass,

.   .   .

and you were someone else being there,
her legs around you, her body, in luminous
motion, repeating itself as if to remember
one unsayable thing. And you understood then

that this was what would blaze in your skull
years after your life was over—the promise,
this turning near, this falling close to heaven,

the moments when your body became a bridge,
an invitation, a window through which climbed
the sweaty angels—other people, good companions,
good tumbling into your arms, a place

where every once in a while, the invisibles
would undo their homespun robes, lie down and
fuck in your bones the way they used to

all day in full view of the sun,
when they were mud-colored, muscular gods,
when the whole world was Egypt.

a reenactment of a real love poem

NADIR LASANA BONAMI

*M*onday,
     me & mawiyah 'r' cuddling beneath a multicolored comforter. it's 1:17 a.m., a toupee-wearing weatherman is whining on television: "the wind chill has dropped tonight's temperature to 7 degrees." we're snug & warm like hibernating bears in the comfort of our unowned home. the arctic breeze is painting the house with ice as we exchange today's trials & tribs like church members, testifying in the name of the Lord. mawiyah's in her last days of pregnancy, we've been newlyweds for 2 months/14 days & i'm happier than an emancipated slave.

mawiyah: how was your day?
myself: it was cool, i talked to saddi on the phone for a good little while.
mawiyah: what was you & boogly talkin about?
myself: writing. i was saying he should write pieces like e. ethelbert does. you know how ethelbert write all those phat-ass love poems abt women he been with. i was telling saddi he should do that too, but he said no, he don't want all his biz in the street.
mawiyah: that's right, he shouldn't do that.
myself: what you mean he shouldn't do that?
mawiyah: i'm saying he shouldn't exploit those women by writing abt them without their consent.
myself: girl you crazy. nothing's wrong with writing love poems abt those people.
mawiyah: shut up. you never write love poems about me.
myself: what you talkin abt? i don't see your poetry pad being overflooded with love poems about me.
mawiyah: i write about you.
myself: yeah, right. maybe i'm not romantic.
mawiyah: hmph. maybe you're not.
myself: you don't think i'm romantic?
mawiyah: sometimes.
myself: ok mawiyah, you want a love poem, i'll write you one.

. . .

i played the interrogated role well, but mawiyah's seed, whether it was for argument's sake, or simply a subconscious attempt to motivate me to woo her with my writing, was already planted. why don't i write love poems to my one & only love? that simple question would grow into a serious question the next few days. a question which was starting to grow some answers on top of its puzzling branches.

1

i loved the 1st time i heard flatus explode from your person. we were sitting on the bed watching a john woo film, or was it an eastwood western, or maybe it was *The godfather* 1 or 2. hell! we probably wasn't watching no video anyway, we mighta been listen to "etta james" groanin, or was it "trane" blowin, or maybe it was "harold 'never singing' melvin & the blue notes lettin "teddy" hollar & beg on "i miss you." whatever we were doing, the bomb from your body startled the shit out of me. i was always the loud & common culprit cuttin huge ones in bed. in fact, when you did it, i questioned myself for a semi split second if that noise from your rear was my body performing an involuntary ventriloquist act. it wasn't. you fractured wind, & while i'll be the first to admit it wasn't no mango incense, it still was beautiful to see you let yourself go like that.

2

"my head hurts." your tone was weightless against the heavy chitter chatter that bore down silence in the crowded bookstore. a day after your due date, we were standing in line waiting for cash back on some used textbooks (another make-some-extra-loot-on-the-side attempt by yours truly), then you started complaining abt headpains. "you need to sit down," i said, surveying the congested store for a nowhere-in-sight seat. "i'll sit outside," you murmured, rubbing your forehead like limbs with rheumatism. "i'm not lettin you go outside by yourself. come here baby." i pulled you towards me in a slow-ward motion, my hands were clutching the sleeves of your coat, when suddenly your eyes began to flutter. you lost consciousness. you slipped through my firm hands, landing gingerly on a hard floor. i broke your fall. "call an ambulance!" someone shouted. the voices were dancing in & out of my ears behind me:
"she fell, a pregnant lady collapsed in the store, call an ambulance!" "is she your wife mister?" "did she land on her stomach!" "is she okay?" i held your palm while kneeling on the floor beside you. "nadir, did i fall," you asked with a voice that knew innocence, "no baby, you didn't fall." not

knowing if you were fully conscious i lied. only when you immediately asked me the same question again, i realized you were conscious. "nadir, did i fall out in front of all of these people."
god, i could have kissed you on that runned down carpet for sounding so cute. after fainting at 9 months pregnant in a bookstore, the first thing you were concerned abt was did you look crazy in front of a bunch of strangers. i said, "yeah baby, you fell out in front of all these people, but fuck 'em, they don't know us." the security guard reassured me that the ambulance was coming, i reassured her, as well as the paramedics, as well as the nurse, as well as the doctor, that you landed on your side. we could soon find out that you were simply a little anemic. i was scared that day. i just never told you.

3
in this cold world, i now believe in letting the hot & cold water within me run so my pipes won't freeze. i'm speaking abt my voice love. i can't continue to let this world bust me/make me rusty. i gotta keep spittin out what's inside if I want to cleanse what's outside. the reason i never wrote a legitimate love poem for you was because this world kept me clogged up with garbage (that's all movies & books.) & i hate being corny & i hate being white too. so i would always keep my faucet running a little bit. hot/water: sex/sensual lust. cold water: death/blues/life in general. but my scope was limited. of course there have been flashes of expansion in my work. a praise poem abt my great-grandmother. a social representing cold. i now realize that everything in life is real. & i love everything that you share with me mawiyah. from your unannounced spontaneous first fart, to your innocent concerned whisper on the floor in the middle of a textbook store, you asking me a serious question: "why haven't you written any love poems abt me?" the correct answer should've been "because, i'm not free." thanks to you i finally am.
thank the essence of life for making us one
ashe.

Euphoria

SHANNON COOK

Soaring on clouds of grey,
black, wonderful, exquisite sweaty flesh throbs,
making me lighter tighter wet, out of control,
my stomach feels soo tight & jumpy,
ooh soo tight I'm losing control,
it's light and warm,
cringing toes ball up!
muscles lock!

Haiku (untitled)

LENARD D. MOORE

Thanksgiving starlight
entering her full wetness
on satin white sheets

Passion in Paris

GILDA N. SQUIRE

*A*s I sit by my window and gaze out at the warm colors of the sunset, I am reminded of that wonderful evening three years ago in Paris—the "City of Lights," the haven of romance. As I take my first sip of café au lait, I begin to smile as I remember his beautifully glistening dark skin, his gentle but strong hands, and his illuminating smile enraptured by such pleasingly moist lips as he walked toward me on la rue de la Fontaine.

He was my dream man. You know what that is. *That is* the brother that would sweep me off my feet. He would stimulate my intellectual juices with discussions about Picasso, *Les Misérables,* Andy Warhol, and cultures of the world. *He* would be my comforter even when I am at my worst. *He* would be the man who would provide the life, love, and joy that most women spend their whole lives searching for, even when they feel they may never find it.

I saw my whole life begin to change as we walked toward one another that day on la rue de la Fontaine, that quiet and peaceful street. In one warm Parisian night, my dream man swept me off my feet, made pure unadulterated love to me under the moonlight, and changed my entire outlook on passion and romance forever. He brought to life every emotion which laid dormant inside my soul.

My name is Cleo. When I met my dream man, I was a nineteen-year-old student from a university in Virginia concentrating on my studies in comparative literature. It was my first trip abroad to study for a year at the American University of Paris and the Sorbonne and unbeknownst to me, my first trip abroad to discover my own ecstasy.

I have since returned to my native homeland of America with many experiences, one of which helped me to explore the essence of my sexuality—pure pleasure. Thinking back to that wonderful night, I'd like to take you, my new friend, back to Paris with me to recapture those memories of my dream man.

As soon as the plane landed that pleasant spring morning in early June, my thoughts traveled to all of the secret places inside the culture-rich city which would eventually make up my own special "home" in this faraway land. I didn't go to Paris with a fantasy about falling in love or experiencing erotica. It just happened. It happened when I least expected it.

I immediately began to fit into the Parisian culture. I met new friends in my summer classes. I met tourists from all over the world during my internship with the Musée National d'Art Moderne. I enjoyed my salad and wine lunches at the ever-present sidewalk cafés as I gazed at those who passed me by. Most of all, I basked in the world charm and comfort of my Parisian apartment on la rue de la Fontaine, where I took refuge from the world every night.

His name is Malik. When I met Malik, I had just celebrated my third week in Paris, finally starting to get over longing for home and my family. I had decided to go back to my apartment after my afternoon class to relax and have dinner.

As he walked toward me, the smell of his cologne blended with the afternoon air. He walked with such pride. He turned his head with such strength as he greeted the elderly woman on the corner. *"Bonjour, Madame. Ça va?"* As we got nearer to one another, I noticed a slight grin and nod. *"Et vous, Mademoiselle. Ça va?"* *"Tres bien, merci, Monsieur,"* I responded, hoping that he would not encourage me to continue the entire conversation in French. He didn't. He did, however, invite me to dinner that evening after we chatted for a short while.

I spent the entire afternoon preparing for my evening with Malik. I must have changed my color scheme at least a dozen times. Red slip dress. Black pantsuit. White sundress. Flirty pink cotton piqué short set. Jeans and a tee. Finally deciding on a very simple silky "white night" slip dress with comfortable sandals for walking, I opted for minimal makeup and jewelry and tossed my shoulder-length brown hair atop my head to form a sassy coif.

Malik arrived at 6:00 P.M. sharp. As we walked to the Jasmin metro station, we held hands and casually talked about our life's ambitions. He wanted to become a doctor so he could help to heal the world. I wanted to become a novelist so I could help people to temporarily escape their worlds. Such different dreams, yet a fantasy intertwined. I wanted him. I knew he wanted me.

After dinner at an elegant French restaurant near avenue de Victor Hugo, we decided to walk toward la Tour Eiffel to enjoy the natural light of the stars and moonlight. It began to rain, so we weren't able to see the stars clearly. We moved away from the crowd and found our own little private place on the lawn.

It was at this very moment that Malik kissed me for the first time. First, on my cheek. Next, on my neck. And finally, his soft lips and warm tongue found my own. The rain began to beat down on our faces while we embraced and kissed for what seemed an eternity. Malik then gently caressed my wet breasts as he pulled me atop his masculine form. As I began to explain to Malik that I was a virgin, he politely wrapped his tongue around my nipple, which caused me to gasp. I attempted once again to tell Malik my secret, and he forcefully covered my belly button with his lips. By now, I began to feel a welcoming moisture which replaced the burning sensation I felt in my stomach.

Malik and I continued to explore one another as we left no limb untouched and no hollow place undrenched. It was the first time that a man had turned my body into his own fountain for nourishment and fulfillment.

As Malik moved inside of me, I closed my eyes and held on tight. As his breaths came quickly and mine kept in time with his, I squeezed him so tight that I thought I had suffocated him. His body was virtually lifeless as he continued to hold me. I opened my eyes slowly as I wondered what expression his face held as warmth filled both our bodies. He whispered in my right ear, "I know your secret."

There was that charming smile, those strong hands which never left me, and those soft lips which kissed away the tears of passion when I opened my eyes for the first time. For a few short moments, Malik and I had forgotten that we were a short distance away from the euphoria of tourists visiting the famous Eiffel Tower, despite the thousands of raindrops. We didn't care that we didn't know one another's life history. What did matter was that we had found and enjoyed one another, even if for a short while.

Malik and I continued to see one another on a regular basis throughout the summer and fall that year. We attended numerous exhibitions and celebrations of the city. We shopped at the Galeries Lafayette. We took long midnight walks along the Seine. We attended performances at l'Opera. And we had many more sensually magical moments along the way. Malik was my first love and I was his. Our futures began to combine as one, and it all began on la rue de la Fontaine.

By the spring, Malik and I were inseparable. The warmth which filled my body for the very first time that past summer had found a familiar home inside of me. We found many ways to make one another warm, and we couldn't imagine that the day would come that the warmth between us would not be there. But it was soon time for me to return home to America. I had successfully completed the three semesters at American and the Sorbonne. My time was up, but I had fallen in love.

As Malik and I whispered our final good-byes at Orly Airport, we promised to call one another frequently. As the months and years passed, the phone calls to and from Paris became less frequent. Were we trying to move on?

It is peculiar how the simplest things in life, such as the warm colors of the sunset, can take me back to my Parisian days and nights with Malik. As I take my final sip of café au lait, I notice the tiny droplets of rain falling through my window and onto my face, arms, and legs. The telephone rings. *"Allo, Mademoiselle. Ça va?" "Tres bien, Monsieur,"* I cautiously respond.

I can *feel* Malik's grin. I can *see* his beautiful dark skin. I can *grasp* his strong hands. He's standing right here next to me even as we speak to one another many miles across the Atlantic. The rain continues to fall . . . stronger and stronger.

man

E S T E L L E   F A R L E Y

I see him from the window
Axe in rhythmic motion
Splinters fly
While wood yields to his will

His back glistens with sweat,
Physical exertion
That does not involve me.

Maleness not defined
by last night's passion
but what goes on below.

lotion

DANITA BECK

"Funny, she's usually so flexible and she has trouble reaching her back."
Your mind wonders as your eyes wander across her body. The journey
over her mountains and peaks, her valleys and plains, and her two round,
rolling hills is breathtaking.

The jasmine scent that once filled the room now clings to her warm,
moist flesh. The heat that's under your collar might be from the steamy
bathroom, or it's the lady. At her request and with her promise once
again to "gladly repay your kindness" you towel-dry her back. Suddenly
she turns. The swift surprise causes the towel to fall while your startled
hands linger frozen in the small space between you.

"Darlin'," she drawls, "you can't dry me off with your bare hands, can
you?"

Your temptation to reach out and grasp the soft coconut halves is halted
as she reaches down to pick up the towel. She places the towel in your
awaiting hand and . . .

"I was just gonna ask you to towel my tush, too."

You finally move, accepting the towel with a quick smile. Slow,
deliberate strokes from the white cotton caress her soft, bronze bottom.
Breathily, she exhales a thank you as she bounces out of the bathroom.
You inhale the steamy jasmine once again as you hold the warm towel to
your nose.

The silence is shattered by a horn-blown melody. You awaken from your
dazed journey. You follow the lady's lead and exit the bathroom. As you
enter the next room, an image softer than a sun-warmed cloud awaits
you. On the bed of feathers that once captured your attention, she now
sits. The tune pulsates, throbbing without the beat of a drum. The

atmosphere if now replete with jasmine as the lady applies lotion to her skin.

Her hands hypnotize as she squeezes the cylindrical container. She has forced the white cream out of the hole. The fingers frantically move back and forth as she heats the lubricant. Performing as if their routine was choreographed, the hands glide across the stage that is her luscious landscape.

First she smooths the cream onto each arm. The hands dance with joy as their attached arms are stroked. Drip, drip, dripping onto her awaiting hand, more lotion comes from the bottle. This time she rubs her shoulders, massaging them before moisturizing her neck and throat and collarbone and, finally, her breasts. Her nipples stand up as she touches their tops. In a slow circular motion she works white cream into the skin of these smooth coconut halves. With envy you watch her squeezing her breasts. As your excitement grows, the horn begins to wail. Her stomach receives brief attention before she refills her pleasure-giving hands.

White streaks are rapidly spread from the toes to tops of thighs and you wish your eyes could feel as well as see. Like migratory birds her hands flutter back to her legs. She shows off the flexibility that impressed you so as she brings each knee to her chest while working on her lower limbs. The toes are rubbed and stroked to her satisfaction. Ankles and calves are caressed and kissed to test the smooth texture. The knees are kneaded to perfection. As she leans back the light settles on her breast to dance and glimmer for your entertainment. She strokes the thighs from bottom to top, from front and around to each side. She raises a leg, revealing a portion of her chubby cheek, to rub its backside.

After repeating this process for the other leg she returns her fleeting attention to the firm object standing next to her. She pours more moisturizer onto her awaiting legs. The chill makes her squeal but the saxophone screams due to the heat. Her arms and legs dance to the music. The hands rotate in circles clockwise then back, up and down and around the leg. The limb extends and retracts while her toes point to the sky and then lower their aim to stare at you. A furious crescendo plays its final note as she removes her hands from her shapely glistening legs.

. . .

The music slows down, she rises. Once more she grabs the bottle and turns away from you. She quickly rubs the lotion all over the round, rolling terrain of her bottom. Bending, she arranges the covers to crawl into bed. You assume she has forgotten you and . . .

"I can't reach my back, can you put some cream on it?"

Suddenly the music stops. You try to hide your excitement as you walk to the bed. Now it is your turn to grip the long, lean bottle and squirt it's contents onto her back. While you are stroking, she turns.

"It's so hard. You might hurt me if you don't put that thing away," as she slides into the satin sheets.

You place the saxophone on the floor before you are repaid for your kindness.

thinking 'bout you

BROTHER YAO

your octave:

the day's mercy
singing

rain

a drop of wetness

in the curve of a collarbone
kissing your neck
or in the valley of a hip
singing your thigh

i have been thinking 'bout you
all day
my lips curled in an *O*
blowing harmonies

soon, again

KYSHA N. BROWN

anticipating your caress

I lie facing the door

and smile wet

kisses in secret space

answering machine

L E S S L I E   W .   C L A R K

delusions of grandeur
windowless panes
of broken glass
filter down upon
my bare flesh.
arousal my primal
fear and solitary
soul mate.
mottly skin testimony
to tattled tales
of torment.
silken threads of
tastes of
times tossed
between these
threadbare
torn sheets
burn my thighs
into open
submission . . .
of what?
sighs suppressed
sucks & sucks
of margaritas
lightly sugared, not
salted to suit
my tastes in
a perfect fit of
embellished
hot.
how dare you
defy me and

deny my
stage the
pleasure of your
performance
upon this polished
wood!
have you—I must
frenzyous actions
hammer mercilessly
into
your hands
hold me aloft.
on tiptoes I stand
as my . . .
yesssss.
melts
down.
beep.

to leave a message press 1.

1.

send my love to your wife.

beep.

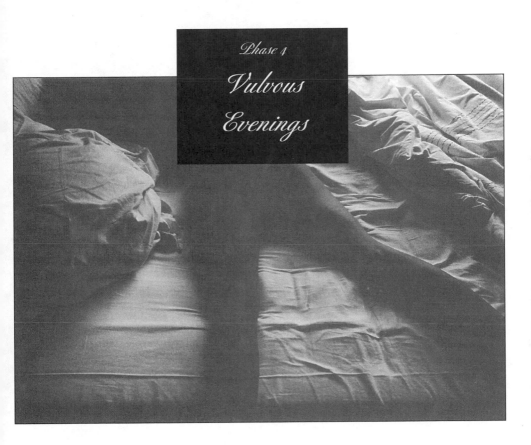

Phase 4

Vulvous

Evenings

*W*e move not for ourselves but for our own oneness, now moved away from all social definitions and acceptable parameters, moved away, indeed, from all those things that we know into the zone of what we know not but now must have.

For Helvettika in her untitled poem, the vestiges of a little S&M still linger like the smoke of your father's pipe. Elle's "will always" shows the erotic lingerings even after the corporeal lover is long since gone. Black eroticism is timeless and a perfect beginning to tie up the evening as Reece Auguiste's "Polish My Pearl" delves, dives, and dishes desire with the dirt of doin' it, doin' it, doin' it well—with more than one person. Perry Holmes's "Pussy Ann Trouble" conjures the video essence, convincing us visually of what Hughes Jones convinces us of chronologically in "Forty-five Is Not So Old." We meet the archetypal, hyper-sexed black scion in Playthell Benjamin's excerpt from *Tall Tales from the Life and Times of Sugarcane Hancock: The Phallocentric Memoirs of a Sweet Colored Man* as he pours sugar from his cane into the trunks of an ebony and ivory twin set. Love-child, with her acidic fuck-me-in-the-face views from "Train Me" leads into a "Merging" with Niama Leslie JoAnn Williams as she longs for kisses of every size, stature, and structure. Several of the phases of "Wind in the Cane" blow past us with the fragrant smell of sex well spent in Chezia Thompson Cager's long, narrative poem, and we close with "Blaspheme!" from Jade D. Banks, bringing eroticism one step closer to being revealed for what it is: a necessary religion.

Untitled

HELVETTIKA

cuffed to my bed in
xcitement
chiseled fingers of
chablis
channel
down into still
shadowy waters
intermingling images
flick endlessly
out. and out. and out.

delirious songs
play
lazily
in this
finely tuned . . .

chained
against my will

will always

E L L E

for chuck

there is something beyond
his play by play account
of some chick's derriere
licking the insides
of his t.v. screen
but there is no word
for this thing
like chocolate icing
teasing my tongue
or hot fudge sundaes
on a September morning
or the heavy green smell
of a freshly cut lawn
a turquoise boa
dragging the
small space
of a pelvis
but I do not know
the word for it
that keeps him merging
with my mirrors and dreams
as the thing
is
deep
inside him
and will not
let me
go

Polish My Pearl (excerpt)

A screenplay

REECE AUGUISTE

FADE IN:

1. INT: PYRAMID HOTEL-ROOM. DUSK.

CLOSE ON:

We see an eye looking through a spy hole in the wall. Full of excitement and urgency, the eye darts around the edges of the hole as if straining to see something, anything.

The VOICE of the NARRATOR is heard:

> NARRATOR'S VOICE
> I've spent the last three days looking
> without seeing. The room is empty and
> cold. My problem is I have a desire too
> terrible to bear yet too dangerous to let
> go. My desire is to see every thing that
> God sees and to feel every sensation that
> he feels. But most of the time I gaze at
> emptiness yearning for relief. I can't
> sleep . . . until I see what God sees.

OPENING CREDITS
Music: Piano Man by Count Basie / Billy Eckstine
Time-lapse Shot.

1. As the southern sunset disappears behind the horizon overlooking the Mississippi river, WE SEE Memphis's skyline awash in an intense, impressionistic and luminous veil of golden light.

2. As the city's neon lights hit the skyline WE SEE coming into focus lines of moving traffic and an oncoming trolley on the junction of *MAIN STREET* and *UNION AVENUE*.

3. *BEALE STREET* comes alive in a mirage of sensual lights and shadows.

CAMERA MOVES, exploring and revealing curious faces, a horse-drawn car-
riage and Handy's statue towering over the throng of moving figures.

4. CAMERA CRANES upwards the side of the Pyramid Hotel to reveal
through an open window a black man restlessly strutting up and down the
length of his room.

END OPENING CREDITS.

2. INT: PYRAMID HOTEL-ROOM. NIGHT.

ANGLE ON:
WE SEE a young black man naked from the waist upwards standing at
the window. This is FELIX, in his 20s, shaved head, with two days of facial
hair growth.
Felix MOVES from the window and jumps onto the bed. He rests his
eye against the spy hole in the wall and looks into the other room.

FELIX
(whispering to himself)
C'mon, c'mon my little angels, come
into the light.

Frustrated, Felix lights a cigarette, inhales deeply, glances at his watch
and places the cigarette in an ashtray.
Felix lowers himself on the bed. He wraps himself in folds of sheets and
begins to explore his erotic zone.

CLOSE ON:
As Felix contorts his body between the sheets his face becomes a mirror
of sublime ecstasy.

OFFSCREEN:
WE HEAR the sound of footsteps, light laughter, then of a door being
opened and shut, followed by a faint cacophony of voices.

PULL BACK TO REVEAL: Felix as he moves towards the spy hole in the
wall like a cat in pursuit of its prey. He rests his eye over it.

CLOSE ON:
Felix's face lights up in ecstasy.

FELIX
(whispers to himself)
Oh God! The waiting is over.

CUT TO:

3. INT: HOTEL ROOM. NIGHT.

FELIX'S POV
WE SEE an elegant bald-headed black woman, in her early 30s, coming from the bathroom wrapped in a bath towel. She carries her statuesque body like an offering to the gods. This is Constance.

CONSTANCE
(chuckles)
If only they knew!

OFF SCREEN:
WE HEAR the sound of joyful laughter.

CONSTANCE
What's so funny Jasmine?

ANGLE ON:
WE SEE a black woman stretched across the bed writhing with laughter. This is Jasmine. She wears her hair in an afro and is decked out in a 70s fashion outfit.
Jasmine kicks her platform shoes off and sits up.

ARISTO'S POV
The Mirror

WE SEE Jasmine and Constance's reflection in the mirror as they kiss, touch, and tease each other. Very playful.

CUT TO:

4. INT: FELIX'S ROOM. NIGHT

WE SEE Felix pull away from the hole. He lowers his body onto the bed in a semi-foetal position and begins to masturbate.

CLOSE ON:
Felix's face becomes a mirror of ecstacy. He begins to fantasize.

FELIX
(talking to himself)
Oh Constance! You're mine. . . . I adore
you. Ooooh, goddess of love, I take you.
You're my holy sacrament, I. . . . I. . . . I. . . .

MUSIC:
WE HEAR Louis Armstrong's rendition of "La Vie En Rose" drifting in from the other room.
Felix lights up even more. He starts singing the words of the song while he continues stroking his dick.

FELIX
Hold me close and hold me fast,
the magic spell you cast, this is
La vie en rose

When you kiss me at one side
and though I close my eyes I
see La vie en rose . . .

PULL BACK TO REVEAL: the room—Felix stops masturbating. He lifts his body up the wall and places his eye over the spy hole.

CUT TO:
5. INT: HOTEL ROOM. NIGHT.

MUSIC: "La vie en Rose." Armstrong.

FELIX'S POV
WE SEE Aristo, semi-nude, dancing in front of the mirror, while Jasmine

and Constance, entwined in each other's arms, are watching him from the bed at the other end of the room.

> JASMINE
> *(teasing)*
> What's up Aristo? You like what
> you see?

> ARISTO
> *(dismissive)*
> Surprise me, show me something
> I don't already know!

Aristo glides across the floor like Bill T. Jones, picks up his cocktail glass and starts nursing it.

ANGLE ON:
Constance buries her head in-between Jasmine's breasts and starts stroking her between her legs. Jasmine responds affectionately.

> JASMINE
> *(appreciatively)*
> Oooh, that feels real good!

> CONSTANCE
> All it takes is a little imagination,
> right Aristo!

Aristo's oblivious. He is spellbound, watching their reflection in the mirror.

CLOSE ON:
Jasmine turns to Constance and whispers in her ear.

> JASMINE
> *(as if confiding a secret)*
> You see, Aristo likes the power of

mirrors. That's his thing, strangely it's
mine too.

Jasmine playfully buries her tongue in Constance's ear. Constance leans
her head to one side and momentarily surrenders to Jasmine.

CONSTANCE
Honey, tonight we need more
than mirrors.

ANGLE ON:
Jasmine moves over to where Aristo is sitting.

JASMINE
(urging him on)
I think our goddess wants you too.

Aristo looks up at her and then glances across at Constance.
Aristo drops to Jasmine's feet and kisses her legs upwards to her thigh.
Jasmine swings around and lowers her body into a chair.
She wraps her thighs around Aristo's body and pulls his head to her
crotch.

ARISTO
(he breathes in)
It smells like New Orleans in spring.

Jasmine lifts his head from between her thighs and wipes her wetness
from his mouth.

JASMINE
She's waiting for your love.

ANGLE ON:
Aristo looks at Constance. She waves him over.

(A beat)
Aristo goes to her.

CONSTANCE
I adore these nights with you.

Aristo slips in next to her.

ARISTO
It's at night that we can really
offer ourselves to each other.

Constance rolls her tongue up his neck.

CONSTANCE
I wish we could make love at midday,
every day.

Aristo chuckles at the thought.
Constance strips off his boxer shorts. She starts to massage his groin, stroking it and rubbing it.
Aristo cups her left breast in his hand. Constance pulls his head downwards and places her taut nipple between his lips.
He surrenders to her completely.
(*A beat*)
Aristo turns to Jasmine.

ARISTO
Play me a kiss, you know
the one, by the God
Satchmo.

ANGLE ON:
Jasmine complies with his request. She selects a CD and puts it on.
MUSIC:
WE HEAR "Kiss to Build a Dream On" by Louis Armstrong.
Jasmine begins swaying to the music like a reed in the wind.

JASMINE'S POV
WE SEE Aristo as he gently parts Constance's legs and presses his fingers inside of her. Constance cups Aristo's head in her hand and pushes it downwards to her crotch.

CLOSE ON:
WE SEE the back of Aristo's head moving in all directions as he licks and sucks her wetness.

CONSTANCE'S POV
WE SEE Jasmine lower herself on the chair. She stretches her legs apart and starts masturbating,

CLOSE ON:
Jasmine's face
OFFSCREEN:
WE HEAR Aristo and Constance's passionate screams.

CUT TO:

6. INT: FELIX'S ROOM. NIGHT.

CLOSE ON:
Felix retreats from the spy hole.

ANGLE ON:
Felix throws himself onto the bed and rolls along its length.
He begins to fantasize aloud

> FELIX
> Oooh Jasmine, take me like you take
> the night. Stroke me and. . . . take me
> inside of you. . . . I feel your wetness
> dripping. . . . dripping. . . . caress me
> with your tongue. . . .

OFFSCREEN:
WE HEAR sensual cries drifting in from the other room. The hoarse screams increase in volume until they reach a climax.

CLOSE ON:
Felix is hanging off the side of the bed masturbating to the erotic noises coming through the wall. He masturbates until he explodes into a pounding monumental orgasmic scream.

FELIX

Whip me . . . oh Jasmine . . . more . . . more
take me and whip me . . . . .more Jasmine
aaah . . . . . . more . . . . . . oooh God . . . . . .

Felix slips off the bed and collapses on the floor panting like crazy.

(A beat)
Felix rolls across the floor.
Felix glances at his watch. His vision is blurred.

CLOSE ON:
The watch—Time reads 9:15 P.M.

ANGLE ON:
Still panting, Felix looks up at the white-painted ceiling and blacks out.

FADE TO BLACK

Pussy Ann Trouble

PERRY HOLMES

O my God
What have I done?
Hypnotized by her eyes
True to life sprung.
A blind fool
While playing her game,
Vicious and delicious
Pussy Ann Trouble is her name.
Loving is hard,
The Bang is softer
But pussy and trouble
Is all she had to offer.
So pretty I confess
I inherited all her faults,
Another man's freak
By laws of nature I'm caught.
Causing a rip in my life
Needing to leave on the double,
Digging her hole
Until my senses fold
Accepting my Pussy Ann Trouble.

Forty-five Is Not So Old

HUGHES JONES

*I*t was 1:30 in the morning. Lucinda was half a jigger away from inebriated as she held a double shot of Seagram's and 7UP poised before her glossy, hot-pink painted lips. Precisely at that moment, Lucinda made up her mind "since I'm going to die eventually, I might as well live tonight," which meant she was not going home alone tonight. In fact, she wasn't going home at all, at least not to her own home.

Billy must of thought she was a fool. "Away on business," or so he had said with feigned casualness. Lucinda knew. Even as she had allowed herself to act like she believed him when he said he had to go to Portland for four days, she knew, maybe he really did have some business to do there, but for sure he was sleeping with Sandra with her little narrow ass. It didn't matter that Billy had left Thursday during the day and that Sandra was at work on Friday, answering the phone when Lucinda called on some pretense or the other. "I know something is up," Lucinda mouthed right before the cool liquor crossed her lips.

Just thinking of that little ninety-six-and-three-quarter-pound strumpet made Lucinda angry because invariably it made Lucinda think of when she was much thinner. Lucinda silently surveyed herself in the large mirror behind the bar. *One hundred fifteen pounds was good to go, but that was at least eight years ago.* Her eyes growing increasingly glassy, Lucinda silently surveyed herself in the large mirror behind the bar. *One hundred fifty-five pounds really ain't that heavy. Besides I'm tall and have big breasts. How is it that these little skinny wenches can get men so excited, what's to it?*

"Furthermore, the slut has buck teeth. What in the world could skinny Sandra possibly do for William James Brown that he likes better than what I do for him?" Lucinda wondered as she took another slow sip of her mixed drink. "I don't look bad—for my age. Hell, in fact, it's not really age. It's experience. I look good to say I'm as experienced as I am."

Lucinda smirked as she thought how Sandra couldn't massage Billy Jo's feet like she did, then wash them in a little antique porcelain washbasin— *I bet she doesn't even own antiques,* dry them with a ultra-fluffy, teal-colored towel, and then slowly suck his toes as her fingernails crawled up and down the soles of his size-eleven feet. And for sure, Sandra had no clue of some of the more stimulating thrills Billy Jo's big toe could arouse. Like when Lucinda felt really risqué, really felt like lighting up Billy Jo's little firecracker in her sexy night sky, after cutting his toenails with a clipper and gently buffing the edges to a smooth evenness with an emery board, after washing them in warm water with scented soap, after tenderly drying them and sucking them as he lay back on their bed, after massaging his feet with baby oil, and as it got good to him, after all of that Lucinda would climb up on the bed and slowly stroke her pussy with his big toe, stroke it until she was wet. God, a woman didn't know what she was missing if she had never reached a climax with her lover's toe tapping on her clitoris. What did that inexperienced child know about sophisticated lovemaking? Lucinda took a long sip of her drink.

Lucinda thought about how pleasantly surprised Billy Jo always seemed whenever she dropped in on him at work. With a toss of her luxuriously coiffured hair, which had been crafted into a gleaming and glistening, jet-black, lengthy, chemically treated mane which languidly lay across her shoulders, Lucinda remembered how it had been the last time she turned on Billy Jo at his office.

"Billy, I was in the neighborhood. I was on my way to that little boutique I discovered, you know the one I told you specializes in silk batiks, and as I crossed Poydras I felt this twinge like a little spark of lightning." He had looked at her partially annoyed but also partially pleased as she stroked his male ego. "I couldn't wait. So . . ." She slid seductively around his desk. "I decided to stop here."

Lucinda reached down and slightly opened Billy Jo's bottom desk drawer. She propped her leg up on the edge of the drawer as she took his right hand and cunningly glided it beneath her skirt and up her thigh. Lucinda shuddered involuntarily as she expertly guided his fingers into the curly mass of pubic hair and the moist flesh of her mound. She tensed her thigh muscles when his fingers reached her clit. "Yes, yes, I needed that," she salaciously whimpered while throwing her head back and squeezing her eyes closed with the same intensity as the forceful contractions caused by Billy Jo's fingertips dancing on the head of her clitoris. Lucinda savored the first trickles of what would soon become a musky flow. And then his phone rang. It was intrusive Sandra reminding "Mr. Brown" he had an appointment in ten minutes.

"That's enough," Lucinda said, pulling his hand away, "for now." And then she remembered his astonishment as she bent over to slowly suck her moisture off his fingers. "We can't have you smelling like pussy when you shake hands with the movers and shakers of industry."

When Lucinda completed tongue-washing each finger, she reached into her mauve silk purse, which hung from a silver metal shoulder strap dangling off her hip. Moving aside her black satin panties which she had removed in the parking garage, she withdrew a pink linen handkerchief that was embroidered with her initials. Before she finished drying his fingers, there was a knock at the door.

"Come in."

As Sandra entered, Lucinda ostentatiously finished her task with a flourish, waving her handkerchief, "there, all clean, all dry."

After daintily refolding her handkerchief and replacing it in her brightly beaded pouch. Lucinda slowly kissed her husband on his clean-shaved cheek, paused to close the bottom desk drawer, and cheerfully called out to him over her shoulder as she sashayed past Sandra, "Have a good meeting, honey. We'll finish ours tonight."

Pausing at the doorway, Lucinda pirouetted coyly, "And, Sandra, you have a nice day. Okay?"

That little narrow-ass secretary didn't know anything about how to administer sexual quickies.

While she was lost in the reverie of remembering the sexual games she often played with Billy Jo, an impeccably dressed young man sat on a stool one removed from Lucinda. Attracted by the resonance of his masculine baritone ordering a cognac, Lucinda turned to look directly at his massive profile. She sniffed and caught the faint whiff of an expensive cologne. He was ruggedly handsome.

"Hi." She smiled at him.

He looked at her briefly, Lucinda saw the almost imperceptible survey flicker as his eyes started at her face, moved quickly down her body, strayed briefly to her behind—she sat up straight and slightly arched her back—and down her legs, and . . . nothing. He turned away without even responding.

She wanted to throw her drink at him. Instead she decided to annoy him. "I said, hello."

He grunted, turned his head, and pretended he was ignoring her. Lucinda hated to be ignored.

She got up, slid onto the stool next to him, and ignored his ignoring her. "My name is Lucinda."

"Okay."

"And your name is?"

"Jawon."

Oh god, what a common name, Lucinda thought, he probably doesn't even have a college degree. Lucinda's liquor continued the conversation, "Jawon, that's nice." Pushing her purse aside, Lucinda leaned forward on the bar's leather lining. "Jawon, I'm conducting a survey. Would you mind if I asked you a couple of opinion questions?"

Jawon grunted without looking at her.

"I take that grunt to mean, 'oh god, why doesn't this old bag just leave me alone with her silly questions. I'll answer one or two, but she better make it quick.' "

Jawon was slightly taken aback by her boldness. He turned to get a second look at this woman. Lucinda leaned back slightly, crossed her legs, and did not bother to tug down her worsted wool dress. Noticing her broad, soft, calf-leather black belt with the gold buckle, Jawon accessed she was probably some kind of leather freak who liked to tie down men or spank them with riding whips. Nah. It's not worth it, was his final appraisal.

"If our ages were reversed." Lucinda leaned forward again, bracing her flawlessly made-up face with the back of her exquisitely manicured hand. "If I was a mature man and you were a young attractive woman, would you be offended if I brushed you off without so much as a civil hello?" Sporting a self-assured smile, Lucinda looked directly at Jawon, awaiting his answer.

Acid cruelly dripped from Jawon's thickly mustached lips. "I think you ought to be at home baby-sitting your grandchildren instead of out here trying to rob the cradle."

"Aha. Well Jawon, ten years from now, I hope you're not sitting on the other end of this question, and if you are, I hope the lady whose attention you're trying to get is just a bit more understanding than you are now. That's all. You may go now."

Jawon backed off the stool and walked away, leaving a dollar tip on the bar and no further acknowledgment of Lucinda. Lucinda turned to face the mirror behind the bar and in reflection caught sight of Roderick, the genial bartender, standing discreetly to the side dressed in black slacks, crisply starched white shirt topped with a hand-tied black bowtie, and a black-and-white-checkered vest highlighted by a metal name tag that mirrored the bar's multicolored neon- and fluorescent-lit interior. There was neither smile nor smirk on Roderick's lips, nor did his eyes give any indication that he had watched the drama unfold. Without bothering to look directly at him, Lucinda sat her drink on the dark wood of the bar and finally addressed

Roderick, "Well, Rodney, don't just stand there. Freshen my drink, please."

As Roderick moved toward her, Lucinda glanced at her watch. It was almost midnight in Portland. Lucinda mischievously decided to call Billy Jo and disturb whatever little excitement in which he was engaged. Before Roderick could pour the freshener, Lucinda waved him off. "Rodney, I've decided to go home instead of sitting here and getting my feelings hurt. Be the gentleman that you are and call a cab for me, please."

Lucinda never, never ever drove her white Lexus when she went out alone to paint the town. A solitary woman cruising down the avenues late at night was like flashing a baked ham in front of hungry bulldogs. Any man that she might meet would pay more attention to her car than to her and assume that where there was a Lexus there was a big bank account that they might access. Besides, it was safer this way. Not that she had ever done much more than flirt—just to see if she still had what it took to attract a man ten years younger than she. Most of the time . . . oh, why think about it.

Pulling two crisp new twenties from her purse, Lucinda waved them at Roderick. "I assume this will cover my tab for four doubles and also adequately provide for your well-being."

Roderick nodded affirmatively as he received the bills with a smile. His clean-shaven head was oiled to a soft attractive sheen and were it not for the gaucherie of two gold-capped teeth, Lucinda might have found him attractive as well as personable. "Will there be anything else I can do for you?" he asked Lucinda in a charming tone that implied he was both a trustworthy listener and a resourceful procurer.

Lucinda's liquor got the better of her normal disinterest in what other people did or did not do. "Does diabetes run in your family, Rodney?"

"Not that I know of. No, I don't believe so. A little arthritis is all I've ever heard about, but then my folks are from the country, out Vacherie way. Don't a day go by they don't walk at least a mile and all their food is fresh, home cooked."

"You're fortunate, Rodney. Did you know the treatment for diabetes is deleterious to the libido."

"So I've heard."

"Watch your diet young man, we wouldn't want your libido going south before you're sixty-five."

"Ah, no ma'am. *We* certainly wouldn't want that to happen."

Roderick had been idly wondering if she was single or out for a fling, or both. Without her having to say anymore he knew that she was grieving for a husband or lover who was no longer sexually active. Someone called to him from the other end of the near-empty bar. Roderick waved an acknowledgment to the customer while he was wrapping up with Lucinda. "Is there a particular company you prefer?"

"Company?"

"Cab company."

"No. How would I know? I don't usually take cabs."

"Okay. I'll be right back." Roderick walked briskly down to the waiting customer, served him, reached under the register, pulled out his portable phone, and rotely dialed the White Fleet number as he walked back to where the matronly woman sat.

"A cab is on the way. The dispatcher will ring me when they're outside."

"Such an efficient young man you are."

"Thank you," said Roderick with a bow of his bald head.

"Rodney, one more thing."

"Yes. At your service."

"Might I use your phone to make a quick long-distance call?" requested Lucinda while removing another crisp twenty from her purse along with the note page on which Billy Jo had written his hotel telephone number. "My husband would just love to hear from me at this particular moment." Roderick took the twenty with his right hand and handed the phone to her with his left.

"Take your time," Roderick said over his shoulder as he moved to the far end of the bar.

"Mr. William James Brown, please. He's a guest." Lucinda smirked at the thought of calling Billy Jo from a bar. "Hello, my lover. Wherever you are."

"You know where I am. I gave you the number and you called it."

"I miss you."

"I miss you, too, honey."

Then there was an awkward silence as Lucinda waited for Billy Jo to indicate interest in her. And waited. And waited.

"Other than missing you, I'm doing all right, thank you," Lucinda finally broke the silence, not bothering to mask her sarcasm.

More silence.

"I'll be home late Sunday night."

"Should I wait up?"

"You don't have to."

"Billy Jo, why do you . . ." Her words trailed off into a stiff silence. Something was in her eye. She paused to dab the edges of her left eye with the heel of her hand. "You know where I am now?"

"No, I don't Lucinda. Where are you?"

"I'm sitting in a bar, but I'd rather be somewhere with you."

Silence.

Something else was in her eye now. "Billy, I just want to make you happy. Be good to you . . ." Lucinda abruptly stopped babbling. "You see you've got me babbling. Would it excite you if I told you I wanted you so much that we could make phone sex right now. And . . ." Lucinda paused. "I started to say something really naughty, but this is a mobile phone and anyone could be listening."

Silence. The liquor kept her talking long after she normally would have stopped.

"I'll be forty-nine next week and in another four months or so you'll be forty-six, and that's not so old. I was thinking maybe some other medication might . . ." His silence was not making it easy. "Are you sorry that I couldn't have children?" As Lucinda questioned Billy she instantly regretted saying anything and wished that he would say something. Anything. "Billy are you there?"

"Yes, I'm here."

"And I'm not."

"Lucinda, I think you've had too much to drink."

"It's all right. I'm catching a cab home."

"See you Sunday night, honey."

Lucinda held the phone to her ear long, long after the dial tone sounded following Billy Jo hanging up. As Lucinda lowered the phone from her ear, Roderick moved toward her. Before she could hand the phone back to him, it rang and startled her. She almost dropped it. Roderick grabbed it, also grabbing hold of her hand in the process of securing the phone.

"It's okay, I've got it." She left her hand nestled in Roderick's as he used his free hand to expertly hit the talk button, shift the phone to his ear, and answer, "Hello." While he listened to whoever was talking, Lucinda tightened her fingers on Roderick's hand. "Thanks. She will be right out."

Roderick hit the talk off button and leaned on the bar without trying to pull his hand away. "You cab is outside."

"Is it?"

"Yes, it is."

"Rodney, you wouldn't be interested . . ."

"I don't get off until four and I've already promised . . ."

"Just kidding," said Lucinda unconvincingly as she reluctantly released his hand. "Have a good night."

Lucinda slowly descended from the stool, studiously attempting to maintain her balance and walk as straight as she could. Roderick shook his head. "The world is full of lonely people."

Meanwhile, in Portland, Billy Jo lay on his side in the dark, Sandra firmly massaging his back.

"That was Lucinda."

"What did she want?"

"Nothing. She was drunk."

All the Things You Are (excerpt)

From Tall Tales from the Life and Times of Sugarcane Hancock: The Phallocentric Memoirs of a Sweet Colored Man

PLAYTHELL BENJAMIN

We came to party too. And, as soon as we sat down, the raspy voice of Soul Brother #1 jumped out of the speakers and commanded us to "Get up! Get on up! Get on up! . . . Stay on the scene/like a sex machine . . ." We were out on the dance floor faster than a speeding bullet; moving, groovin, doin it to death. All the girls were dancing like they were dying to do the nasty; Solange and Gretchen were doin it too. I was dancing between them, doin the Dirty Dog. My shit was a little outta style but I was down wit it and couldn't quit it. I had never seen Solange really party on the dance floor before and she was something else! The girl threw her hands in the air and shook it like she just didn't care.

And Gretchen, tossing her long blond hair in time with the music, put her hands on her hips and let her backbone slip. Mezz Mezzrow, Johnny Otis, Elvis Presley, the whole fraternity of white Negroes would have been proud of her. While she was not a well-trained dancer like Joy, Gretchen practiced the groove religiously, dancing along with the Soul Train dancers on television every Saturday morning. She had discovered the source of the funk and her shit was authentic on the dance floor. Both of the ladies moved with a cool grace that resembled a series of elaborate poses celebrating unrepentant vanity. Although I pretended to play past it, I really dug the way everybody was checking us out. . . . Gretchen and Solange were the belles of the ball and I was their one and only.

When we got back to the crib it was afore day Christmas morning. We were still in a festive mood so Gretchen went in the kitchen to make coffee and hot chocolate, which she served with French pastries Parisian style. I broke out my own goodies, rolling a thick stick of Cheba Cheba, which was still the rage in cannabis sativa, then passed around the golden spoon filled with the breakfast of champions. It was Christmas, and we had had such a grand time the night before that none of us wanted to get undressed. So we lounged around groovin on Charles Brown crooning "Merry Christmas, Baby, you sure did treat me nice."

After awhile Gretchen got up and changed the record. The mellow, sophisticated funk of the Spinners strutted out of the box and the wispy, romantic tenor of Phillippe Wynn replaced the bluesy barrelhouse baritone Le Grand Charles. "Tommy Bell and Linda Creed have done it again," I said, paying no homage to the tuneful twosome as the sheer pertness of the melody and poetic resonance of the lyrics swept me away. They had barely begun to sing the first chorus of "I Guess I Must Be Falling in Love" when Gretchen walked over to Solange, took her by the hand, and led her out on the floor to dance.

"I just looove the Spinners! Don't you?" she said, looking Solange dead in the eyes, smiling her brightest smile.

"Oh yea mon! Ah love dem too . . . I'm a big Spinners fan," Solange testified, throwing her head back saucily and starting to swing her bodacious butt to the rhythm.

"Wanna join us?" Gretchen asked halfheartedly.

"Nooo . . . I think I'm gonna sit this one out. . . . The two most beautiful, sexy, and stylish ladies in New York are struttin their stuff and I got me a ringside seat . . . I ain't goin nowhere . . . I'm all eyes. So yhall just go ahead and shake your thing; shake it till you break it!"

They were hardly paying me any attention. And as the dance developed it was almost like I wasn't even there. Both of them were really fired up; you could tell from their glassy eyes. The smoke and coke had them wired and they were dancing around each other in a circular movement, sometimes making eye contact and other times closing their eyes and funkin to the music like they were lost in the groove. As the ladies danced I got the impression that they were executing some choice moves just for me, sexing it up, shakin it to the east, shakin it to the west, shakin it to the one that they loved the best. Whenever I'd catch one of them looking at me I would grab my swollen swipe and shake it menacingly. That would inspire even more radical moves although they did nothing to acknowledge it.

"We better go to bed because it's getting late and we're invited to dinner over at Boogie Woogie's house tomorrow, remember?" Gretchen said after dancing to a couple of cuts from the Spinners album.

"Who's Boogie Woogie? Have I ever met him?"

"Naw, you'd never met him. And once you meet him you won't have to ask that again . . . 'cause you'll never forget him! Woogie is a fascinating guy."

"I'll bet you know a lot of fascinating people because yhall know what they say: 'Birds of a feather flock together.' "

"I'm going to get ready for bed, you coming, Solange?"

"I'll be there in a minute." As soon as Gretchen left the room Solange came over to where I was sitting, kissed me on the lips, and whispered with a hint of fascination in her voice: "You really liked seeing me and Gretchen dancing together, didn't you? Ah mean, we got you pretty excited, huh?"

Being the well-seasoned freak that I was, I recognized an opening when I saw one and decided to make the most of it. Like the Philadelphia party-people always say: "You never know where the next star freak will come from!" I had learned so much about Solange since that exchanged look Friday when I first saw her in Paris, singing like one of the heavenly hosts while Toots wailed like Gabriel on his trumpet, serenading Our Lady of Paris with sacred music. At first I though she was an angel. Then, after I peeped her spirit dance at the concert in Greenwich Village, I thought she was an African earth mother/goddess. Now she was a fly girl prima donna, and seemed to be gettin flyer all the time. The funny thing is, she really was all those things.

So from where I sat, the situation looked pretty fluid. Everybody had a hidden agenda, but I was the only one in the room who had peeped every-body else's hole card. Part of the reason why that was so was because I was involved in secret conspiracies with each against the other. But beyond that I was the player in the crew. That's why it didn't take me very long to figure out that there was nothing wrong with Solange's back. She had feigned a back problem in order to conceal her real problem: me and Gretchen sleeping together while she lay in an empty bed down the hall. Gretchen was so blinded by lust she couldn't peep it, but I dug what was goin down early on in the game. I just decided to play past it because, although she didn't know it, Solange was heading right down my alley. Now I had her right where I wanted her.

The way I figured it, once she and Gretchen hooked up and got it on, none of this would matter. And if it turned out like I suspected, they would be so enamored with each other that I would have myself two wonderful wife-in-laws again. To tell the truth I expected to experience something different, something more, when Solange and Gretchen finally savored each other. Afraid that I might blow my opportunity and miss the magical mo-ment, I hazarded a confession.

"Do you really wanna know how I felt watching you and Gretchen dancing with each other? . . . Huh?

"Ah would love to know, ah asked you, didn't I? . . . So come on, tell me now."

"You better watch what you ask for, 'cause I just might give it to you."

"You know what ah think? Ah think you're uptight. Me say me can't believe it! The great Sugarcane, scared to speak his mind. . . . Cha!"

By taunting me like that, Solange played herself outta the pocket and right into my hands. "Okay, you asked for it . . . so I'ma give it to you straight. Yes, I dug watching you and Gretchen dancing with each other; how could I not? . . . After all, you know I'm a very visual person and I love women. You even spoke on it a coupla times yourself, snappin on me about how I love to look at pretty women on the streets all the time. Well, you and Gretchen are the two best-looking women in New York for my money. And I get real excited just thinking about two beautiful women like yhall making love to each other. . . . I love to watch it almost as much as I love fuckin, and you know how I love to fuck, I ain't gon tell no lie. . . . There! Now you know . . . I'm a bona fide freak! . . . I guess you bout ready to run outta the room screaming now, huh?"

"You really think ah born yesterday don't you? . . . Ah know men like stuff like that. Even Ron, with his square self-righteous self, useta try to hint around about stuff like that. One time he even showed me some smoker films with women in them to try to get me interested. See, there was this girl ah knew from college who sand with us on some gigs, and she was always saying things that made me think she was hittin on me. Ah wasn't sure whether it was my imagination or what. So Ah asked Ron to watch her and tell me what he thought. Well, he concluded she was trying to get next to me alright; but instead of gettin vexed, the mon became intrigued and wanted to help her. He got all these wild ideas about having two wives and tried to justify it with that Crislam nonsense!"

"Damn! The more I hear of the inside story on that boy the wilder he gets. But I havta say, on that question the boy is a man after my own heart. Everybody can't play that game, though: you got to be qualified to satisfy." I carefully studied Solange's body language for some clue to her deeper feelings as I took another toot and passed the golden spoon to her. I could tell when the cocaine assaulted Solange's brain because her eyes caught fire.

"But he wasn't qualified . . . Ah had no desire to do that for him," she said with a wry smile. Then she looked out the window over the Hudson River, to the cultural wastelands of New Jersey, and said matter-of-factly: "Ah would do just about anything for you though . . . you're my dream lover." Casting her eyes down demurely, her smile took on a wicked tinge as she confessed in a slow deliberate manner: "If Ah was ever gonna make love to a woman . . . it would be somebody who is beautiful, elegant, smart, charming, and sexy . . . somebody like Gretchen."

I could feel brother Johnson step to attention in my pants as the meaning of Solange's words sank into my head. Before I could get myself together enough to say something slick, Gretchen waltzed into the room and practically ordered Solange to bed. "You better come on to bed, girl, we've got a busy day ahead of us. We've got a dinner date at eight and you've got a concert to sing at midnight. So you need to at least get off your feet and relax. You must really be tired. I know that coke is telling you something else, but take it from me, you need to relax your body. If you come on in the bedroom right now I'll give you a massage."

"Now that's an offer Ah can't resist, girlfriend. It sounds like just what the doctor ordered. Let's go."

"You can come on in and join us for a while if you want, Sugar," Gretchen said with a wink.

While Solange headed for the bedroom, I was sending Gretchen silent signals behind her back. Forming an O with my thumb and index finger, I pointed to Solange and pantomimed a dramatic "yes!" Gretchen looked puzzled and surprised but her face wore a happy smile as she slid out the door behind Solange. "Tonight might just be the night!" I said to myself, taking a drag off the Cheba to cool out the coke just in case it really was the night and I was called upon to do double duty. Looking at it in retrospect, however, I know that whatever drug I was fired up on didn't matter, because if Solange and Gretchen locked asses my dick would stay hard under any circumstance. It would have taken a nuclear attack or a willful act of the gods to blow my hard-on. Even now, almost two decades later, my dick still gets hard just thinking about Christmas morning 1976.

I sat there in the living room for a while, thinking about the various conspiracies I had engaged in to move events to their present stage. It was interesting how things had turned out. Solange had faked a malady in order to keep me out of Gretchen's bed, and Gretchen had welcomed her into my spot without question because she was itching to jump Solange's bones. I had encouraged and guided it all with an invisible hand. Now it was time for the big pay-off. Just as all the pieces of the puzzle were falling in place, I remained uncharacteristically cautious. . . . It still seemed too good to be true.

After about twenty minutes I got up and eased back to the bedroom. I couldn't hear what was going on because the music was too loud and there was a speaker in the bedroom. When I got near the door I approached it cautiously, trying not to call any attention to myself. Solange was laying on her stomach with her eyes closed, purring with pleasure as Gretchen massaged her. She had hiked Solange's gown up high enough to manipulate the muscles in the small of her back, exposing her long fine ebony legs and beautiful bulbous butt, which was tight as a drum.

From where I was standing, I could clearly see the puffy chocolate fudge lips of Solange's pussy. And every few seconds those lips would spread reflexively and reveal a shiny pink inner sanctum where true joy resided. I could feel the crotch of my pants stretch when I squatted down to get a better view of her juice box and peeped a thick splotch of do-it fluid casually oozing out. That was all I needed to see to know for sure that Solange was ready to be taken.

Gretchen heard me come in the room and turned around to meet my gaze. I gave her the okay sign again and pointed to Solange's gooey pussy. Without pausing the intricate movements of her hands, she continued to knead Solange's muscles while stepping back far enough to get a good look at her pussy. The minute she saw how it was snappin and frothing and carrying on, a blush came over Gretchen's skin that was almost as pink as the interior walls of Solange's goody gap. She looked around at me again, as if seeking further instruction. I nodded and gave her a thumbs-up. From that moment on, Gretchen began to make her move.

At first she seemed to be playing past all the signals that it was time to turn up the heat. I had begun to wonder if she was gonna choke, just bitch up and lose her nerve. Slowly but surely Gretchen worked her way down Solange's body, massaging her gluteus maximus muscles while marveling at their generous dimensions and near-perfect symmetry, then moving on down to her thighs. When Gretchen gently pulled Solange's thighs apart and placed the tip of her index finger directly on her swollen maiden's head it was so sensitive Solange sighed audibly, abruptly raised her butt up off the mattress, and clutched the sides of the bed. Gretchen quickly placed her free hand on Solange's butt and held her in place while she massaged her clit in a circular motion. Soon Solange started winding her pelvis, giving her some then moving to the dictates of Gretchen's finger, helping her to make her feel good.

"You like this, sweetie?" Gretchen asked with a growing aggressiveness and authoritative air that I had never seen her exhibit in carnal matters. But then again I wasn't around when she did her thing with her "clients." On those occasions she was very much in charge. Perhaps she was becoming hooked on the adrenaline rush of the power trip. And, of course, there was my own example, which she had observed for years.

"Yes! . . . Yeeeesss Ah love it," Solange testified with feeling.

"Can't you feel it all over . . . Huh? . . . I wanna make you feel good all over, sweetie."

"Ooooooh ya doin it . . . ya doin it . . . Oh gosh man! . . . Ah feelin it all over."

"Tell me how it feels, Solange . . . and call my name; I want to hear you tell me who's making you feel so good."

"Lawd, Ah feelin it! . . . It feel sooo good. It feel like a buncha little hot and cold electric worms crawlin all over me body . . . Oh . . . Oh! . . . Good gosh mon Ah feelin it good!"

"Tell me who's makin you feel so good Solange. . . . Tell me!" As her voice grew more demanding, Gretchen increased her hand speed so dramatically it looked like she was fanning that pussy to keep it from catching afire.

"It's you! . . . It's you, Gretchen! . . . Oh Lawd, Gretchen, it's you that make me feel so good . . . ooooooh baby!

The room was lighted by candles and there were many dimly lit spots. I was standing in the shadows holding my swipe in my hand, squeezing it through the fabric of my pants. I really wanted to take it out, but once the bald-head champ got loose things could get confused, cause he'd wanna play the scene like sex machine, sticking his head in everybody's private businesses. That would be an unforgivable breach of etiquette, the tasteless antics of a greedy amateur, an action bespeaking a crass impetuosity unworthy of a seasoned cocksman like me. For the essence of the art of the ménage à trois is the joy of observation, and I was the epitome of the highly refined voyeur. As I've previously confessed, I was a big-time peep freak who was capable of experiencing real eyegasms. And watching Solange and Gretchen get it on was a continuous eyegasm.

All of a sudden Gretchen stopped cold. From the urgency of her body language and the panic in her voice, I could tell that Solange was about to get off. "OOOh nooo! . . . Don't stop! . . . Please don't stop now . . . Ah feelin it, ah feelin it goooood, Gretchen . . . en." But Solange's desperate pleas fell on deaf ears, for Gretchen was unpersuaded by her impassioned cries. While refusing to tease her boy in the boat any further, Gretchen made it clear that she was not done with giving Solange pleasure. Bending over, she kissed Solange's smooth black buns, then pulled them apart and blew hot breath up her butt.

After conducting a cursory inspection to see if there was any hint of residual defecation, Gretchen buried her face in Solange's stetaphygic derriere and proceeded to ream her rectum with a hyperactive tongue that danced about like an open flame. Solange cried out in ecstasy as she tried to crawl away from the nonstop action of Gretchen's kinetic tongue. But Gretchen grabbed her by the thighs and refused to allow her to escape. At times like these Gretchen reminded me of "Rectum Roz," a tall tan dancer lady I useta know. Rozland had big juicy dick-suckin lips and would right-eously polish your know, but she was rumored to prefer the rectum as a hole. The word was if she liked you Roz would suck your asshole mucho pronto. Gretchen wasn't that kinda booty bandit, though. She just got the urge every now and then. But she was fascinated by Solange's big fine African ass.

When Gretchen finally turned Solange aloose she lay there trembling, grittin her teeth, and mumblin over and over "Ah feelin it . . . oooOOOO Lawd! Ah feelin it." As soon as she could collect herself Solange sat up in the bed abruptly, as if she had snapped out of a trance. She was looking woozy, her page boy bang falling in her eye, scratching her head as if she was trying to get her bearings. Later on she would tell me that she felt as if she were at the beginning of an out-of-body experience. But at the time it wasn't clear what was going on with her; I thought she might be about to faint or something. Through it all Gretchen was sitting on the side of the bed staring at Solange with a slightly silly/slightly cocky smile that struck me as part self-satisfied smirk and part genuine euphoria over the pleasure she had given Solange, a lady whom she dearly loved.

When Solange peeped how Gretchen was staring at her she just smiled a starbright smile warm as the Caribbean sun, leaned over, and ran her lithe ebony fingers through Gretchen's silky blond hair, shook her head in won-derment, and announced: "You somethin else, girlfriend. . . . You're dan-gerous! . . . I'm halfway scared of you." Then she gently pulled Gretchen's head over and kissed her for real, I mean they were swappin slobs for days. It turned me on so I almost went over the top and coughed up the stuff of life. But at the last minute I thought of ice fishing in Alaska again, and played it off, managing to hold my water. It was a damn good thing I did too, because the best was yet to come.

"You don't know how long I've been wanting to do this. Girl, you don't know the half, believe me," Gretchen said as she planted passionate little kisslets on Solange's luscious lips, which looked especially delicious when moistened by the heat of passion.

"Well, you should have told me how much fun it would be, girlfriend! I'm really havin a ball . . . How bout you?"

"Listen, sweetie, I can't even describe how good you make feel . . . I just know there's no poet beneath the skies who can describe the beauty of it."

"Oh what a wonderful thing to say! . . . You're quite a sweetie pie your-self, and Ah really dig you,"

Solange had a look of genuine admiration as she gazed deep into Gretchen's smoky blue eyes—which were clouded up from generous doses of cocaine, champagne, and Cheba Cheba. She ran both hands through Gretchen's hair, tilted her head back slightly, and swallowed up her tongue with her enormous lips. Gretchen looked like she was in heaven as she vigorously returned the kiss. A few moments later, after they had disentangled from mutual embraces, Gretchen looked my way and thanked me for my part in getting her and Solange together. Solange grinned spacily and concurred. Then they sorta sat there making eyes at each other, grinning and being all touchy-feely the way girls are inclined to do. It was a good thing I had a super ego, because the way the ladies were getting into each other would give alotta dudes a big hangup; they wouldn't be able to handle it. But I kept telling myself that I had the dick; plus, after all is said and done, I had the best head too.

"I'll be back in a minute" Solange said as she dashed out to the john.

"Hurry back, sweetie!" Gretchen called out softly. "Havin fun?" she asked, turning to me with a smart-alecky smile.

"You better believe I'm havin fun . . . I'm sure that nobody in here is havin more fun than me. . . . How about you, are you satisfied now?"

"Not exactly, but I'm getting there. I'd like to suck those pretty tits of hers for starters. . . . She is really scrumptious!"

"Well you've got the power; right now you can probably do whatever you want with Solange . . . Looks like to me she's been havin big fun, and I believe she's hungry for more. So it's on you."

"Look, I'm not complaining; I'm having a great time . . . Do you have any herb rolled?"

"Yea, I rolled a couple of joints when I was out in the living room. Here, take a toke."

I fired the herb up and handed it to her. We were sitting there sharing the joint when Solange came back in the room, stepping like she was walking on air. I offered her a toke but she passed it up. I got up and hurried into the living room to cop some blow. Although I was only gone for a brief moment, when I returned Solange and Gretchen had grabbed each other again and were kneeling in the center of the bed, mommy hugging and sucking each other's tongues to the beat of the band. I stood quietly in the doorway and watched, thrilling to the pulse of multiple eyegasms inspired by the bacchanalia before me. I knew this was the same kinda stuff that the Bible claims destroyed Sodom and Gomorrah, but it still didn't keep my dick from getting hard!

Looking at it in retrospect, I still think my relations with my ladies were far more honorable than the way George Washington and Thomas Jefferson treated their white and black women. My ladies were with me by choice; I had neither the power of the purse nor the coercions of law to force my will upon them. And I employed no chains, except those amorous chains that fettered their minds, inspiring them to joyfully do my bidding. While I admit that there was some deception in our relationship, the ladies were as deeply implicated as me. And, when compared to the constant reports one hears nowadays, about Catholic priests buggering innocent young boys and parents fornicating with their children, our behavior was exemplary.

I felt almost as if I had profaned a holy ritual when I gently pulled Solange and Gretchen apart. But they just laughed and offered up their noses for me to fill with happy dust. After a couple of stiff blows they started licking each other's tongues again. Gretchen had dropped Lady Day on the box. She was bending blue notes and warning "You don't what love is." Her wise and wispy voice sounded as if she possessed some special wisdom in affairs of the heart. Maybe Lady was right. Perhaps we didn't know what love was, but what was going on between us was some kinda wonderful. As the ladies kissed, each fondled the other's breast.

I could tell that Solange had become damn near addicted to the feeling she felt when I sucked the milk from her breast, because after awhile she seemed to crave it. Pulling away from Gretchen, Solange sat up straight in the bed, stretching her arms above her head as she yawned, causing her tits to jut out as if demanding attention. Gretchen cupped them in her hands lightly, admiring them with hungry eyes. Digging the way Gretchen was fixated on her boobs and, no doubt, reflecting on the joys of her magical tongue, Solange reached inside her gown and pulled out her chocolate D cups, holding them in her hands while silently staring in Gretchen's eyes. Conspicuously proud of their beauty, she rubbed them lightly, titillating Gretchen while enjoying the feel of her own hands.

Gripping her breast firmly, Solange raised the nipples up so that they were pointing directly in Gretchen's face and squeezed them. When the first droplets of creamy milk bubbled out of her elongated nipples, which reminded me of black Spanish olives, Gretchen's eyes lit up like Roman candles. Solange's offering appeared to excite Gretchen as much as it excited me. She was so turned on by this beguiling spectacle of female prowess her adoration was palpable.

"You like them?" Solange inquired.

"Ooooooh yes, they're beautiful! . . . I love them," Gretchen gushed as she leaned over and slowly licked the milk from Solange's nipples. Carefully removing Solange's hands, she took hold of her breasts. They looked like two rolls of dark gourmet salami in Gretchen's delicate alabaster hands, and she handled them like they were priceless jewels.

For the next few moments Gretchen gazed admiringly at the big black tits, lightly massaging them and licking up the milk drops that trickled out, causing Solange to squirm around and break out in goose pimples. It was obvious that she wanted to take her time, prolong the wonder of their first experience. For Gretchen had lived the experience countless times in the virtual reality of her vivid imagination. She chilled as long as she could, but when the temptation became unbearable, Gretchen fastened her lips onto one of Solange's juicy nipples, closed her eyes halfway so you could only see the whites, and vigorously suckled it while emitting a cacophony of sighs, gurgles, and moans.

Solange held Gretchen's head in her left arm, stroking her fine golden hair with her right hand and softly kissing her forehead. When she felt that Gretchen had had enough milk from one breast, Solange pulled her hair with a tender but firm insistence and reminded her: "I've got another tittie you know . . . Here, try this one . . . Ah betcha you'll like it just as much." This time Solange cupped her tittie in her hand and fed it to Gretchen like she was a baby. Watching them, I couldn't help thinking that the attraction between these ladies spoke to some unspoken truths that lay buried deep in the closet with all the other silent racial skeletons of American civilization.

I wondered if Joy, and all those other upper-class southern white women who had suckled at the breasts of black women in the first years of life, harbored any desire, no matter how repressed, to do it again when they were around beautiful big-titty black women as adults. After all, their black mammies were often the first encounter with true womanliness these white girls experienced. Now that many of these fine white ladies had meta-morphosed into rabid womanists who preach the gospel of women lovin women, should they not love black women, who first suckled them at their breasts? The more I thought about it the more it made perfect sense. I could tell Gretchen was on fire and wondered how wet her juice box was. So I stuck my hand under her gown and it felt like a bowl of mush.

I reached over, took Solange's hand, and put it directly on Gretchen's pussy. She quickly started finger-fucking her with a vigorous artistry that belied her amateur status, like the way Moses Malone came right out of high school and became a star in the NBA, she was an overnight sensation! Of course, I had long been fascinated by my observations of women who I knew were virgins to the girl-on-girl experience yet seemed to know exactly what to do once they laid down with a woman who really turned them on. Solange was no different. In fact, as the morning grew older, she would prove to be uniquely talented in yet another art.

Solange soon found Gretchen's boy in the boat and commenced to tease him. It was not so generously proportioned as her own, but very sensitive. Which, as I have previously counseled, is the crux of the matter. It didn't take much time before the ladies started conniving to be the first to suck the other's pussy. It was a fantastic sight to behold! Gretchen tried her level best to lick and suck her way down to Solange's juice box, but Solange would have none of it. She grabbed Gretchen by the hair and firmly pulled her head up, crushing her mouth against hers in a deep tongue kiss. Then she flipped Gretchen over on her back, crawled on top of her, and started licking her tits with great inspiration. Gretchen's taunt pink nipples looked like raspberries in a bowl of hot chocolate when Solange wrapped her lips around them.

She smiled and looked up at Solange in wide-eyed wonder, stretching and purring like a white tiger in heat, spreading her long ivory legs until they appeared to swallow Solange up. When Solange made it really good to her she would draw her legs up around Solange's back and prop her pale feet on her dark mahogany butt. Gretchen was already pretty wigged out when Solange started kissing her way down to glory, so it wasn't surprising that she fairly screamed when Solange reached her joy button and enclosed it in her steamy mouth. No sooner had she taken Gretchen's clit in her mouth than she paused, looked up with an expression of innocence, and humbly confessed:

"Ah don't really know what I'm doing, not the way you do. So I'm just gonna do what feels good to me and hope you like it . . . okay?"

"It's all right here, sweetie," Gretchen said, nodding down toward her open legs as she smilingly pulled the lips of her pussy apart, exposing her boy in the boat. "All you've got to do is wrap those wonderful lips of yours around this and suck it gently. And don't be afraid to let your mouth get good and wet. It cuts down the friction when you tease it with your tongue. But you'll get the hang of it because I can already see that you've got a magical mouth. . . . You've got that touch."

"Cha! . . . You're the one with the magical mouth. I'm just glad I'm makin you feel good, cause Ah bet you've had the best. At first Ah started not to even try this; Ah feel like such a novice. But you make me feel so good Ah wanted to do you too. Ah wanted to try it even if Ah didn't get it just right."

Solange kissed and nibbled the insides of Gretchen's thighs before she made her way back to the pussy proper. And when she did, she started to lick it. She licked around the rim with the very tip of her tongue, then licked right down the seam, smack dab in the middle, stopping intermittently to deep-tongue the pussy. She had Gretchen about ready to jump out of the bed before even touching the joy button. That's why Gretchen grabbed her by the back of her head and held her like her life depended on it when Solange swallowed up her boy in the boat like the whale swallowed Jonah. But as soon as she got a good grip and the rhythm of her tongue struck the right beat, Gretchen released her head so quickly it was as if she had touched a live electric wire. Now it was Solange's turn to restrain Gretchen from running away.

She looked like she was swimming a backstroke, flailing her arms about, trying to push away from Solange's red-hot mouth. There was a look of hysteria in Gretchen's eyes when she discovered that she couldn't escape Solange's grip. For her part, Solange seemed inspired by Gretchen's response to her artistry and stepped up the action. Gretchen grabbed Solange's head again and screamed, "AaaaaEEEeee!!" Then, with a quick and vigorous twirl, she slipped out of Solange's leg lock and jumped completely off the bed, landing on her feet like a cat. She looked down at Solange—who seemed shocked—and tried to explain her behavior.

"Look, sweetie . . . I'm sorry," she said, shaking all over and trying to catch her breath. "But you were about to make me come and I don't wanna go there without you . . . It's so much more beautiful if we come together."

"Hey, that's a great idea, Gretchen. Yhall should come together right now, over me."

"Listen to him! You may not believe this mon, but we forgot you were in the room . . . Ah sure am glad you're alright, girlfriend, for a minute you had me really scared."

"Oh, I'm so sorry," Gretchen cooed. "I didn't mean to frighten yooou. I just had to get away quick or you would have pushed me over the top. I know a better way to come that's more fun. Here, let me show."

"Go ahead. I'm here to learn . . . whatever you think Ah ought to know, like the song says: 'Teach me tonight.' "

"Okay, first you've got to turn over on your back. . . . Now I'll turn this way and we can get at each other with no obstructions."

Gretchen flipped her leg over Solange's head and positioned her pussy dead in her face. It put her in the perfect position to suck Solange's pussy too. It was the position widely known among the freak set as 69, and I've never seen it performed with more fervor. Gretchen was on top and when she stuck her head between Solange's legs, carefully stretching the skin that hid her clit with both hands, she was startled by the generous proportions of the robust boy in the boat staring her in the face. She stared at it as if she were hypnotized, diddling it with the same fascination with which she had fondled her breast.

Clearly, Gretchen had never seen a clit the size of Solange's when fully inflated. This was her first glimpse of the elongated spear tongue that is the special gift of many Africoid women. I don't want to leave a false impression on this point, however. For while I have observed the jumbo clit most often attached to black twats, I have occasionally seen some pretty impressive ones on white gals too. Gretchen had a nice one herself, but it looked like a fat little pimple compared to Solange's, whose size and coloring reminded me of a freshly steamed mussel popping out of it's shiny black shell. As Solange gnawed on her joy button Gretchen bawled and babbled until she started returning the favor and her mouth was too full of hot quivering flesh to cry out.

Soon they were both trying to cry out with their mouths full, creating a buzzing sound that brought to mind a swarm of honey bees. The real screams came when their twats began to pop while releasing the forces of orgasmic eruption. It was a holy experience and they made joyful noises as they came. Solange started coming first and Gretchen soon followed. Before I knew it I was hollerin and screamin too. As my hand filled up with jism, I knew I had shot my load and that would be it for me. I would be no trouble to anyone that night. But it was all the same because the ladies had worn each other out and collapsed with smiles of satisfaction on their faces.

Train Me

LOVECHILD

Treat me like the slave I am
throw me to my knees
hang SLAVE around my neck
lasso me with your leash
and walk me, Mistress
I follow behind
in the circle of your feet
like the dog I am
train me
til I submit to your pleasure
crop-whip my ass

welt my legs
make me abide
the strap-on punisher
between your thighs
slap it against my face
my lips
force me open
push it down my throat
cocksucker that I am
invade me til it jerks my lungs
then drag me
slam me
over your wooden table
lock my bit
tilt my ass in the air
slap lard in my asshole of perversion
make me beg for my mistress to
fuck me
buck me

shuck me
like a good little girl
like a hungry virgin
like the nasty whore I am

Merging

NIAMA LESLIE JOANN WILLIAMS

I long for purple kisses
kisses I don't have to wet my lips for
kisses that come after a sweaty night of lovemaking
kisses that make my tongue tired
and my nipples rise.

I want to dance with you
and feel your stomach on mine
lie with you and feel the musk rise from your skin
lie with you at my back, our knees touching.

I want to taste your chest
swallow your insides as I lick the sweat from your skin.
I want to bite off little pieces of you
and hide them for safekeeping.
I want to hear your voice over the phone and moan in agreement to all
   of
your
questions.
I want the dog not to be able to tell our secrets apart.
I want to mingle our blood in an ancient rite of passage
then tend your wounds with my tongue.
I want to drink the sight of you in long, small sips
then wiggle you against my teeth.

I want your heart to share my rib cage
and your stomach to digest my food.
I want to wake up tasting what you ate for dinner.
I want to wake up and not tell my sweat from yours.

I want an eternity together, love.

Wind in the Cane (Parts III and IV)

CHEZIA THOMPSON CAGER

Part III

As wishes were
comments on uncharted
emotional terrain
I take your pulse
in my mouth
and know that your effect
to bend me to your will
is so much unsung poetry
on a dinner menu
uneaten
    today
But tomorrow
who can tell . . .

Part IV

Your natural arc
into my pelvis
is like onto a
tornado wail's veracity
It's hard and fast
because your masked need
slides into purple orchid
velvet slipper
like an old shoe
that knows your shape and size
Are we fucking yet?

I mean are we
spin-toe slue-footed

walking on the ceiling
Are we slip-sliding
dew-covered all over
on your mama's floor
while you talk and weep
and do push-ups in and out
in and out and tremble
without shame in my arms?
Or are we thumb-wrestling
at the navel in 100 degrees heat
no air-conditioning
To your heart saying "Stop"
and your back saying
"Fuck You!"
As I ease to the side
to play seesaw
with your greyhound legs
stallion hips and designer red knotted hair
because it feels divine.

I see that ugly face
you make
coming . . .
Are we fucking yet
or did you decide
it was time to make love?

Blaspheme!

JADE D. BANKS

My mouth hungrily searching for yours

My pelvis aching, stimulating

I cry out "Jesus!"

But hope to God He doesn't hear.

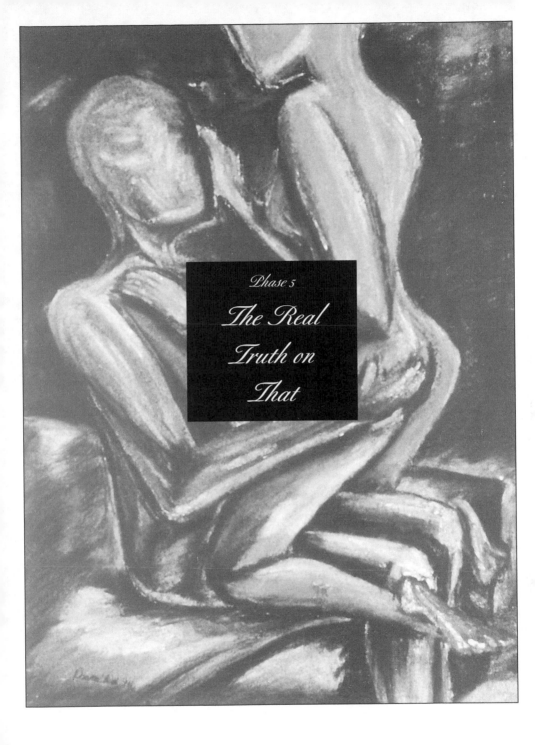

Phase 5

The Real

Truth on

That

*D*ue to the very simple fact that Transitional Generation blacks (TGs) have no paradigms for existence, they take for granted what took their forebears four hundred years to invent. In the erotic realm this is especially true, when one considers how inventive the African made into a slave had to be to keep any semblance of eroticism amidst the degrading sexual practices of slavery, and how carelessly TGs take their erotic quirks so senselessly for granted, ignoring the power of the everyday erotic. The writers in this section slow down their contemporary selves long enough to drink deeply and long of their composite erotic history.

Andre Mollet pours "Gentle Raindrops" on us in a raging late-night storm. Jerry W. Ward, Jr., in "Dreamwork/Eros Sections" supplies a philosophical view of the playing fields of Eros as Janice W. Hodges takes us for a ride in the backseat of '64 in "Red Lights" and Ajuba Joy in "Nzinga Astral Travels" takes us on a telepathic flight. We go to the bone in new ways in Tim Seibles's "Marrow," and Randall Moore's "Hands" traverse the thoroughfares of our sexual ambiguity as "sweetness" is drained from Jade D. Banks's tender inclines. None of us will be so lucky as to have a friend who has a mother like "Winnefred's Mother" by Glenn Joshua, and Anthony Barboza, with his tongue-teasing excavation in "Profile This," tours the plains of petition while Kazedge is "timed" on the slickened railroad tracks of self. Sharon A. Lewis asks us to see "His Side"—the untruth of a good man scorned by the devil herself, while JZB bestows ancient "Cherry Blessings" upon our sacred flesh—silken petal by silken petal. In Estelle Farley's "Teenager's Bedroom" we commit . . . seductively and selectively . . . the most criminal act of bustin' curfew. Do you need assistance with the truth about yourself? Then let Gilda Squire reveal your truest self with the help of "The Assistant." Honoree F. Jeffers is filled with "Sugar," while Niama Leslie JoAnn Williams envisions desire of the highest—and blackest—grandeur through "Cutting," a woman's silent plea for permanent seduction with each nick and cut. Also included are "So Close to Hell" and "Tout Proche de L'Enfer" by Amanda Townsend. After all this, even the real truth must be tempered with an erotically religious "Conversion: A Most Religious Experience" by Saddi Khali.

These writers give you the real truth on their erotic experiences—not the dead TV clichés from your favorite cable channel—because they have no choice but to do so; this leaves you no choice but to read them.

Gentle Raindrops

ANDRE MOLLET

Stormy lovers
Raindrops of passion,
Thunder rolling
Lightning flashing.
Not quite a hurricane
Just a tender shower,
A few moments alone
Making love on a bed of flowers.
Wet as an ocean
Flowing like a stream,
The things we imagine
In a deep-sleep dream.
Music is a heartbeat
A tune never turned off,
Caressing like a breeze
Blowing so soft.
A flux of rain
Mending our souls,
Raging through the night
As our love affair unfolds.

Dreamwork/Eros Sections

JERRY W. WARD, JR.

i

*T*he dream comes to you as a tantalizing shock. You see yourself with brilliant clarity, a nude in Nieman Marcus under the gaze of expensive eyes. You are a bold transgression caressing leather: ah, the perfection of buttered baby skin. A warm liquid bathes your legs. Your body is in progress through this silent film. No one can speak. No one can tell. You are absolved of the guilt to confess, to strangle with words the moment to which your fingers have prompted you to come. This is sanctified experimentation.

Such is the work of Eros, the grounds upon which the erotic spreads into all the spaces love would leave unfilled. What has love to do with a tongue exploring the unnamed depths of Chocolate Death? Your tongue glides in and out, into the pliant tissues of silken flesh and out to leave oil of orange on your breath. The innocent purity of love is always already admitting impediments. It wants to erect barbed-wire fences between your body and your mind. It wants to forbid the most sensual zones. It aborts the memory of delicious achievements. It freezes the fruit in the pearly bud. Eros will have none of that. Eros spreads everywhere to satisfy your exquisite curiosity.

ii

Anything so bold as to funk the funk's funk must be black, a reckless and ungendered desire for more exposure of the half-seen: the flesh glimpsed through the slit of a skirt, the muscle in its briefest ripple under the bondage of a shirt. More exposure not full disclosure. And thus the erotic announces its opposition to admissible evidence of the pornographic. The erotic champions elegance and concealment so that imagination can take creative control. Pornography, the tired utterance of harlots, is like the refrigerator of blues song: it can't keep anything. So it spoils by leaving nothing for imagination to imagine. Privacy is negated as pornography invites the world to stare into the bedrooms of our soul. You want, and definitely need, privacy in your hottest seconds of orgasmic abandon when the healing comes like the New Birth soprano climbing into what's here to stay until it's time for you to go . . . and "go" is stretched out into an explosive pitch. But there is such a thin line between the transparent and the translucent, a narrow opening where the sex that is not says don't touch, just appreciate. Or, maybe, baby, just listen! You don't want to violate your welcome, because maybe the next time it will be yes, yes, a hundred thousand times yes, as the regularity of tick-tock is splendidly modulated in the pleasure of tock-tick, tock-tick, tock-tick. The erotic guides her/his mouth/hand to tickle all the right numbers.

iii

You are hyperventilating and sweating, strawberry juice on a bed of swan's down, regretting the finitude of positions. There are only so many you can attain. Only motion, not position, can let you journey to infinity. Pure unafraid motion-sound associations becoming image becoming a physical reckoning that cradles back to unsounded sensation or whips out into an alley called joy and pain. The erotic is mimesis. Though your mind is sometimes as white as noise, it is always embodied in the movement of jet-black sand. She/he is the body in motion, a boundless aesthetic potential: he/she is juice undamned, flowing through the least opening it can find. In that nanosecond of crystal clarity you are anointed and ordained. Sanctified experimentation complete.

You are Eros.

Red Lights

JANICE W. HODGES

thumping heartbeats
rush red lights
thrusting rhythm
stains the night

Nzinga Astral Travels

AJUBA JOY

He speaks in sentiments of depths,
too deep to deny a fantasy of
What if!

I ask my heart beating slightly faster than his own

What does he want?
Who is this Soul brother catapulting
lyrical litanies my way
placing me in a subliminal trance
utilizing only
the oxygen stored in my blood
for I have ceased to breathe,
caught in his web of
expression,
dangling with the nature of passion.

The order of things in my life
is temporarily in suspended
animation.
I know the feeling of love lost,
love's giving,
love's receiving,
love's lies,
love's eternal
murmuring

I reach for Imhotep's wish, the hope, the dream of
love, power,
peace and ease.

. . .

Nzinga recognizes she is amiss,
Gliding forward to a new calm,
with syncopated thoughts of being loved
Godly,
        held warmly,
           listened to intently,
             massaged deeply,
               kissed tenderly,
                 respected highly.

Remembering ancient memories, they take
flight,
fused with nova heat and uncanny delight of no
words,
        Only submission.
He reads her telepathic whisper.

It's what you do, that makes you free

He enters her Warm Organized Meticulous Body (womb)
    and is
nourished;
    He feeds from her Nile and she responds with paroxysmal
      pleasure.
        They exhale, they stay, Oya! Oya!

She asks again who is this Soul brother?
What does he want?

I awaken in my king-size bed with no king in
it.
   Whew! that was deep!
   Hmmmmm! Astral traveling again Ajuba?

I just need ten more minutes before getting up to
face
the internally oppressed and the racist for the
day.

Marrow

TIM SEIBLES

I suppose it is too late to say there is a lesson
in the way a woman's eyes take over an evening,
how her legs move all the tall ships in my blood—

and this thread pulled taut around my belly,
the liquid spool of her hips finding the book of praise
inside me: how old must I get not to feel it

opening like a door in my chest. Inside me
there must be an abandoned city where only
one man lives walking around looking for company,

while inside him someone else calls out
in some other solitary place. To the marrow.
I think this keeps being true.

I have opened my eyes every day for 38 years
and I am not much wiser, no matter how it all pours in,
but so often and unslowly the world is simply the face

and fluid gate of a woman coming into view.
I can't say anything else about it: these open streets
and lamplit avenues; the beautiful names gathering

along the tongue's front edge, a surge of something
like a prayer for someone to touch, loneliness,
my lungs almost holding on to the air—her mouth
delicious, her legs, one moving next to the other.

Hands

RANDALL MOORE

He has strong hands. Hands that caress my innermost thoughts my outermost sensations.

With these hands he makes love to my mind, to my heart, to my body, and my soul.

I dream of his hands, strong . . . stroking the nape of my neck, the small of my back, the skin on my face.

His hands, causing my mind to travel to places that I never dreamed I'd go. Wanting him to take me . . . there wanting him to take me . . . now.

I write these words and I feel his hands holding me down, holding me safe . . .

I caress his hands feeling his energy through every pore, through every fingertip. It's hard to resist taking him in my mouth, feeling his energy on every tastebud, stroking him with my tongue, feeling him run down my throat. Ever so gently he fills me, makes me want more . . . I watch his reaction; am I drawing energy from him, does he feel me feeling him? I wonder.

It's all spontaneous, him, me, us! Why is it happening so fast? Why do I feel this way? Two months ago all I wanted was . . . Now, I think of his hands, his fuck. It's like a fever. It's not a fever I want to get rid of . . .

Take it slow they say . . . I'm trying, but his hands hold me, I long to feel his hands hold me, moving me . . . It takes over me, my physical, mortal, and spiritual being.

Do I . . . could I possibly have the same effect . . . It's not safe to let this show. Does he see, he sees everything else. I'm afraid, but it feels good. Will he protect me, will he shelter me? Can I ask him these questions and still have him? I wonder.

I keep thinking of his hands, why do they turn me on? I daydream of hot sticky nights, honey, fruits (the really juicy ones), ice cream, and whipped cream. I hear pleasurable sounds screams of delight surround me. Damn, don't go there . . . Sometimes I think, sometimes I wonder . . . am I transparent? Does he have an insight that few people have? I don't want to know. My mind keeps wandering . . . back to his hands . . . strong . . .

they make me feel safe why do I trust him, what is it in his hands that makes me . . . it fills me completely . . . Happiness, something I haven't felt in a long time, I thought I was, but his hands . . .

Caressing me, making me . . . go there, that place only his hands can make me . . . go. I'm sitting here now wondering why he's not here. I miss his hands, the touch . . . the feelings are aching to come up and out . . . His hands . . . they evoke undescribable, relentless, dramatic . . . I daydream . . . they explore . . . touching me places I didn't know existed.

His hands, I wish, I want . . .

sweetness

J A D E   D .   B A N K S

your palms grip my hips

your lips at my tenderness

my life force rushes to you

Winnefred's Mother

GLENN JOSHUA

After spending a lifetime of doubting the usefulness of celebrating national holidays, I think I found out the true meaning of at least one of them right after a spectacular Thanksgiving dinner.

Winnefred's mother and I walked into the living room to join Winnefred and her father as they watched the football game, and as Winnefred's mother sat next to me on the love seat, the lightest brush of her fingers fell squarely on my crotch. Winnefred and her father sat across from us on the sofa, hypnotized by the screen. Normally, the move would've been written off as purely accidental, but by then I kinda knew better.

That's the way it had been all afternoon.

Winnefred's mother glanced in the direction of her husband and daughter before leisurely patting my thigh. "Winnie, this here's a fine young man," she said. They didn't hear.

Winnefred and her dad were big Cowboy fans, and her father, in particular, who'd been talking NFL to me throughout most of the meal earlier, was now geared up for gridiron action.

It all began one hour before.

"Let the boy eat, Larry," Winnefred's mother had said to her husband while we all ate. But I suppose he didn't feel comfortable mentioning anything unless the conversation was on seemingly manly fare. Like pro sports, for instance. I mean, realistically, we couldn't rhapsodize about his daughter, which was actually the only thing we had in common. No way, brother. I could just see it. Heaven forbid he would ask me . . .

"How did we meet? Yes sir. Winnie and I met in World Civ. She sat next to me for two months wearing nothing but those spicy, tight-ass things your credit cards probably paid for. Oh yeah, and your daughter used to raise up them big fine legs every so often to give me a flash of pantie whenever I would drop my pencil on purpose. You know, we'd toss out a little eye play and a stupid grin or two every now and then without ever saying a word to each other. Then one day before midterms, she'd asked me if I could help her study the Glorious Revolution. And that night, it was.

"Anyway, now that Winnefred has fallen in love with the dick, I guess she just had to invite me over for Thanksgiving dinner. That was cool because I didn't have anything special planned today. You see, my parents flew up to Seattle to spend the holiday with my aunt and uncle, so I said, Sure, why not? I mean, who can turn up their nose to a free meal, and a free fuck to boot? I know I can't."

Winnefred's father had rambled on between bites of turkey and dressing. I stayed silent, tripping on my ready responses if or whenever he felt like bringing up Winnie. But he never did. Winnefred's father, with fork in hand, took a glance at his watch and began to titter. Dallas was playing Green Bay at home at three, and Winnefred's mom had to hurry to make sure all the food was set and eaten in time for the game. Despite her flurry, Winnefred's mother had everything in perfect order.

The meal, to say the least, was interesting.

"More giblet gravy, Kevin?"

"No, ma'am," I replied. Winnefred's parents were on opposite ends of the table, with me and Winnefred in the middle.

"How is your turkey, Larry?" Winnefred's mother asked her husband, but Winnefred was in the process of questioning her father on Dallas's 3–4 defense, so he left his wife hanging.

Winnefred's father turned and asked me, "How do you think Emmitt's gonna do today, Kevin?"

"Emmitt? . . . Smith?"

Winnefred rolled her eyes.

"Ol' number 22's gonna kick butt today, Daddy," she chimed. "I've been catching all the games in my dorm all season." Winnefred gazed adoringly at her father before spooning a shaking clump of cranberry sauce.

Winnefred's father nodded to his daughter before trying me out once again. I was met with a scrutinizing eye.

"So Kevin, who's your favorite team."

Off the top of my head I blurted out, "The Buffalo Bills." When Winnefred gasped I realized my error and suddenly wished I'd simply played dumb.

Three weeks ago Winnefred and I were in my bed watching ESPN's Sunday night game. It was the Chargers against the Bills.

"Turn the channel," Winnefred had said.

"Whattya mean?" I was massaging a penis still humming from a recent bombardment of both honey and teeth. "I thought you liked football."

"My daddy says the AFC isn't football." Winnefred was on my stomach as I lay upright on my bed's headframe. Her hands tugged my chest hairs before reaching for the remote control. "My dad told me that the AFC stands for the All Fag Conference, and any God-fearing man who prefers the AFC over the NFC might as well call himself a fag too."

I remembered lying in bed chuckling benignly at her statement that night, but later, as I sat there at the Thanksgiving Day table, I could feel the tension closing in around my throat like a well-worn pair of Winnefred's panty hose.

"The Buffalo Bills, huh?" Winnefred's father muttered. A swift look to his daughter spoke a thousand words. He wrinkled his brow, inspecting me like I was some strange unidentifiable growth billowing up from his dining room chair.

Winnefred's father never spoke to me again.

"Is that the team Shaquille plays for?" Winnefred's mother made a valiant attempt to save me. I saw Winnefred mouth an "Oh my God" under her breath. "Just pass the dinner rolls, please, Mother," Winnefred said out loud. Winnefred's mother slid the platter to her daughter, who was already once again reminiscing on Dallas's glory years of the seventies with her father. Winnefred's mother resumed her attention to me and asked about my hobbies, lighting up when I mentioned listening to jazz and reading popular novels. The woman knew nothing about football, and it was becoming clear her primary concern and focus throughout the meal was on me. Her matronly politeness was evolving into something close to spirited flirting. But at that time I shook it off because I really couldn't be sure.

Winnefred's mother had a petite, shapely little frame, and I found myself watching her body dart back and forth into the kitchen during the meal, returning with trays of more tantalizing goodies cooked with great expertise and care. All the while, Winnefred's mother engaged me in witty conversation, oblivious to her husband and child's one-sided topic.

"What is your major, Kevin?" Her large, probing eyes had now moved a shade beyond idle chatter. They waited impatiently for me to speak. Her eyes were alive, addressing my active imagination, "Kevin. I'm hungry . . . Even with all this food spread out before us. I'm still . . . ravenous."

Kevin, you're tripping, I thought.

"This is my last year of finance. My graduation is next May."

Winnefred and her father had forgotten us, enchanting themselves with a myriad of football stars and post-season playoff predictions. Winnefred's mother saw that her husband's plate was almost empty.

"How was dinner, Larry?" she asked him. In response he grunted what I assumed was an affirmative, followed by a loud putrid fart.

"Daddy, how gross," Winnefred teased. Her laugh was mischievous. "I can't believe you."

I couldn't believe it either. Winnefred's mother, who surely should have been embarrassed by her husband's flatulent flare-up, paid it no mind. She asked me if the food was all right.

"This is the best Thanksgiving meal I ever had," I replied, almost to myself. Winnefred and her father were pushing away from the table.

Kickoff time was in five minutes.

Beneath the cacophony of rustling furniture and anxious movement, Winnefred's mother took my hand on the table. She squeezed it.

"I want you . . ."

"Huh?" I looked up, startled. Winnefred was out of the dining room. Her father trailed close behind. I turned my head to Winnefred's mother.

"What did you say, ma'am?"

She laughed. "I said, I want you to help me with my finances in the future. If you can spare the time."

"Sure. I'd love to." But by now I was getting confused.

"You see," Winnefred's mother went on in a chirping singsong, "there are a few shortcomings in my life that just aren't adding up." She threw a lasting look on her husband as she said that. "And I may need a hand in making sure certain things fit."

Winnefred's mother caressed my hand. "Kevin, I believe you might be just the one who can help me."

I gagged on sweet potato pie. I pushed away from the table as she gave me a pat on the back.

"Are you okay?" She straddled me, grasping my head next to her bosom. Our coupling took me by surprise, and in my haste to maintain balance I grabbed the first thing I could, which turned out to be a firm but yielding middle-aged behind. My hands recoiled like I had touched something hot.

Well. It was definitely *warm*.

Unfazed, Winnefred's mother stood between my legs, rubbed my shoulders, and cooed, "I can't have my handsome guest choking to death in my dining room."

"I'm all right," I croaked as soon as I could find my breath.

Seeing that I wasn't in any immediate danger of expiring, Winnefred's mother returned to her seat at the head of the table. We were alone. Winnefred and her father were in the living room, glued to the game. By the intensity of their shouts and cheers, they didn't seem to mind our absence.

"I can get you a glass of water, Kevin, if you want." Winnefred's mother cupped my face in her concerned palm.

"No, ma'am." I grinned sheepishly. Then I gave her a smile that was sexy as hell. Winnefred's mother was just too eager to throw one back. She obviously wasn't minding our absence from the living room either.

"Kevin, would you mind helping me clean up in the kitchen?" Her smile was excruciatingly sweet. The intent, unmistakable. Her eyes sparkled with an energy and sophistication foreign to me until that day. She led the way and I followed; her humble assistant, her willing instrument of facilitation.

The dishes were stacked high, and I rolled up my sleeves to get down to business. Winnefred's mother had the faucet running. I stood next to her at the sink, catching an abrupt scent of feminine heat mixing pleasantly with the smell of Palmolive dishwashing liquid.

Winnefred's mother was a head shorter than me and had to look up to make sure I caught her eyes when she spoke.

"Kevin," she said. "You wash, and I'll dry." Before I could work my mouth to say, "Fine with me," she had knelt down and unzipped my jeans with one fluid movement. I looked over my shoulder toward the kitchen door, expecting either Winnefred or her father to come in for chips and beer at any time during a commercial.

"What are you doing?"

Winnefred's mother gave me an impish smirk and pointed to a dirty dish. "Wash it. Wash it clean for me, Kevin."

She whipped out my dick and I commenced to washing the hell out of that one dish for five minutes straight. I was washing that sucker so hard you would've thought Winnefred's mother had served oven-fried shit on it instead of oyster dressing.

"Kevin! You're missing the game!" It was Winnefred calling me from the living room. "What are you doing back there!" Upon hearing her daughter, Winnefred's mother assumed an urgent rhythm in sync with my supersonic circular arm motions.

"I'm washing dishes!" I yelled out.

"Gladys!" Winnefred's father shouted. "Leave them dishes and let that boy come in here!"

Winnefred's mother stopped sucking and giggled like a coed. She held me in her hand long enough to murmur, "Sorry, Larry. He's coming in here."

"Gladys. Do you hear me, woman?" Heavy footfalls began moving toward us. I panicked and tried to pull away, but Winnefred's mother had the whole situation in hand, and she wasn't letting go.

"Come on, Kevin. Hurry, baby." She moaned before devouring me in her mouth again. I could imagine Winnefred's father passing through the dining room, the intensity of his steps sounded like he was approximately seven paces away from opening the kitchen door. I was close but not close enough. I wasn't going to make it.

We were busted.

"You can do it." Winnefred's mother took a breath and urged me on. The footsteps kept approaching, and I wildly began searching for an escape route. The kitchen window was just my size. That's when I heard Winnefred scream.

"Daddy! Deion just intercepted!"

"What?" I saw the kitchen door open slightly before he stopped in his tracks and about-faced it back into the living room in two seconds flat. Winnefred's mother didn't miss a beat. The shouts and hollers in the living room went well with me scoring the play of the day just as Deion scored his.

Two minutes later, Winnefred's mother and I joined Winnefred and her father in the living room just in time for the second quarter. We watched the Cowboys pound the Packers all afternoon, but by far what was more thrilling was when Winnefred's mother, who was sitting next to me on the love seat, would secretly stroke a dick still recovering from the oral thrashing it was subjected to a few moments ago in the kitchen.

During a commercial break in the fourth quarter, Winnefred glanced my way with a familiar glint in her eye, very much reflective of her mother's.

"Would you like to go someplace after the game, Kevin?" I didn't say anything at first. But I can only imagine how satisfying my smile must've looked to her right then. Here I was, full as a tick from the meal, buzzing from an endless supply of Budweisers, my favorite next to Heineken, and almost totally recovered from the after-dinner set with Winnefred's mother. The beer in my left hand was fresh and ice cold. I took a sip, sort of sorry it wasn't Old Milwaukee, 'cause at that point, it sho' didn't get no better than this.

"Anywhere is okay with me," I finally said to Winnie. Her mother gave me a firm pat on the thigh.

"Winnie, Kevin can drop by anytime, you hear?" She glanced triumphantly at her daughter. "He's such a big, fine young man." Winnefred smiled as if she knew something her mother didn't, and Winnefred's mother I suppose did likewise.

Awhile later, Winnefred and I got up to go. Her mother already had my coat in hand as we walked through the foyer leading to the front door.

"Winnie, don't let Kevin be a stranger." She then turned to her husband, who was catching the post-game show.

"Larry. Kevin's leaving," Winnefred's mother said. The man gave me a halfhearted wave from the sofa, and I could only shake my head and wonder how a guy could be so into Michael Irvin when he had one of the best wide open receivers in the conference right underneath his own roof.

"Hope you enjoyed it," Winnefred's mother whispered to me. Her face was pressed next to mine. She deftly tickled my dick one last time before pulling away. "We'd love to have you back, Kevin. How does Christmas sound?"

I didn't want to push my luck knowing that, as it was, I was making a getaway by the skin of my teeth. But bless her heart, Winnefred's mother was insisting. "We will be expecting you for Christmas dinner, won't we, Kevin?"

"Only if you let me help you with the dishes," I replied sincerely. I bid Winnefred's mother farewell, already counting the days before I'd return to make my Season's Greetings.

While walking to the car, Winnefred asked me if I was ready for some "holiday pussy," and I looked up into the clear sky and offered up a solemn testament of thanks. The meaning of Thanksgiving was brought home, and to this day, it has remained one holiday that I will always cherish.

I'm not even gonna talk about what Christmas means to me.

Profile This

ANTHONY BARBOZA

On the heels
up the ankles
calves be real
thighs is steel
romp rump hump
protruding
got to stop
to nose gram
slide my ham
lick the crevice
That's heaven in your heaviness
pause and rest
drawing up the spine
in time
palms guide
slide ride up and back
to shoulder-hold
Treetop
coconut brown round
round over & down
temple crest
glide on the nose
eyes doze
pools deep piercing
sign of heat
brow break yes shake
shake
Breath and smell
nose knows open
lip style
thirst

sucking
stop to burst
Tongue swirling
lashing
Lips be thrashing
juicy retreat
to chin & down
neck to the collar
bone—yes more

meat
Circling O's black
satin feats
double treats my eyes
meet
down & round
A belly bounce then a hip
every ounce buttons
wait-quake-breathing
sighs
I approach the navel
grasslands tingle
fire glowing black coals
of gold
Beyond that land
my lips
my hands
my dick
in the nick
The head done rise
plunging tides
I'm lost
Holy heaven does open
Suddenly! a sound
a murmur
building into a cry
another sight
up again with
esteem & mean

a scream
sweet
retreat
rehearse
Without a curse
I must stay
come home coming
Now that is hard
Yeah soo hard
but I must continue
down sweet soul smelling
Wind blowing sure makes me think
purposes put in ink
on land the sand
beach heat
Head high the thigh
and another thigh
thick black ruby
rush up up
up again
Shaft shift
Stiff dick dip
a lunge a plunge
Yes juicy fruity
berries the blackest
be in grasslands
grown
a moan
Once given once shone
Better meat I have
not eat.
for thrice I treat
then retreat past knocking knees
and shin bones licking feet
with telling tales
tricks of heat
profile with style
is complete!
Now I must go

with a leap
Back up to grasp
What I have caste
I remember—a member
Do you hear?
I forgot the ear.

timed

KAZEDGE

for emory

out of himself
and into me like
a wet locomotive
curving the tracks
at 2:45 a.m.
back arched
cutting against the fog
edge against my mist
he is on time
always on time

His Side

SHARON A. LEWIS

*N*athan, did you hear my question? Do you want me to repeat my question?"

"No, I heard you the first time. I am still madly in love with her."

"Is it lust or love?"

"Both!"

"How can you still love her after all that you've told me. Have you forgotten that she's the most self-centered, egotistical, manipulative . . ."

"Please stop!"

"Have you seen her lately?"

"No. I rang the doorbell, but I walked away. I just could not begin to release all the hostility that has generated over the last three years. She says that she's ready to change. All of a sudden she wants to hear me out. Normally when we talk she's doing all the talking; and I'm trying to control my anger so I don't say a word. Finally, when I interrupt her, I barely complete a thought before she's blaming me for everything that has gone wrong in her life. Over the last three weeks, I've driven by the house, but I just can't bring myself to wait until she opens the door before I walk away."

When I'm alone, I keep remembering how I felt when she charged five designer suits and a round-trip ticket for herself to Maui on the American Express right before she told me that she quit her job to return to school. I almost lost my cool when I saw the charge bill for $6,000, due at the end of the month.

Sharon always compared me to her ex-lovers. I trusted her Christian faith and spiritualism so much that I did not question her about how she knew how much money those guys grossed. She knew enough about where they shopped, vacationed, and what they wore to constantly compare my Brooks Brothers suits to their Armani's. She would say that if Sean or Arnold had my education and position that she would have already graced the covers of *Jet* and *Ebony* magazines.

I thought that a woman as young as her, with as much as I gave her, would truly appreciate me. But she held my every effort and many gifts in contempt. She never said thank you for the pearls that I individually hand-picked while on a trip to China. I know for certain that no other man ever gave her anything but a bad back and vicious attitude. You would not believe the clothes that she was wearing when we first started dating. Her clothes looked like she was looking for any man to just make an offer.

I could understand if she was not happy at one job or maybe two jobs, but during our three-year marriage, Sharon changed jobs seventeen times. Of course she needed a new wardrobe for each job whether it paid minimum wage or sixteen dollars an hour. She seemed to be very hostile that my job was so secure and stable. I could sense her total irritation about how I could set my own hours and get off whenever I wanted. She did not realize that I worked long and hard hours many years before I met her. I'm beginning to believe what my friends said, which was that all she knew was that I was a lawyer, and she started seeing dollar signs while planning how fast she could spend it all.

On one occasion that I sent her a dozen roses, the delivery man arrived at my office saying that the woman did not want my flowers. But when I finally agreed not to accompany her to her reunion, then she started doing wifely duties again. I struggled with the kids, the house, and my job for a week while she rested and played with her friends.

I have always enjoyed the festivities surrounding Christmas until I got married. Lately, I have dreaded to look at the final tallied dollar mount. For instance, last year I already had fifteen blends of suits in my closet that were all paid for and in good condition. She bought me, and actually she did not buy the suits because I paid the bill in the end anyway, but she carried home four new suits for me. That couple of hours of shopping cost me $3,400. Now count up all the shopping hours possible during the season and you can imagine how the final amount replaced my love.

I don't understand it. She never wanted to keep the kids home with her or take them on her errands. She refused to buy them clothes or toys or to go to their games. Many people thought that I was a single father. Recently, a woman recognized the kids with her and asked if she was the baby-sitter.

She always had a hair or nail appointment. She had a personal trainer although she did not have a gym membership. I don't even want to think about where they worked out. She was too busy to accompany me to family cookouts at my parents' home.

I certainly do not miss her jealousy. I had to fire the best secretary that I have ever had because Sharon said that Becky was staring at my butt. I had to change cleaners since supposedly the female employees at one cleaners were calling me too often about my suits and the starch in my shirts. Our phone number has been changed so often that my business cards do not list my home number. She would not go to church because the women at all four churches that we joined as a family were trying to seduce me.

She blamed me and the kids for her not getting into professional school and not being able to hold down a job. It took me a long time to realize that Sharon cared about nobody and nothing except herself. With cautious eyes I've watched her manipulate my emotions of love yet denounce my lack of feelings.

I stood by while she cussed out my barber, my brother, and flirted with my best friends, but when she started treating my mother with contempt, I could not help but put her out of my life. I listened to her excuses about why the baby got burned with the curling iron as she sat on the phone with her friends.

I've shouldered the blame for her not being happy with her jobs even though I know that if she didn't party so hard in college, she probably would be where I am now or at least on her way.

She constantly reminded me that I was not the first man with whom she was intimate, nor the first man to propose marriage to her. But I was also not the man who beat her in her face with his fist nor did I ever give her any reason to stay up all night waiting for me to come home. I made sure Sharon knew that I wanted her from the first time I ever saw her. I loved the way she smiled. I craved her body from the beginning and I still do even after two children.

I sat at work thinking about her eyes and her smell and her lips and her legs and her breasts. I couldn't wait to get home and do to her everything that I fantasized. Then I woke up and realized that I walked out because she made it too hard for me to love her. Now she says she's ready to let me love her. I just don't know.

Cherry Blessings

J Z B

She loves sensuously.
With mouth, tongue, and tears.
Warm jasmine oils, candlelight, and bubble baths.

She loves with her whole heart.
With blackberry preserves his mother made.
Beet juice. And sorghum molasses from home
which make their even sweeter bodies
melt into their oneness.

She loves innocently.
With the energy that always leads the sun
back to the east and allows the child
to love even in death.

She loves with cherry blessings which promise
to ripen soon and assure her that the
wisdom of the moon and the sacred sounds
of the sea gently guide the fruits of her
womb on their pilgrimage.
They whisper:
Be patient. The trees, the earth, the moon—the stars await
our arrival; all the universe is on our side.

She loves with each breath, each pulse, each beat of her ancient heart.

Teenager's Bedroom

ESTELLE FARLEY

Parked
Lights off, engine silenced
"Momma said come home straight from the movies."
Hand dance begins, buttons undone
"Don't kiss me there"
Marvin Gaye's on radio
Breathing on sync
Heavy, hot weight
"Where's a Stevie Wonder song?"
Window fogs
Cocooned space
Fingers fight then conspire
Luther Vandross begins.

The Assistant

GILDA N. SQUIRE

*T*he board meeting was finally over. Four long hours of presentations, negotiations, and voting had taken its toll on Damion. He was ready to relax, just plain chill. These meetings always had this effect on him, and he sometimes wondered why he had gotten himself into this business of music. What he most enjoyed though were the people who he worked with on a daily basis. Those *fine* Nubian sistas who graced the hallways of the record company with their beautiful skin, meticulous clothing and hair, and manicured hands. Damion could have claimed any number of these women as his own because they too admired his six-foot-one chiseled frame which always was clothed in Armani or Tommy. The handsomely shaven head and deep brown eyes only added to his daringly good looks.

There is, however, only one woman for Damion—Tabitha. Damion and Tabitha have been working together in the public relations department for three years. Tabitha is a slender, very chic young woman whose life consisted of work and more work, that is until her mind shifted toward Damion. He had heard several of his colleagues laugh and talk about the "freaky shit" they were doing with their assistants. And he knew that he and Tabitha had to be careful, what with all the sexual harassment controversy taking front and center. *None* of it compared to what he and Tabitha shared, *especially* after these lengthy meetings.

Tabitha walks into the office. Damion is already there sitting on the desk *sans* shirt and pants. He is wearing that CK underwear that Tabitha likes so much. As she locks the door behind her, she slowly begins to unbutton her blouse. By the time she reached the desk on which Damion had planted himself, there was a heap on the floor of their tossed clothing. Damion had taken care of the phones; the lines were switched to voice mail. "You have reached the public relations department. I'm sorry that we're unavailable to help you . . ."

Damion pulls Tabitha up to him, lifts her onto his lap, and puts her on the desk. He wraps his hands around her ass and softly squeezes it. Tabitha forcefully wraps her StairMaster-trained legs and thighs around Damion's small waist. She could feel his long, lean dick really good now. Yeah . . . just like she likes it.

Tabitha reaches farther across the desk, knocking over the container of pencils and pens. There was that bottle of white wine her hands were searching for. She gently pours some on her breasts as Damion kisses, sucks, and licks the sweet wine off her honeydew skin. He follows the trailing wine with his tongue as it reaches it final destination between her legs. This is his favorite part. The white wine and her natural juices flowing together between his lips absolutely make his shiver.

As Damion takes possession of Tabitha's most private treasure, she flinches and sighs as she opens her legs wider with her heels clinging to the edge of the desk. His tongue quickly flickers up and down and side to side on her clitoris. Tabitha lets out a deep moan and then a silent scream that only Damion can hear. And when Tabitha can't take anymore, she grabs Damion's head and gives him the signal that it is time.

They quickly change positions so that Damion is now on the desk. He thrusts his hard penis into her drenched vagina. Neither could wait for the ultimate excitement which is ahead. Tabitha quietly tells Damion to just sit back and relax. All those hours on her StairMaster proves to be beneficial. Her legs, thighs, and hips are ready for the work. She pumps long and hard until they explode onto each other.

For a few short moments, they lie draped over the cherry wood executive desk covered in perspiration. They had missed lunch. Well, sort of. There is another meeting at 4:00 P.M. They quickly shower together in the office's private bathroom. After they are fully clothed, they give each other a complete checkover to make sure all is in place.

As Tabitha leans on the desk and glides on her mod velour lipstick, she yells out to Damion, "That will be all, Damion. Thank you. Oh, and get me the director of promotions on the phone and cancel my dinner appointment for tonight."

"Yes, Ms. Johnson. Consider it done," Damion responds.

Just another dull day in the office.

Sugar

HONOREE F. JEFFERS

You are my candy.
The sweetness when you come, so
colorful the taste.

Cutting

NIAMA LESLIE JOANN WILLIAMS

he woke up with his arms around her waist and his knees tucked into hers. She smiled at the warmth and worried that the arm he'd placed underneath her might have fallen asleep. Too many times she had felt that particular stiffness, those uncomfortable twinges. She wished him no discomfort. She wanted his life to be easy, sweet, hard. That was the problem. She loved a man who needed to grow up.

She tossed that thought out and closed her eyes, reveling in the intimacy of his touch. She loved sleeping with his knees tucked into hers. It made him more than her lover, it made him a man who wanted to be exactly where he was. She concentrated on the pulse in his legs. She moved his arm from beneath her. She rubbed the moist brown skin. Brought back circulation, blood. She thought about biting him when her eyes fell on the letter opener.

She blinked.

It was too close to the bed—how had she let that happen?

And then they began. The knife thoughts. She picked up the letter opener in her mind, the black-handled letter opener, much beloved gift of a friend, and brought the gilded point into contact with the palest part of his forearm, the underside, the side that got the least sun, the part where you could see his veins most clearly. She always pressed the point slowly, between interminable ticks of the kitchen clock. The first spurt of blood always surprised her, then caused her first deep breath of freedom. After that, she pressed harder, faster, and deeper, severing the vein, bleeding him slowly into unconsciousness. He never stirred, never felt the pain, because she drugged him first. There was a firm air of premeditation about the whole procedure. She had knives in every room now and the letter opener by the bed—that was the final straw. Soon she wouldn't be dreaming this. Soon she would be answering to policemen and psychiatrists about why she had slowly bled her lover to death. At first she had fantasized drinking the blood from one of her best flutes, but had acquiesced to the feel of his warm blood on her skin, permanently staining the sheets.

The phone rang.

She started, shook her head to clear it, made sure the letter opener was still a safe distance away. He murmured and turned in his sleep, his knees no longer tucked.

The caller did not leave a message.

Her day was beginning and he was still alive.

She told herself the knife in her purse was for protection. She never imagined pulling it on someone. Then her boss walked in.

"How's the book coming?"

She grimaced. "It's at the publishers. This is the fourth time I've told you."

"Oh! I'm sorry. So many faculty to keep track of. I forget. That's the thing about you, Sara—you always do what you envision. A four-hundred-page edited book out while still a graduate student, a book of interviews the very next year, and now your dissertation, fully rewritten for a wider audience, at a publisher. And they all started with a little idea in your head. I might actually have to recommend you for tenure."

Sara forced herself to keep a straight face. "If you like."

"And so gracious!" The department chair forced a smile.

Sara didn't. "It's hard to smile with a knife in your back."

The department chair's face finally reflected the naked envy she felt. "A warning?"

Sara's face was expressionless. "No, just an observation based on experience."

The false smile returned. "Oh, well then. I suppose I will see you at the faculty meeting? Nine A.M. sharp."

"Yes, nine A.M. Now I really have to get back to these papers."

"Always the work! Truly destined for greatness. Press on, Sara, press on!" The department chair bustled out with an energy as false as the positivity she feigned.

Sara sighed. Why couldn't she have knife fantasies about that witch who hadn't published anything in twenty years? Sara's brilliance and success daily assaulted the chair, who'd had a fast rise twenty years ago before leveling off into mediocrity. To make matters worse, the students loved Sara. She treated them with respect, like they had brains that actually functioned. Plus she intrigued them. Her lectures were often ciphers she challenged them to solve. The combination was deadly. She and the department chair had been enemies from day one.

But the knife thoughts only came at the wee hours of the morning when she woke up in his arms or postcoitally, when she lay back to revel in the feel of his sweat on her skin. Then she would think of taking a small silver blade and drawing a fine line across his throat, angling the blood to fall just to the left of her face, carefully darkening the sheet and not the pillow.

He wanted to marry her and she was very afraid.

"What's this doing in here?" He held the letter opener up for her to see.

"Oh! I, uh, decided to open my mail in bed yesterday. You know—combining two of my favorite pleasures—bed and the mail."

He laughed. "I thought you had strict rules about opening the mail only in your office." His brown eyes twinkled. "Are you gonna bring those ignominious piles of organization in here?"

She took the letter opener from him, blade first. It was almost a snatch. She was sweating.

"No," she said sharply, "I was just—indulging myself while you were out yesterday. Don't worry; I won't break our rule. No work in the bedroom."

He smiled. "Don't sweat it." He laughed, looking at the beads on her forehead. "Literally. We all slack off sometimes."

She frowned, then took a deep breath. She didn't want to look at him as she spoke. "Don't tonight, though, okay? Remember, we've got to save for the wedding and the honeymoon. All sets of parents are broke."

He didn't even look annoyed. "I know, I know. We're only going cruising—no buyin'. I just need my Friday-night fix."

"Okay." She smiled. "Thank God for Sheila. At least she understands the components you get excited about. I'm still using the system I bought ten years ago."

He walked over to her and put his arms around her shoulders, drawing her to his chest. "Theodore doesn't understand why Sheila and I love cruising computer stores either. What can I say?"

She held the letter opener tighter, stroking his back muscles with it, her eyes closing in anticipation.

"Just don't buy anything, okay?"

"Okay." He jumped. "Hey, watch that thing, will you?"

Her eyes snapped open.

He squeezed her tightly and she hated herself for nagging. She loved him, and he spent too much money. He only had a master's degree to her Ph.D., and was doing nothing with his brilliant filmmaking skills. He taught high school music and convinced himself he loved it because at least he'd completed the certification process. He was not even envisioning his potential and was spending just enough to make her uncomfortable. And she was going to marry him because he was her first mature love. She knew she wanted no one else. But it meant a lifetime of parenting him and hating herself for it. So she slipped into fantasies of bleeding him, of killing him in a way that allowed her to feel his warmth to the end. 'Cause he made love like no man she had ever known and believed in cuddling after.

It was about so much more than body heat.

"I almost stuck him yesterday."

The room was dark except for the candles on the altar and the light in Asha's eyes.

"But you still love him."

"I stroked his back with a letter opener. I almost drew blood. There were fine scratches on his skin this morning. I saw them when he got out of the shower. I'm going to kill him, Asha."

Asha did not move. Her stillness betrayed a peace that could terrify. Sara had grown used to it, desired it for herself from the moment she had met the priestess.

"You're not listening to them, Sara. Close your eyes and listen."

It was All Hallow's Eve. Not significant for Sara or Asha, a Yoruba priestess, but Sara knew it was the final night. If she didn't emerge with answers tonight she would leave him. The letter opener had felt too good in her hands the night before.

She closed her eyes as Asha instructed and watched the candle flames flicker through her lids as Asha had taught her. Soon she was in the flicker, a part of it, following the flames' dance with movements of her own, her head to one side, her arms free, body elsewhere. She was attuned to the white candles now, it had been easier this time, and soon Obatala would speak to her in a vision.

Her foot stamped. The candle flames flickered madly.

"Stop fighting him, Sara."

She moaned in protest and flung her arms.

"Be a part of the flame. Give up your soul to him, Sara. Only Obatala can save you. Use your head."

She stomped again. Asha blew out one of the candles and Sara winced, crumpling her body.

"Concentrate on the center candle, Sara. Become its flicker. Give up your soul."

Her left foot lifted, then stopped in midair. She squinted. The flame that she saw through her eyelids flickered then went out and she was in total darkness. She screamed.

"Obatala is with you, Sara. Follow him."

She was frozen in motion. The candles continued to burn, Asha had not extinguished a single one, but she was in another room, another world, in darkness. Her left foot brushed against something warm. She knelt to feel it. At the second touch, she knew it was Andy's body, drained of blood. She wailed. She heard Asha's voice as if from a great distance, but could discern no words.

Her wail turned into a deep sighing, but she was not allowed even that. A force yanked her into a room of blazing sunlight and white walls. In this room her mother sat on a couch with her father. They were embracing, a smile on both of their lips. Sara felt an overwhelming rush of anger and ran forward, fingernails bared. She ripped at the image of her parents until they no longer embraced but stood back to back on separate sides of the room, frowning. She grimaced with satisfaction then turned away, in search of the dark room with the warm body of her lover. She did not find it, but the room of blazing sunlight slowly dimmed and the warmth of Andy's body began to envelope her. The warmth was heavy, burdensome, sweet. She let it grip her heart and paralyze her limbs. And then she began to keen in earnest, for she knew it was his soul passing away.

"I'm sorry," she said, tears on her cheeks, the knives from every room collected at her feet. They were sitting Indian-style on the living room floor on the Nubian-women rug they had made love on when first moving into this house.

"For what?" He looked bewildered.

"I have no models," she said, "so I wanted out at any price. I couldn't love you, be with you, share your life, because I'd never seen it done."

"But the knives, what did it mean?"

"I wanted to be one with you, but in a state where you couldn't hurt me. My parents' marriage dissolved long before I was born. I saw only bitterness and resentment. So a future with you was impossible, inconceivable, unless you had no power to hurt me. Unless you were dead."

"What!" It was a soft, bewildered whisper. He looked at the knives, one for every room in their two-story house. Then at her. She could feel his confusion, the return of a deep sense of betrayal.

"But I fought it," she pleaded, brushing his cheek with her fingertips. "I kept going to Asha until the dreams were clear to me. Until I saw what they hid. My scars. My anger."

He looked at her steadily for a long moment. "You never saw a happy marriage, did you?"

"No," she said, her eyes full, her fingertips still on his cheek.

"So you couldn't imagine . . ."

"No," she whispered, "I couldn't."

"Strangled by a fear of the unknown, your dreams struck out."

"Yes!" she exclaimed. "And I was terrified because what I dream I do. But the warmth. The warmth of your body never left me. It was in all the dreams. So I pressed on and made Asha's teachings work. She and Obatala saved us."

"And my life."

"And your life."

"My god." He ran his hands over his face. "The scars," he said. "The scars of childhood."

"Old demons never die. Until you bring them out into the light. Especially a flickering white candle's light."

"Thank God for Asha."

"Yes. And for you."

He looked at her, a reservoir of distrust and sympathy still in his eyes. She picked up the first knife and flung it into the fire. She flung them in one by one and watched the flames attack them. When she picked up the treasured letter opener he stopped her hand.

"No," she said. "It must go too. I almost drew blood with it."

He was silent. She tossed it in and watched the black ceramic base crackle and sputter. She burst into tears. He held her for a long time that night, but the warmth was slow in coming.

So Close to Hell

AMANDA TOWNSEND

You take my breast
in your mouth
and the ache that it transmits to my thighs
transports me onto the altar of infinity
so close so close to hell
you lick me
and I remain suspended
on my empty mountain of drunkenness
and as your tongue searches
for the center of my submission
you sacrifice me to the entire universe
so close so close to hell

Tout Proche de L'enfer

(French translation)

AMANDA TOWNSEND

Tu prends mon sein
dans ta bouche
et la douleur enflammée
qui s'elance entre mes cuisses
me transports sur l'autel de l'infinite
Tout proche tout proche de l'enfer
Tu me leches
et je reste suspendue
a ma montagne vide d'ivresse
et comme ta langue
cherche le centre de ma soumission
Tu me sacrifies a l'univers entier
Tout proche tout proche de l'enfer

Conversion: A Most Religious Experience

SADDI KHALI

i'm peering at you
     over book pages
         & in the silent sway of candlelight
          body oil makes your nakedness
          look like 'judgment day'
when sinners like me
  pray   (in repentance)
   hoping our clash
   earlier tonight on christianity
   hasn't deprived me my place
          where angels dance
          behind the gates
          of your double inner heaven

. . . woman   if you want i can be moses
standing at the sea of your thighs
  dying to be born again within you
        to be baptized
          in your sacred spaces
        to be saved . . .
i have seen the light   (the candlelight)
& i beg that you spread your gospel
                all over me
      deliver me from temptation
       show me your scriptures
       your places of worship
    please   woman   in the name
           of all that is holy
           open your faith to me

      baby   it's hell out here

. . .

. . . for i know that God is a forgiving one
　　　& i say grace
　　　　to pledge my devoutness
　　　　　at your altars
where you've anointed your body with oil
where i can dwell

　　　　　　in the house of your love
　　　　　　forever

　　　　& ever

　　　& ever . . .
　　　　　amen.

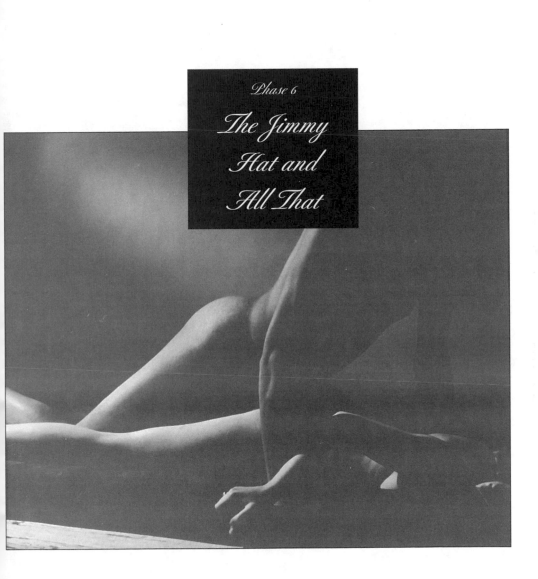

Phase 6

The Jimmy
Hat and
All That

*N*ow it is clear that we can never go back to where we should have never been. So we learn to live with the accoutrements that must go with our sexual selves here at the end of this hard-hearted century. Indeed, our protectives and toys must become essential parts of our erotic experiences, so much so that they cannot be imagined without the experience and the experience cannot be imagined without them. What then can writers make of the cyber-erotique?

This so-essential phase of Learjet level eroticism, raised to such lofty levels that sex—both carnal and cerebral—are erased from the linens of each page to become mental poltergeists only to be released through our loins. Kalammu ya Salaam ushers us into the safety-decade with two haikus that allow us to be as close as we can be in numbers 131 and 135 of his erotic series of images. Rae-Ree Richards's excerpt from the novel *I Wish Cotton Was a Monkey,* "Dirty Diana," shows the innocence of a young male's first brush with the erotic, and "these nights are not important" by StarrStarr skirts the edges of brash seduction as Liv Wright prodigally chases down "The Wandering Lover" in the most abstract way possible. "Monica," by Cheri Daughtery, makes us understand the new term of "bi-genderical" and blurs this new word in sheets of satin, as Joy Doss envelopes us in her "Circle of One." Estelle Farley awakes "Living in a Memory" and provides us with a perfect beginning to tie up the evening with Jerry W. Ward, Jr.'s "Miss Rose," as both narrator and object of desire drink in the fullness of the arcane. Lana Williams serves us "In the House" on her mother's fine bone china as you and I, dear reader, partake sips of "Intimate Times" with Janice W. Hodges. "These Bodies" touch intimately but do not touch in these days of sexual safety, as Tim Seibles so beautifully writes. For Nightingale in "SweatBurns" the vestiges of a little S & M are still timeless, while we are burned "Acid Black" by the Friday-night cavorting of Scott Jackson's pseudo-sexuality. In double-edged ode to the hell . . . and joys . . . of "Celibacy," Xavier restrains and releases without touching. Finally, Willie James King completely covers and brings to coital closure our safe-sex section with "Dear Lord, I Lift the Covers," wherein the narrator prays for the frustrated strength not to autoerotically release his seed in anger only.

We make love not of our time but of ourselves.

Haiku #131

KALAMMU YA SALAAM

I tongue touch your flesh
flower, spring sun slow sucking
rose to trembling bloom

Haiku #135

my butterfly breaths
flutter caress the female
flesh of your dark door

Dirty Diana (excerpt)
From I Wish Cotton Was a Monkey

RAE-REE RICHARDS

Willie Mitchell was crazy, ugly, and downright nasty. He was the kid in school who always wore dirty clothes, never combed his hair and went barefooted whenever he was not made to wear shoes. They lived about eight houses down from us on Delmar Ave. In a nasty duplex with overgrown grass. Even in the ghetto, there was class division. He had a sister named Diana, who was about three years older than us. And on top of everything else, she always smelled bad and wanted to fight. I was in the fourth grade then, and was always small for my age. There were only about four bullies that I actually encountered in my life. In rank order they were Dirty Diana, Raymond Claxton, Gil MacDonald, and Marvin. But she was very special because she was the meanest, ugliest, and by far the most confusingly frightening of them all. She was my PAR-ADOX, a metaphorical monster that plagues any live organism. I didn't understand. . . . My father would always tell me "never hit a woman," strange words coming from a man who made it a convenient habit. I took his advice to heart, even then in the face of such contradiction.

One day I was coming home from school when Diana, just for the hell of it, had decided that she would charge every kid that came down the street for the right to pass on their way home. There she stood, in the middle of the sidewalk, in all her wildebeest fury. I've never been one to respond well to intimidation, and to this day, one surefire way to ensure a quick-draw contest with me is to threaten me, but the only difference now is that I use the weapon of intelligence instead of my fists. I had the feeling in my stomach again as I approached the woman-beast that warm and fateful sunny afternoon. Word had already gotten back to me from all the kids that she was out of her cage and making a show of her strength and power. All my life to that point, I had battled for my little spot in the sunlight, free of intimidation, fear, and vulnerability. I would soon come to realize that Dirty Diana was only the beginning of this inevitable struggle. I'd had enough intimidation from the teachers at school that day and sometimes, like Rosa Parks, all it takes is the right combination of timing and mood, and enough becomes enough in our day-to-day struggles to mask the desperation of survival that consumes the powerless. Like most other angry Negroes, she took her anger out on other, 'less angry' Negroes. I was angrier than either of us could have ever known. In Rosa Parks–like fashion, I walked steadily down the sidewalk toward the house, which unfortunately was on the same side of the street as hers. It didn't matter which side I had chosen. THIS was about POWER and CONTROL. . . . This was about the ghetto insanity created by hopelessness and helplessness. It was about not breaking the rules and realizing my place in the food chain. This was about Diana having claimed her territory, and about me being an outsider. THIS was about my dealing with the hand I had been dealt in life, now and forever. . . . It was now or never. . . .

Diana had claimed the whole street anyway, at least for those under a certain age. She stood steadfastly in the middle of the sidewalk as I steadfastly walked into my destiny. "Whea my mummy?!" She loudly stated when I was within three feet of her rotting, bulking carcass. I didn't say a word but looked straight into her beaming demon eyes and stared silently. Again she asked, "Whea my mummy??!" I don't know if it was a premeditated strategy or fear that cut off my vocabulary, but I simply stood there and continued to stare at the PSYCHOLOGICAL REINCARNATION OF ALL MY PSYCHOLOGICAL MONKEYS. "You a fool an I'mo make you pay, muthafucka!" She breathed in fiery-hot stank breath. I needed a tourniquet to stifle the flow of deadly oxygen that desiccated all living organisms near and far. "Kiss me muthafucka!" she raged. "Since you won't pay me, kiss me, bitch!" I was stunned!! Was this her way of saying she liked me??!! I wondered, God forbid. . . . Taking steps that led to nowhere, I had run into the arms of SATAN himself. . . . I could no more kiss those horrid lips than kiss the GRIM REAPER. . . . NOOOO!!" I screamed, from way back in the crib. . . . It (SHE) rushed toward me in a streak of brown lightning, surprisingly juggernaut for a creature of Sasquatchian proportions. She grabbed me in a headlock which seemed MARVINISHLY familiar. I wondered if she and Marvin had gone to the same bully-training school to learn that technique. "You gone kiss me or you gone die!!!!" she ranted again and again. . . . A pungent, almost herblike smell greeted me as she squeezed my head between her massive tree limb of an arm and her gelatinous polyester-encumbered flesh. It was dark, in that hole beneath her armpit, rotten and dark. . . . It was going to be the end of me. "NOOOO you animal!" I shouted, simultaneously wondering why in the hell I would insult the one THING that held my life in ITS hands. . . . It was my way of clinging to some degree of dignity and respect in a system in which I had no power or control. It was stupid, it was sad, it was all I had. . . . She swung me around and dragged me up, under her arm, to the top of the grassy incline that led to their yard. Terror and panic made themselves known. I had seen her do this to other victims. She was going to throw me down the hill!!! I flailed helplessly as she positioned herself in her flinging stance as we finally reached the top of the hill. I could feel the life drain out of my neck as she continued her choke hold. My hands flailed aimlessly as she tossed me around like used luggage at a Third World airport. It would be impossible for me to hold on if she tried to throw me. I could not reach around her massive frame to get a good grip with my opposite hand. I couldn't even begin to try to trip her as I had seen the wrestlers do on Saturday mornings. I couldn't bring myself to bite into her filthy, malodorous hide. My hands waved aimlessly as she maneuvered me about like a lifeless puppet on a string. Something deep inside me told me not to give up, the same voice I had heard in my struggle with Marvin. Something told me to think!— THINK!! She yanked me with one smooth, hard, quick jerk as she let go of my head and neck and for a few brief seconds I saw her evil eyes and a more evil grinning, rotten-toothed smile underneath her buckwheat woolly mammoth head. And right in front of my wandering eyes were two giant mounds of fleshy breasts. . . . As I began to fall backward, I reached out and grabbed for them and for all I was worth. It was a desperate maneuver at a most desperate time. . . . Eureka! I had almost stopped falling backward. By that time a large crowd of the usual onlookers had gathered. I thought I had stopped my fall, and even more important, from being thrown around by this thing of a girl in front of everyone I knew. Wrong!! . . . Dirty Diana and all that pent-up Negro anger that she epitomized toppled toward me and down the hill! She had again managed to grab me, and we snowballed downward and down onto the sidewalk, off the curb, and into the middle of the street! I rolled away from her as fast as I could and managed to gain my stance before she did. I wanted to run, but I didn't. Again I stood there, paralyzed, afraid, mostly angry. I was not about to run away with the whole world watching. Dirty Diana finally managed to stagger to her feet, looking even more cartoonish than normal. She sprinted over to her torn shirt, screaming expletives so loud that I'm sure the people over on Dunlap Street three miles away could hear her. The crowd was laughing loudly and point-ing at Dirty Diana as she ran to the broken-down open duplex screen door. Just inside the door, holding it open, was another creature that looked like an older model of Dirty Diana with rollers in its head. It, too, screamed the same expletive language, and as Dirty Diana ran inside, it kicked and hit her as she passed into that dark dungeon. . . .

I looked around me and the crowd had started to dissipate. All except one figure, Sam Mabon, my father. He quietly told me to meet him at the house as we stared at each other. I knew what was in store for me. No explaining in the world would work. I was going to be punished again for a crime I didn't commit. I was "slowly" becoming used to silently shouldering undeserved blame. I was becoming an expert at adjusting my RAGE INCUBATOR. In all the systems that I had run into or those that had run into me, I was learning to patch my invisible wounds and to keep moving, even if I had to crawl. I had to "KEEP MOVING" . . . and to never give up. I knew the drill. In tangential fashion, I slowly turned and walked toward the white house with the green roof, the one I had learned to call home. It was the beginning of the loneliest walk of my life. . . .

these nights are not important

S T A R R S T A R R

to waste his juice in drops
as polished diamonds spilled
on a black velvet midriff

this is not important
this lover in my mind
with the winds chasing beneath
my skirts up the opaque dusk
of north broadway

and if eve were created
this very night of what I see
could she say (?)
of those young soft things
idoled
on ancient rusted fords
and greasy old harleys
legs sprawled in minis
and two-inch pumps

the trees aren't the only ones
bearing fruit this evening

these nights are not important

The Wandering Lover

LIV WRIGHT

"I love you less than I love myself,
        but more than I loved all the others"

This was the song that spread from her
when first he spent
his seed.

                            And he
                            rising from her
                            quiet body like
                            a serpent from
                            a stair/stood/

waiting from his
racing heart
to swell.

                            (the moment passes)

And wandering lover

                            (still unmoved)

folds his aching tongue
weaves his wagging way

                through the love wet evening
                down the wind-drawn alleys

he drips his way home
                in silence.

"It is all meek now

. . .

(that which was once sublime)

and words that once lingered
are forgotten
'til another time."

Monica

CHERI DAUGHTERY

*S*he always began her day with a three-mile jog around her neighborhood. This is while back home the kids are taking their baths and preparing for school. Once she drops them off it's back home to dress for the day of hundreds of phone calls, beeps, pages from the secretary, and interviews with her clients. Most of the time exhaustion runs its gamut. So occasionally Monica takes a mind break and when she breaks it's for an erotic journey. You've done it. You're doing it now. Come with her.

All of a sudden she doesn't hear any phones, no vibrating pager, no voice on the intercom instructing her to pick up line five, no it's just Monica and her team of erotic specialists who have designed for her a package in which she can explore her sensual self.

Once they came in with an invitation for her to join them for a massage. Well, she thought to herself, this sure is a sexy-looking guy delivering this message, and wondered if he would be a part of her massage. He helped her put away her things and said, "Follow me." Outside was a long black Cadillac limo and as she stepped inside she knew that she could relax into this experience. Before the door could close, the limo rolled forward. Her favorite jazz musician came mellow from the surround-sound speakers as she lay her head back. The second her head touched the headrest an electric portable bar slid forward with the bubbly already freshly poured. Well, why not take a sip and push your shoes off? With a smile coming across her face, she was wanting to enjoy each moment of this experience. As they approached what looked like an apartment building (it was four stories high) a garage opened and the space swallowed the limo quietly. The driver/ messenger was at her door opening it and as she tried to slip her shoes back on he said, "Leave them." Then he leaned in to help her from the car but first he lightly pinched her nipples, just a slight pinch holding them for a brief second or so, just slight enough to bring them to a hardness that showed through her silk blouse. He then took her by the hand and led her from the car onto plush carpeting (in the garage) into the building. Once inside she found out that it was a house and magnificently decorated in all the shades of sensuality. No sooner had he closed the door than there appeared three people, one man and two women. They must be the masseurs, she thought, quietly thinking which one she would choose. Well, let's see, the woman to her right was a real beauty (real dark features of a mixed-Mexican or -Spanish descent, lovely black eyes that said, I would like to be your masseur; she had a name tag that displayed her name as Wonda). Next to her was this guy, African-American, large hands, large lips (I wonder how those lips would feel?). His tag said Croso. The other woman was short, smiling, and kept rubbing her hands together as if she had already began to massage Monica's body. By then her driver/messenger, and now masseur, was back in the room with just a large towel around his waist. Well, now he is going to make this a real easy pick for me and in her mind she chose the driver/messenger/masseur as her special one, and she didn't even know his name yet. As she started to ask, he told the short woman to "Give her a bath." He looked at Monica and said to "Follow her." She led and the others all followed us to this bathroom that seemed to take up the entire second floor. When they stepped into the room each one of the four began to dance, slow and easy–like, the music flowed true to their ears and they made such beautiful rhythm, and one by one each one would come to Monica and effortlessly unbutton a button, unzip a zipper, touch her hair, run a finger across her breast, stroke a knee, so before she could tell them which one she wanted to massage her they had her totally naked.

Again a command from the driver/messenger instructed the short woman to "put her in." The woman took her by the hand to the Jacuzzi that she knew could easily seat six and undressed herself so quickly that it seemed like they never stopped moving to the waiting water, as she led her up the bath stairs, rubbing her hands together, preparing to give Monica her much-needed bath. The smell of the bath oils was intoxicating. The woman guided her to sit down and then she began to wash her. The woman began at her feet, and what a delightful sponge—yielding yet rough—the strokes were firm yet soft. The sponge kept moving up her leg to her thigh, around her prize and over her buttocks, lingered at her navel (slight trembles began in Monica's sensitive region and she let out a low "aah"). As the woman continued up her torso to her breast, she felt another sponge at her feet and another at her back and another on her face. All these hands had joined them in the water; all the hands were rubbing her and feeling her and releasing her. She was going to try not to come just now but with all the rubbing and the wonderful smells and all the hands touching her in all her right places and here that hand seemed to belong. It knew just where to touch; those fingers so big knew just when to probe and just as he was pushing one of those large fingers into her space she took ahold of his arm and rode his finger like she was riding a stallion, and—

WHY IS IT ALWAYS ONE EMERGENCY AFTER THE OTHER? WHO'S PROBLEM IS IT, ANYWAY? WHO TOLD YOU TO SEE ME? WHERE DID THIS STACK OF PAPERS COME FROM? PROBLEMS, PROBLEMS, PROBLEMS! WHY CAN'T SOME NICE PERSON WALK INTO THIS OFFICE RIGHT THIS SECOND CARRYING A CARD WITH INSTRUCTIONS ON IT. AND WHAT THE INSTRUCTIONS SAY IS, HI YOU GORGEOUS WOMAN YOU. WHAT YOU WILL HAVE TO DO IS BE WILLING TO FOLLOW THE ENCLOSED INSTRUCTIONS. THE WORDS WILL ONLY APPEAR IF YOU DESIRE TO FOLLOW THEM WITH ALL YOUR HEART. TAKE A MOMENT AND WISH TO BE IN A PLACE WHERE ALL YOUR NEEDS ARE MET BEFORE YOU CAN THINK THEM. BACK TO WORK.

Circle of One

JOY DOSS

The rain ebbs and flows with the rhythm of our bodies . . .

We are immersed in our love and ourselves
A pleasurable drowning in love's deep waters
Drenched in passion's liquid heat
Soaked in each other's emotions . . .

Preorgasmic sounds filter thru the air
Mingling in quiet euphony
Our expressions of lovemaking dance around us
And envelope us in a circle of one . . .

As we simultaneously reach a paramount
Our bodies mold into one form
Flesh to flesh
We look at each other
And our mutual satiety speaks for itself
Unburdened by lofty language
Our love is inexpressible except with our bodies . . .

Our eyes reflect an intimate cognizance of each other
Our eyes reflect our sincerity
And submergence one within the other
Body and soul
Our eyes say "I love you."

Living in a Memory

ESTELLE FARLEY

Palms pressed downward
fingers centered

Searching for the place
He took me to so many times

Eyes closed—remembering
Breasts rise

Cursing his name
Back arches upward to meet . . .

Miss Rose

JERRY W. WARD, JR.

Possibility invites.

I come clean
as a whistle
as she moves

Mysterious
her wonders
to perfume.

I drink in passion,
her milk of paradise,
full-flavored joy
of her secret lips.

Her hands
inscribe my shoulders
like branding irons of desire.

Anointed, my mind
slips through my tongue
into the wombworld of eternity.

In the House

LANA C. WILLIAMS

Where they lived,
carrying delicacies
like liver pudding
on engraved silver trays,
while somebody fanned plumes
in the corner.

Later, after brandy and port
from Father Randolph's crystal,
they crave sweet desserts.
So, there, in the middle
of the finest, polished,
most solid oak,
covered with Missus's
French lace,
she acts like holiday turkey.
Golden brown and juicy,
spread-eagled,
for guests to spoon
her giblet gravy stuffing.

Intimate Times

JANICE W. HODGES

Sometimes I'm afraid
to move underneath you.

There's a little bit of fear in excitement.

Meaning
sliding back and forth between us
carrying words in boxes on its back
wrapped in ribbon, wicker or steel,
reminding us we're two.

There's a little bit of fear in anticipation
feeding my motivation
to do things
women, wives and mothers do.

Courage
comes from not thinking

so I listen
with quiet ears
to our future in my sac,
and the clock ticking on the nightstand
muffled by your breath, steadying
sawing it and out.

Chillbumps scratch the sheets like sandpaper
when I realize
my security is in the hollow of your back.

These Bodies

TIM SEIBLES

for Nia

i touched your belly once   remember
in the hallway of that white university

right there
hands whispered secret plans
to the future inside you

right there
i reached a revolution thru your navel
& cradled the rage of your daughter-to-be

i felt like an astronaut exploring your full moon
my antennae rubbing 'cross your cocoon
before the birth of your butterfly soon

& at the time i'd've sworn we'd never been closer than this
just cuz our shackled shapes
could not recall the kiss of freedom
these frames hadn't followed tree moss & stars
to a promised land

& it wasn't until
right now
two runaway-slave years later
during bittersweet narratives
on this long distance all
that i'm realizing
we
are not these bodies

.   .   .

'we only live once' is bullshit   baby
we've been here before

why waste time talking of man & woman
when really we be soul-filled traveling souls
vacationing in young black skin & earth flesh

us two
with more luggage
than we can handle

let's leave these cheap hotels where the room service sucks
& go home
escape this place
& go home
disguise ourselves in incense smoke & daydreams
& go home

we are not those bodies
we are spirits
wearing jackets for this world's cold
come on
if we huddle close we can keep warm

we are not dreaming
we are flying
higher than birds
(mortal wings would only weigh us down)
we are not dreaming
we are the air we breathe
inconceivable & formless
we are not these bodies

we are the sun
shining too close to earth
we are the sun
& not these bodies
we just put on these old things
to man-&-womanifest god in the flesh

. . .

you & i
right here
making change

old proverbs
becoming
new meanings

we started this a long time ago
remember, sista
distant worlds ago
remember
long alternate planes before my past palms
gave the present to your future-filled womb
remember . . .

so right now
right here
until we leave these bodies
turn in our room keys
& are called home

let's
just
be . . .

ONE . . . TWO/GETHER

Sweat Burns

NIGHTINGALE

sweatburns
into the
furrowed lines
i have etched
delicately with
my nail art.
her tiny hairs
curl
angrily
on the nape
of her neck
as we latch
legs like crickets
in a monsoon
flood
waters pour
down her throat
as she dunks
down
for my
ice
cube
i am so thirsty.

pour me a cup of you,
girl . . .

Acid Black

SCOTT JACKSON

*T*o be sure, tinnitus is coming like an uncaged beast. I can hear it rumble down the steel tracks and wooden ties like an old, familiar friend. That heavy ringing comes every Friday night when I cast aside the scarlet silk tie and the maroon Florsheims and set my sights on achieving some more ethereal state of stupor; some bohemian escape into freedom masked in free-flowing clear and amber liquids.

I hit the mean streets an hour after sunset with my chief partner in crime Gabriel in his anonymous foreign car. The getaway car, on more than one occasion. It has a little bit of punch and blends effortlessly into the background when the situation demands. Just like a whispering ghost in traffic; hiding in plain sight.

My dinner of old chicken and slaw was spartan and I scarfed it down in the same amount of time it took me to change my shirt. I needed something a little smoother, a little cooler for the nighttime culture of carousing. Dressing for the scene was like costuming for a play; every color, every texture held significance. I decided to go purple—the regal color that stands out even in the dark. A loose-fitting violet cotton shirt with jet-black pants and a heavy pair of equally black boots just in case there was trouble.

Of course, I washed down my fried chicken dinner with a cold Rolling Rock wrapped around a pair of No Doz. Those are my legal, lawful beauties. A leftover habit from when I worked the overnight shift at the radio station back in my college days and needed a pick-me-up around four in the morning. Speed was too unpredictable and far too illegal, not to mention costly. But every sensation, including hyper-alertness can be gotten right over the counter at the local all-night drugstore nowadays. Why bother with the shifty-eyed types on the waterfront when you can buy a slightly lower-level methamphetamine at any grocery store? Everyone needs a little boost now and again, hence my legal, lawful beauties.

There had been a time when I would have scoffed at any drug save for alcohol and maybe a little nicotine now and then, and although I don't expect my No Doz to act as a gateway drug to heroin any time soon, I know that I need to be careful and map out my parameters for drug use now and forever. However, that bit of psychological cartography can wait until tomorrow morning when everything is less urgent.

Gabriel left his house five miles north of mine the same instant I removed my barely warm chicken from the oven. Nine minutes later he was in my driveway and I was closing the apartment door behind me, a second Rolling Rock in my hand and a half-empty bottle of my legal, lawful beauties in my jacket pocket. I thought for a second about grabbing a box of condoms out of the glove compartment of my own junky car and rooting around for some more pills, but decided against it. In an emergency, I could buy either of the two while I was out.

I get up to go to work at six in the morning Monday through Friday. I use the pills when I go out on Friday nights to counteract the depressive nature of the alcohol I'm sure to imbibe and make sure I don't drop or drag around midnight. Midnight is when the fun really starts downtown and I need to be alert. Need to know what's going on. Can't be caught half asleep. And with the No Doz, I can roll around until seven or eight in the morning. Sometimes I have. I once went thirty hours on a handful of No Doz and a bottle of gin. Gabriel and another friend had been passing enormous joints, but I was just as happy as a baby with my bottle of Gordon's.

Gabriel hasn't even completed his turn into my driveway before I'm out the door, giving a second and final look at my own car and its possible contents. I fling open the door and we say our "wuzzup"'s with a palm slap. I'm ready for the night. Gabriel is always ready. We go south. To the big city. Like soldiers.

Our first step is to pick up Doughboy at his truly raggedy place across the street from the mental health center where my sister Amani works as a counselor. The crimson streaks of twilight have already eroded into that sensual acid black of Friday night and the air feels like rain. Neon screams of red and blue mark the boundaries of the thoroughfare, serving to entice those nighttime crowds. We roll slowly down one of the city's busiest streets; three twisting miles of businesses and homes, with alternating African-American and Jewish enclaves. With the radio turned up loud and the kicker in the trunk barking out thunderous bass lines, we are seeing and being seen. Just like everyone else creeping down the street with their windows rolled down.

We come to a stop in front of Doughboy's building and cut the music. After we stroll over the lawn of exotic weeds, Gabriel pounds on the unlit doorbell. Doughboy answers the insistent buzz, greeting us each with a bottle of Killian's Red. Every microbrewery in the world is brewing red beers nowadays, but Killian's remains my favorite of that class. Maybe because I'm a fan of Coors, the Killian's parent company. Back in New York, Coors was plentiful—available on tap at every corner bar—but here in this city it is sometimes hard to come by.

Killian's is also the first red beer I ever had—at a bar when I was nineteen. There's something to be said for the first times and first loves.

The three of us scale the rickety wooden staircase to Doughboy's third-floor apartment, jammed with walls and ceilings slanted at mad, impossible angles. Sharp edges abound. The architect was a lunatic.

Before I even make it to his auburn Salvation Army couch, I'm feeling decidedly electric. I've already finished half the bottle of Killian's in the short time it took to climb those creaking stairs. I kill the bottle while Doughboy chooses the perfect pair of boots and makes sure every three-foot strand of hair is in place and ascertains that God is truly in his heaven. A pretty anchorwoman on the infotainment show screeches at me from the battered thirteen-inch television in the corner. I want to tell her to shut up, to concentrate her efforts on real news, but she wouldn't hear me so why should I bother? She'll prattle on about trivia, but no one watching cares what comes out of her lips. They just wonder what they taste like. Is that cherry lipstick? I wonder, I wonder. And I'm not the only one. But curiosity is a murdering fool, especially when it comes to the fairer and most unfair sex.

As if by black magic, another cold bottle of Killian's appears in my right hand. Already opened, too. Must have been my favorite elf Gabriel, watching out for me. And who am I to complain? Free beers don't grow on trees. Never look a gift horse in the mouth. I take a long draft . . .

. . . Sean O'Grady's is a terrible yuppified watering hole on the city's newly gentrified east side. I'm not sure if there's an actual "Sean O'Grady"; I hear that a consortium of four Italians actually owns the restaurant. But everyone likes to drink in a bar strangely reminiscent of the Emerald Isle.

Even with a gentrification that magically transpired during my years in New York, there's still a pocket of strip clubs and abandoned factories in that section of town. But Sean O'Grady's typifies the overall new ambience. I don't like it. A lot of wood and even more gaudy Coca-Cola signs from an era gone past, when Coco-Cola came only in those shapely, erotic bottles. O'Grady's tries to seem as if it has been in the same spot for a hundred years, consistently catering to the city's most pretentious cliques through peace, war, and depression.

I think it was Doughboy's idea to stop there. He was hungry, and besides, he never misses an opportunity to shake up more established types with his unique appearance. But we pass muster with the bouncer without a problem and I beeline to the bar, uncertain of whether or not Gabriel and Dough are at my heels. Not really caring, either.

The bored-looking fellow behind the bar serves me my Budweiser in an unwieldy leaded glass tumbler. I know the bar doesn't use tumblers for the atmosphere, it's their tricky way of skimping on the fluid ounces served to the unwashed masses. My guess, it's a ten-ounce glass and they're charging twelve-ounce prices. The ten-ounce estimate is generous; if may be as low as eight and a half. No tip for him, are you crazy! If you serve drinks in decent-sized glasses, then you've earned a tip.

I can't understand it. Beer from the tap is always a moneymaker because of the size of the kegs and the economies of scale. There's never a need to cheat the customers.

Maybe I'll switch to mixed drinks. Doughboy is drinking ale and Gabriel hasn't strayed too far from Rolling Rock, so a pitcher for the three of us is out of the question. Buying a pitcher for three men who know their way around a bar is almost as difficult as ordering a pizza with people who like different toppings. A lot of "well, what do you want?" and "are you sure that's okay?" But I don't make enough money at the radio station to knowingly get cheated by buying thimblefuls of beer, so this will be my one and only draft. Mixed drinks or bottles will be the order of the night.

Too much goddamned wood in here. Waitresses are hustling hither and yon, in prerequisite white shirts carrying prerequisite platters of allegedly spicy buffalo wings. They'll lean over at just the right angle when serving you drinks so maybe you'll buy some more to get another look at that freckled flesh. You'll follow the line of her bra strap with your unabashedly wandering eye and she'll let you. Nothing on God's green earth is by accident, especially a woman's smile. She's hiding something and you will never find out what, no matter how clever you may think you are.

I want to leave O'Grady's and try my fortunes elsewhere, but Doughboy orders the calamari from a wiry redhead with a quick smile. I hold up my hand, a silent indication that I'll be drinking my dinner.

Calamari. Why would anyone eat squid? The entire concept seems dirty.

We sit, weekend warriors with nothing in common, and toast the seamier side of life where we grew from boys to men. Our demeanor and our toast is a mockery of the wiseguy stereotype. You can almost imagine those sixties mobsters in the back of a Brooklyn social club, clad in brown Italian suits and holding up their martinis, praising the success of the family.

We are something quite different. Not mobsters, but still distinctly street.

Not Brooklyn, but still urban. Doughboy is a street rat through and through, Gabriel is a nihilistic musician, and I am a two-dimensional reflection of a page out of the Bible, like Old Testament God's right hand—working for the good cause but reveling in the violence. The Budweiser in my glass has long since vanished and I refuse to get another draft. I order a bottle of Corona from the redheaded waitress's ample cleavage and entertain dirty thoughts about what I'd like to do with the lime wedge. There's something about redheads that I can't resist. But I want the beer more that I want her. A lot more.

I can count on twelve fluid ounces in a bottle of Corona, *la cerveza mas fina*. Who knows what you'll get in a strange woman. They'll cheat you worse that a bartender with a supply of leaded glasses.

Gabriel and Doughboy discuss some issue, but my attention is focused on the basketball game on a corner television. I can't hear the commentary, but the score at the bottom tells me that the away team is adding to an already impressive lead. The home team has been shaken to its roots for the last three years. Trades, retirements, and player deaths. The world has gone mad: professional athletes are passing away at a greater clip than nursing home residents. Day is night and night is day.

I only know one player on the floor these days; the spunky point guard with more heart than talent and the ability to play above the rim with flair. However, he cannot hit a clutch shot and receives little respect from coaches, fans, or his teammates. The team will miss the playoffs for the fourth straight year. No matter, we will still cheer for the uniform, not the men.

Too much wood, too many yuppies. Four men in the corner still have their ties on and almost all of the women are still wearing their too-mild daytime scents. Pheromones be damned. The skirts are too long, the hair is too severe, the people are too pale, the area is too gentrified, and I need to go. It won't take me but a minute to finish my Corona. But Doughboy eats his calamari so slowly it's almost embarrassing and I proceed to sip my beer instead of guzzle. Gotta go, gotta go, gotta go; it becomes my internal mantra. The team falls behind by an even greater margin. Gotta go, gotta go, gotta go . . .

. . . Zoom Billiards. I have another Corona. Doughboy buys this round, and I dropped a third No Doz in the car on the way over. It's still relatively early, but, thanks to the beers, the night has blossomed nicely into that neon sparkle I love so dearly. I consider bumming a cigarette off of Doughboy, but cancel the notion. There are already enough different types of drugs rollicking in my bloodstream.

This is the downtime between happy hour and the club hour. The time of anticipation. We'll just bide our time shooting stick until the short skirts and hungry looks start walking past the plateglass window. Zoom is conveniently located between a parking garage and a moderately popular dance club, making it the ideal spot to gauge the depth and breadth of tonight's party girls. When the barely dressed club vultures emerge from their slumber and rat-a-tat out of the garage, it will be time to end our game and move to greener pastures.

Gabriel is no good at pool. Neither is Doughboy. Neither am I, for that matter. But we always seem to find ourselves positioned at the corners of some Italian slate table, eyeing the hustlers and the hustled, staying away from both. We've played enough to know what shots simply cannot be made, but that doesn't mean we sink the easy ones. In fact, we go after more difficult ones just to avoid the embarrassment of missing an easy one.

It's nearly all male in here. A gaggle of men, a convention of men, a host of men, a murder of men. The only woman wears a shooting glove and has wrists only slightly daintier and more feminine than mine. She banks home an improbable shot and narrowly avoids scratching. She's too good to be a hustler; she's showing off instead of making money. She should know better. If she allowed herself to scratch, she may have had a chance to take some high roller with a male superiority complex for a little bit of coin.

She is a woman in every physical sense, but starkly androgynous compared to those soft specimens who will soon be trolling around outside, offering their curves to whoever drives the best car and tells the best lies.

I ponder for a moment on the billiard hall lighting. Shaded lamps cast a harsh light on the tables, but the overall mood remains dim and bleak. Better for surreptitious exchanges of cash. The pool halls and the waterfront are the only parts of the city where it is a bad thing to engage in commerce. Back to the lamps. I wonder how long the progression took to the shaded lamps ubiquitous now in every hall. How many people had to say, "I can't see a goddamned thing with this naked bulb hanging in my face!" before the shades evolved. Silly thinking, but somehow right at home on Friday night.

The geometry, the absolute precision of this game kills me. I live by the X-factor, the unknown, the random. Billiards is the crown sport of the ugly science physics, where all is unpredictable, and those who stride boldly within the margin of error reign supreme. I prefer to color outside the lines. I prefer to make the impossible shot where the cue ball curves by force of will, not the application of the proper English. Only that never happens in pool. Although it frequently happens in life.

With a cat-quick shot, I ease the three ball into the side pocket. Study long, study wrong. That's what my mother says. I play the game on autopilot: visualize the shot and stroke the cue. No calculations, no attempt to set up my next shot. It drops with a hint of luck and chaos into the game. And if I am lucky, I look like a truly magnificent player and the hustlers walk away to seek out easier prey.

I scratch—cue ball down low in the corner—and straighten up as Doughboy takes aim on the fourteen. Suddenly, the back-to-back Coronas hit me like a Civil War cannon and the game fades to black. I should have finished my dinner or had some of Doughboy's revolting calamari to soften the blow. But the buzz is why I'm out tonight so it would be bad form to complain.

I'm not sure how we end up at the Eden Club, a strip bar miles and miles from Zoom but only a few blocks from Sean O'Grady's. The unmistakably sour taste of British ale coats my tongue. I wonder if we stopped at another bar between Zoom and here because I don't think Zoom serves Bass. That's the only British ale I'll drink. And I drink enough of it to know the aftertaste like I know my own name. Bass has legs. A pitcher of Bass will keep you buzzed all night and into the day and back into the night.

On one side of Eden is a standard topless bar. The dancers fiddle with their G-strings, but if they take them off, the establishment's liquor license will be revoked in a New York minute. And the beer is where they make their money, so that liquor license is the proverbial goose that laid those eggs.

The men who line the stage are far too shy and insecure to talk to a naked woman without a bottle of beer or a cigarette or both in their hand. They need something to divert their attention; a talisman of sorts to ward off the stark realization that a strange woman's breasts are only so captivating and it is moderately pathetic to pay a hefty cover charge just to meet a woman paid to talk to you. A woman whose job is to make you feel more masculine than God intended you to be.

On the other side of Eden is an all-nude club that traffics in wide varieties of raunch until four in the morning. I must be drunk because, without hesitation, I fish into my wallet for fifteen dollars to see what the bearded man behind the glass counter advertises as an X-rated girl-on-girl show. I've never paid to see a naked woman before; I figure maybe it's time to let my pagan side free. Besides, I've been on my own for such a long time

I can use a refresher course in the basic principles of female anatomy. All I remember is that the body will trap you and the mind will tear you apart. And I think that's all I need to know.

I decide to steel myself before I enter. Alcohol is strictly prohibited at the live show—drunk men and naked women is a combination that is typically a bit too combustible—so I snack on a dry No Doz. Like a dromedary, I have enough drink stored to get me through the show. To get through a series of shows. It's all in the hump. I can last thirty days in the desert.

I wonder what one of the dancers would say if I told her, without provocation, that it was all in the hump. Would she signal a bouncer or try to stroke my ego?

We push through a heavy blackout curtain that stinks of pipe smoke and into a low-ceilinged room alit in reds and purples and streaking acid black. A large television in the corner plays a pornographic movie hopelessly lacking in style and the dozen men in the room pretend not to watch. As if pornography is silly and immoral while what we've come and paid to see is not. No sound issues forth from the television; slurps and groans would seem somewhat inappropriate, even in these surroundings. Those distinctly human sounds have no place in any public sphere.

Doughboy, Gabriel, and I take seats near one corner of the ten by ten stage. They enter into a jocular discussion about the other voyeurs looking blankly around the room. I do not. My head is too light, or maybe too heavy. Thinking seems like such a waste of time. I study the brass pole before me. It's filthy with fingerprints up to about six feet off the cool-looking marble stage. The rest of the pole—up to the ceiling painted black—is tarnished. The stories that pole could tell.

The videotape ends abruptly as an overly muscular and unfortunately endowed man achieves orgasm. Some voice of God announces in basso profundo that the first dancer is about to take the stage and about forty additional men seem to drift through the very walls to see the show. They ooze in like fog. Most are either around twenty-five or fifty. Dirty young men and dirty old men, all looking for the same thing. Trying to find out what kind of clay makes a woman.

The dancer actually looks pretty in the reds and purples and acid blacks. Bright smile. A bit plump, but I like my women with a little weight. Five-nine, one-forty are the dimensions most appealing to me. The woman before me is five-seven, one twenty-five. She'll do.

Men lean forward like puppets on strings as she touches herself. Always seeking a better view of the action. There is no community in this room, just a horde of hungry individuals. Wanting. There is a mad fierceness in the air, and the stink is not of sin or cigarette smoke but pure individualism. What everyone wants to do to this little girl if she'll only give them a chance. But she won't.

The movies lie when they show a bunch of good-natured wild boys whooping and hollering at the dancer, tossing dollar bills and fives and tens upon the stage with reckless abandon. In real life, every dollar bill goes toward a specific purchase; a special view, a personalized view of the woman on the stage. No one overtips unless they've heard from a friend of a friend that if you spend fifty or sixty dollars, a dancer might take you into the back room for additional fun.

But there is no back room.

The silence of this crowd is ponderous. No one smiles. No one even looks full in the face of his neighbor out of fear that they may meet again under less illicit circumstances. Faces are half-covered with baseball hats and fingers holding cigarettes. This is business, and a shameful one at that.

Those movies also lie when they show that one spunky woman in the audience enjoying the show; a harmless night out at the burlesque theater. The only women in Eden are getting paid to be there. And paid well.

I lean back on the chair's rear legs, as ashamed as I should be, yet cruelly fascinated by the grinding woman and the leering vampires surrounding her. The dancer is alone, naked and yet significantly more invulnerable than any woman walking down McKinley Avenue at this hour. On stage, she is protected. Holy ground. Anyone who dares approach her will reap untold sorrows at the hands of the edgy and essentially liability-proof bouncers. You can't tell your wife or your sister or your grandmother that a behemoth at the door of the local strip club blackened your eye. No one will take them to court because that would be a public admission of an adolescent fascination with breasts and vaginas.

The bouncers carry walkie-talkies or radios of some sort but never use them. There is too much tobacco in their bottom lips for them to speak intelligently. There is always a policeman in the vicinity for "security pur-poses" and to ensure that all laws, statutes, and regulations are properly applied, but for some reason, he always appears to be drunk. Without a doubt, there is something questionable about a police officer who, week in week out, stands in the corner watching every show just to earn a little overtime. Sometimes being an officer of the law is its own reward. He can enjoy the surroundings while avoiding the guilt of the rest of us leering monsters.

I sit stock-still in my position, the most primitive mode of self-defense.

If I don't move, the dancer cannot see me and cannot know what I want. She cannot know me. Despite the brightness of my violet shirt, I am camouflaged against the acid black. She parades around the stage, looking at me but never seeing.

The vampires lay their dollar bills along the edge of the stage. They fold them lengthwise like little tents for a miniature army. And for this bargain price of one American dollar, she puts a leg over their shoulders and lets them take a good, long look at what she is. Maybe she'll hook that long leg over the edge of the stage and grind the heeled shoe into his crotch in an excruciating display of pleasure-as-pain. She will run that foot up his thigh and to the promised land where she will stroke. But not for too long. That will cost another dollar.

She moves to the next dollar bill. And the next. Maybe she'll coo at one in five to send them fumbling for their wallets, thinking if only they pay her more, she'll give them what they really want. That mythological back room where they can fall in love.

She looks at Dough's dollar bill and senses, through some extraordinary means, that he will spend money. She makes a production of folding the dollar bill into a one by two inch rectangle and puts one end of the paper in his mouth. She puts her mouth over his, taking the bill in a sloppy mercantile exchange, more than likely condemnable by both the Department of the Treasury and the Bureau of Public Health. But in this carnival of sexual fantasy, nearly anything is acceptable as long as that dollar bill is somehow marginally involved.

My money stays in my pocket. I am invisible, and only those bills will attract her attention. I could be charming or witty or unbearably handsome, but in the end it is only the dollar bills that carry any weight.

After ten minutes of grinding and the most innocuous of simulated sexual activity, the music stops. She smiles quickly, offering a breathy compensatory kiss on the cheek to the patron whose special view was aborted by the ending of the song. Then she is gone with those ragged and sweaty dollar bills clutched to her breast. She earned every last one of them.

One man claps, then stops when no one chooses to follow his lead. He puts his hand to his mouth in a pathetic pantomime of a cough.

Next come two women clad in brown felt outfits designed to give them the haughty look of felines. Out of the darkness and onto the stage, with its brutal assault of white, red, and blue lights. Upon reflection, Eden is just as patriotic as it could possibly be, except for the notable lack of fireworks—literal or figurative. It is so plainly American to throw money at those objects we want the most. With money, there is no need to earn anything—up to and including the love or tender caress of a woman.

But these aren't women; this is the "girl on girl" show, as advertised by the barker at the front door. Again, the booming bass of the emcee assaults the patrons like a slap to the face. He announces their unforgettable names and the countless adult films in which they have been featured. All the titles sound the same.

The emcee insults our manhood in a juvenile attempt to get us to cheer like lunatics. We may be lunatics, but we choose not to cheer.

Even without the requested cheering, the two women strut and sway to a stripped-down remix of a familiar song about cat people. They purr and mewl.

They define beauty in the modern American sense. Long blond hair, slender waists, large, firm breasts, and legs that stretched for years on end. But as beautiful, as sensual as they are, I find the remix much more interesting than the women. Despite the ostensible passion of their gyrations. They each wear the vacant look of someone with nothing and nothing left to lose. There is nothing new to their performance.

But the bare-bones remix—all drums and howls and screeches—gets me nodding without even realizing it.

The smaller one thrusts her breasts into Gabriel's face, his reward for blessing her with the single dollar bill. Her partner jams a hand in his lap. I'm close enough to smell the talcum powder on their bodies. I stop nodding and return to complete invisibility amid the acid black. Gabriel seems remarkably at ease for a young man with two porn stars giving him more than his dollar's worth.

The kittens turn their backs to me and away from my lack of dollar bills. They return to the center of the stage and begin to satisfy each other with paws and whiskers and tongues. Like the dancer before, they will offer an instant of simulated sex for that lone dollar bill.

The vampire seated next to Doughboy drools, then glances around, ashamed. He wipes his chin. I look away, unwilling to share that intimate moment with him. His intensity is frightening and he reaches for another bill.

The dancers leave. Twenty minutes to the next show. The announcer informs us that the kittens are available for private dances and photographs. Twenty dollars for the former, ten for the latter. It's all mercenary. It's all commercial.

Gabriel, Doughboy, and I look at each other, planning the next move.

Now that the beers and pills have had a chance to settle in, I can barely stand. But it is just a shade after midnight so we leave the naked women behind to suck even more marrow out of life. Our fellow vampires swivel back toward the television, awaiting the next video that they will pretend not to watch. Then the next show. Then the next video. They are living proof that all things sensory can become addictive. Figuratively speaking, this was my first taste of crack cocaine. I wonder if I'll want to go back to Eden next Friday. I hope not. But if I do, I will come armed with a score of worn dollar bills. To try to buy my way into that back room.

With Gabriel behind the wheel and doing fine, we decide to try our luck at the New Oasis, a college bar on the very edge of the city. After Eden, we needed to surround ourselves with approachable women with whom we might have a legitimate chance. College girls are notorious for wanting something new and exciting—the flavor of the month—and we are three very different men than the kind they'll find in Economics or French.

Too different, in fact. The bouncer at New Oasis cuts one look at Doughboy and his long hair and says absolutely not. We are not welcome in his bar, no matter how much money we have to spend. Although Doughboy is bigger than the bouncer and Gabriel and I can take on anything, we decide not to press the issue. We just tell him he's a punk and roll out to another bar.

Sometimes bouncers need a reality check that their word is not God's word, but tonight is not that night. Gabriel has been known to push bouncers to the brink, but the night is still too young to waste it fighting and consequently running from the police. Instead, we decide to try our luck at a barely popular dance club called Archives located downtown.

The calculus of party spots in this city is difficult to understand at first. This is not New York or Los Angeles, or even Chicago, where people will wait on line interminably to get into the most popular nightclubs. Here, popularity is determined strictly by the number of people crammed inside, not by the name of the place and any local celebrities in attendance. But once those clubs get overcrowded, people look for a new place to drink. The key is to be ahead of the curve: a club patron while it is on the upswing and nowhere to be found when it gets so crowded that there are knife fights in the bathroom. Archives has been quiet for several months, which means that it is due for a resurgence. We figure that tonight may mark the rise of Archives.

Somewhere on our way to the club, we lose Doughboy. One moment he was in the passenger's seat, the next moment I was. I have the vaguest recollection that he went back to Eden, seeking a twenty-dollar lap dance from one of the busty felines. Depending on where you are, they may call it a lap dance or a private dance, but it's really just four and a half minutes of dry humping. For most strip club patrons, that twenty-dollar bill represents three hours of work, yet they are willing to give it away to have a naked woman grind on their lap for the length of a song. And the dejay always seems to cut the records short.

For twenty dollars, you can get live sex anywhere on McKinley Avenue. However, the McKinley whores tend to look a bit more ragged and desperate than the women stripping at Eden. And, as unfortunate-looking as he is, Doughboy has always had a penchant for very pretty women. So he will spend his twenties in a quest for the back room.

But I have neither the time not the attention span to worry about Dough or his libido. Last call in this state is 1:45 A.M., and that deadline is rapidly approaching. I want time to get to another club if Archives still isn't happening.

We screech into a parking lot around the corner and take off running across the cracked pavement to Archives. The club is a little out of the way, on the cusp of Weldon Hills, which is generally recognized as a "bad" part of the city. Bad for some, but not for us. At least the reputation minimizes walking traffic and we don't have to dodge around pedestrians as we dart to the club.

Fifty minutes to closing. We fast-talk our way out of the cover charge, barge into the club, and stop dead in our tracks. It is immediately apparent that we've seriously erred in our application of the nightclub calculus. The slope of X as it approaches Y does not equal "Archives."

The place is practically empty and a scratchy Elvis song is on the turntable. The few young girls scattered around the dance floor look at us hopefully, but I ignore them for the greater seduction of the bar. I haven't had a drink in more that forty-five minutes, so I order a rum and Coke and guzzle it down. I request another to ensure the quick buzz and leave a good tip for the bartender for the potent drinks. The club rebounds from merely dark to the acid black I so adore.

We still have time. I give Gabriel the look and he pounds down his vodka tonic so we can head to greener and blacker pastures.

We are off to Net, a few miles down the road. No chance to outtalk the cover here. It's the city's most popular club year in, year out, and they make no deals at the door. We pay a reduced cover of three dollars because of the lateness of the hour and enter. Uncharacteristically, I bypass the bar on my first swing around. I'm still high off my fourth wind and the double hitch of powerful rum and Cokes at Archives.

On the floor, not surprisingly, I see my sister Amani with a beer in one hand and a wine cooler in the other. She does me proud; last call could come and go and she would still be set for drinks. Amani is a bit older than most of us in the club, but she is possessed of great beauty and sophistication whereas the rest of the women are a bit haggard from dancing and trolling all night. It looks to me like Amani is dancing with three men, each one trying to outdo the other.

I wave to her and start to move to another area of the floor. She raises the wine cooler in greeting and flashes a truly brilliant smile. One of the men dancing with her looks over his shoulder and sneers, as if to say there's no more room at the inn. I want to grab him by the neck and shake him, but I have to smile at his jealous reaction and I keep walking. Maybe I'll teach him something about manners if I meet him outside after closing. That reaction comes partly from being a protective brother and partly from alcohol-induced aggression.

Amani can take care of herself. She's been doing this longer than I have and better understands the undercurrents of the city's nightclubs. I'm certain that she didn't waste time going out to Archives.

Somehow I sense that Gabriel is no longer behind me. I don't care. There are no rules when we go out; if we get separated, we'll both find our way home. We're resourceful fellows and a sixth sense seems to bind us in times of real trouble. Much like a twin able to feel his brother's pain.

I pick up a lonely-looking woman in white desperate to dance to the latest grooves. The Net plays dance versions of popular hits, so everyone can either find the beat or just sing along. That's why the club stays popular.

It's actually surprising to me that someone so attractive is still available this late in the evening. I don't even ask her name. It's just a dance and I've had my share of vampirism for the evening. I'm not looking to fall in love.

In a solitary haze, I swim through the heavy club air, my buzz peaking. She moves with significantly more grace than I, but I make up the difference in enthusiasm. I can't be sure if my mind is clear and my body is sluggish or vice versa. Ordinarily, I'm an outstanding dancer, but my reactions at this point are just too impaired and I can't tell whether I'm lighting up the floor or making a fool of myself. I put a hand on her hip, more to steady myself than for the human contact. I almost lose her in the strobe light and the pulse pounding in my head. I am grateful for the hand on her hips, that tether me to the world of the living.

The woman in white is replaced by one in a sweater. A can of Heineken is in my left hand, half empty. Unless Amani or Gabriel gave it to me, I've been to the bar and don't remember. I take a few puffs of her filtered cigarette, reveling in the nicotine tickle, and then she disappears back into the crowd.

I dance slowly with a woman in a great blue dress and the club is almost empty. Her hands are groping wildly as this is her last chance for the evening. She whispers an offer in my ear and I politely decline, although her fingers feel very good on the back of my neck and I am enchanted by her breath in my ear. But I do fish a business card from my wallet and slip it, clumsily, into the strap of her dress.

I hope she doesn't call. I don't expect her to. Since my senses are so impaired I can no longer trust my judgment of women and only want to share this dance, this purely platonic physical contact. She won't call, though. She is looking for a man tonight, not Monday night.

Gabriel has definitely left. Otherwise I would see him in the practically deserted club. He may have found a woman himself or he may have just decided it was time to go. Maybe he even went back to Eden to get a private dance and maybe a little more in a mythical back room. There aren't any rules on Friday night, and when I see him again there will be no hard feelings. I would do the same to him.

I find my sister talking to a bouncer near the back door. The three men with whom she was dancing are gone. Much like the three women I had the good fortune to encounter.

Getting a ride with Amani is cheaper than getting a cab, and my pockets are significantly lighter than they were earlier in the evening. She has no real objection to chauffeuring; she sends the bouncer into the men's room to make sure that Gabriel wasn't smoking in one of the stalls.

Amani leads me to her car, and although my head is fuzzy, my balance is still good and I don't think I look visibly drunk. We talk about everything and nothing during the fifteen-minute trip to my apartment.

She drops me off at home, then squeals away to some after-hours party thrown by a friend of a friend. She has invited me to come along, but my night is done. I pass by the television without even giving it a longing glance and stumble to my bedroom, where I make a conscious decision not to undress. Instead, I collapse. The remaining quarter of a bottle of No Doz rattles in my pants pocket. My heavy boots clunk like granite to the oak floor.

Bed.

Sleep.

And the acid black world spins amid and among me.

Celibacy

X A V I E R

CHOKING
          ON
      ROSARY
BEADS
IN
   A
       SEA
   OF
   CUM . . .

Dear Lord, I Lift the Covers

WILLIE JAMES KING

Once more, this morning
I found myself alone, a
frustrated man needing some
one else, but willing to take
matters into my own hand
and not wanting to throw
all caution to any condom.

Too much STD out there for
any man to shake
his dick at.
And Lord, there are those who
have it and are angry about it
and would like to spread it around
until it encompasses this town.

So, I take my penis into my own
oiled palms, trusted, well-practiced
hands, where there's no harm
and fight with the vigor that this
venal take-over requires
to grapple with this giant of
a thing that has a mind of
its own, and attempt to
beat myself lovingly, 'til I am sane.

Angry at AIDS 'cause it is inexplicable,
and doctors
for not being able to explain or defy,
I lift the covers from my
taut blackness and begin
to stroke my silklike skin

until the sensation and all
of my senses blend; a photo-
graphic thought of a girl
I wish I were getting with
each touch, erotic images
that pop up like my proud
penis pointed toward the bare-
bulb ceiling, throbbing as
it always does when it wakes
unruly wanting to do something. I rub, slowly at
first and soon the speed
picks up
as my dick dictates
until I feel all right,
'cause AIDS ain't no angst,
and right now, I don't care
to risk it: That's not the kind
of love I'm willing to die for.

Phase 7

Erotic

Abstractions

$\mathcal{E}$ ven in your worst braggadocio you are unable to describe exactly for the benefit of your friends what happened, how, or why. That moment of divine abstraction happened and it cannot be recaptured in speech. It cannot be recaptured even with the binary opposite of the abstraction. It can only be head-shook, sighed on, lamented-after-the-fact that it is gone and was so good.

Picasso fought and fought against the European interpretations of his abstractions, "disjointed modern life mirrored in the disjointed angles of human figures," and all that. Picasso retorted, "My art is African art; my abstractions are African life." The erotic one's most favorite wish is to be continually, abstractly, undone.

Abstractly, Lovechild answers an eternal question for all women—and many men—in her self-explanatory and evocative piece "Why I Play with My Cunt." All questions are now answered. Calvin Baker's "In Partial Fulfillment of the Requirements" is a fictional treatise on one of the mainstays of the erotic urban—the taxi cab and the titty club dancer. We sup in "Communion" with JZB. "The Ballad of Sadie LaBabe" by Tim Seibles moans and laments carnal psychosis in the archetypal patterns of African-American folk song. "Malkai's Last Seduction" will not be the last time we are so otherworldly seduced by the brilliant writing of Kiini Ibura Salaam. Winston Benons's untitled prosepoem uses abstract indirection to bring the readers to the same coital state as the two protagonists, and we experience the "Chastity" of virginal coitus by Janice W. Hodges, while at the same time being seduced by De Ann Diax's "Seduction." Diax's piece is primed with the indolent inked words of "The Writer" as divined by Estelle Farley. Linda White states the abstract bluntly in "Encountering Ecstasy." As the wings of Lana Williams's "Butterfly" are thrust through the seventies, "The Flower" blooms in a late-night '63 Chevy for Lenard D. Moore. Carol Hill Faulkner shows how "I Long" to come into the space that encompasses you, without the arrogant provocation of "surrogate lovers" by Evangelist Jannie James. Baron James Ashanti expands even further our parameters of abstraction with "*Cajunto Sabor,*" a mystic odyssey into the never-never land of "the credibility of lust(s)," and "A Reminiscence" by Leah Jewel Reynolds that will not let us forget closes our chapter. Our complete tome is finally sanctified by Lenard D. Moore's "Afterword," the stamp of afterglow lest we forget our most recent experiences. Moore reminds us that the erotic is forever, unending . . . and episodic.

Why I Play with My Cunt

LOVECHILD

*B*ecause I was not breast-fed; because my crib was padded and I like the feel of steel; because I was spanked by my baby-sitter; because the kids used to call me half-breed; because my father ignored my mother and fucked the bottle; because my brother jerked off to Aunt Jemima; because my dog was kept in bondage till the day he died; because a whiteboy took my virginity; because I was never taught homosexuality in health class; because the sandman was a lesbian; **BECAUSE IT FEELS GOOD; BECAUSE MY CUNT IS SELFISH; BECAUSE IT'S SELF-GRATIFICATION;** because my period feels like a bullfight; because I hate the smell of pork; because I love the taste of pussy; because I can't fist my own asshole; because I have a lot of time on my hands; because it feels like a baby when I shave it; because my platform heel won't fit inside; **BECAUSE IT FEELS GOOD; BECAUSE MY CUNT IS SELFISH; BECAUSE IT'S SELF-GRATIFICATION;** because my vibrator isn't powerful enough; because transsexuals turn me the fuck on; because scenes from *Caligula* run through my head; because Cinderella wasn't my slave; because it throbs like a dick; because I sleep alone; because of the inevitability of death; **BECAUSE IT FEELS GOOD; BECAUSE MY CUNT IS SELFISH; BECAUSE IT'S SELF-GRATIFICATION;** because Mistress Erotica says I'm a pervert; because three virgins in horsetails whip my dreams; because my double-dong was stolen; because I smoked my last cigarette; because I want to spit-shine Prince's boots; because I hate sloppy blow-jobs; **BECAUSE IT FEELS GOOD; BECAUSE MY CUNT IS SELFISH; BECAUSE IT'S SELF-GRATIFICATION;** because there are no more virgins; because I can't give the government an enema; because whores are too expensive; because I hate the thought of clothing; because I'm the borderline between dyke and boy; because I want to be saddled and trained like a horse; because slavery is in my roots and I thirst for S&M; **BECAUSE IT FEELS GOOD; BECAUSE MY CUNT IS SELFISH; BECAUSE IT'S SELF-GRATIFICATION;** because I can never get enough pussy; because the sound of a woman's voice over the phone enters me like a tidal wave; because when it's wet it glazes my fingers; because I want to be gang-banged by female inmates; because I want to fuck for food and water; because I wasn't born in a chastity belt; **BECAUSE IT FEELS GOOD; BECAUSE MY CUNT IS SELFISH; BECAUSE IT'S SELF-GRATIFICATION;** because I like to fist-fuck a cunt with latex; because I was born a bitch-boy; because I like more than one orgasm; because I don't have to say "I love you" to anyone; because in my genital mind I can fuck anyone I want; because it's healthy; because I'm a vain bitch and only I know how to love myself . . .

In Partial Fulfillment of the Requirements

C A L V I N   B A K E R

*T*he clock's face was cut in half before I had borrowed enough courage from my gin to lean in for a kiss. Music had pushed us together long ago and the slightest pressure from my hands closed a distance just wide enough to hide an erection.

Shana's fingers tightened on my shoulders and our lips finally joined, sealing a pact we had been negotiating silently since the lightning smile she gave me in the cafe. I sighed with relief because my grandmother always said, "If you can't get laid by three, it's time to go home."

We went back to our table and gathered purse, sweater, and jacket, then abandoned the pounding strobe light to the straggling souls who didn't know they had only ten minutes left.

Outside, coquettish gusts of wind lapped at our sweat and we huddled that much closer for warmth as we tried to hail a cab. Finally, an old black DeSoto pulled over and we jumped in behind an old Luo man shrunken by neglect and abuse.

As we negotiated the fare, though, he bickered relentlessly and his withered look dampened the embrace we had curled into on his backseat. We agreed to his price, the few shillings seeming trivial next to his premature age and the insistence of Shana's hip.

As the lights of the city receded and the darkness of Miotoni Road hushed around us, I slipped my hand under her skirt, coaxing her panties around my fingers, down her legs, and finally out the window. The driver's half-dead eyes meet mine in the rear-view mirror and for a moment we were perfectly still in the back, afraid that he had seen the purple lace vanish into the night air.

When his stare finally melted and I was sure that he was trained on the road again, I clamped my hand to the moisture uncovered by fabric that some worker would find on his morning commute, wondering for a second whether he would have the fetish to keep them.

For us though, the lace was irretrievable. When the wind carried her underwear off, it lent a peculiar consummation to what had been, until an hour ago, a platonic relationship. We had both pledged faithfulness to other people thousands of miles away, and from then on, the damage was already done. For a month we had pretended at innocence. But the lace was gone; the pact was sealed.

"Now here," I thought when we met a month earlier, "here is someone I can love." I never told her that thought. In fact, I never would, but as her hips rose to meet my fingers, I imagined that she had been overcome by the same sentiments, that exact same sudden and inexplicable desire that wells from the gut to the roof of the mouth with a frightening quickness and an even scarier surety. The perfume from her fingers pressed into a sleeve that only I could smell and drag from for the rest of the day until the sides of my face ached from smiling.

It rose when I saw her walking across the middle of the campus, the summer grass giving away to graceful and sensuous footfalls. Each step setting in motion an almost imperceptible tremor of flesh and earth.

It rose again two days later, when I entered the restaurant where I was meeting friends for lunch and found her seated at our table. She sat with a grace that was as svelte as it had been when she walked across the grass, and a face that was kind.

Yes, there's love at first sight, but its almost undermined by impotent reason, flagellant doubt, or commitments on another planet.

Desire, though, rose and did not fall.

"So, Walter," she asked after a lull in the conversation, "what are you studying?"

"Linguistics," I told her. "I speak seven languages, and so . . ." But I never finished because Dale, who chaired the literature department at the university and had invited all of us to lunch, cut me off with some fascinating theory about some fascinating fucking thing he had read while taking a shit in Moscow, and Russian wasn't one of my languages.

After polite laughter and a suitable pause, I tried to pick up the thread of conversation with Shana. "So what brings you here?" I asked her.

"I'm a writing fellow."

"Really, what are you working on?"

"Oh, it's a series of poems I started a couple of years ago."

"You're a poet. I didn't think anyone still wrote poetry," I said jokingly.

"That's because you're a theory head," she said, I think, teasingly. "You've probably never read a poem."

A quiet fell over the table as the others picked up on the conversation and waited for my response. I was too tongue-tied to speak and the pause hung there until Jane, who studied comparative literatures, saved me.

"So what are the poems about?" she asked.

"Parts of the body," Shana said then looked at me. "Why criticize when you can create."

I had never really thought of myself as a critic, but there you have it. A battle between theory and art, reason and emotion, desire and commitment. The conceit of my point of view versus her muteness, save some sparse lines—bent through the prism of memory—here and there. A classic love story but for the following simple truth: Not only did Shana not need me to save her from her personal dragon, she hated me on principle. And when principle has taken ideology to the water and forged character what can overcome that?

Character for her meant that poets were good and the machinations of a critical mind were nestled next to adultery on the moral spectrum. She celebrated the universe and added to its beauty, while I forced my fingers where they did not belong to undo the holy handiwork. What can change such a vile first opinion?

Still. Something in my makeup—once it has been bent on a course—prevents me from backing down until I reach the most humiliating of possible conclusions. Loneliness, the condition of being without love, made me pick up the phone three days later, after looking her number up in the student directory. Loneliness, the writer's middle ground between inspiration and paper, made her agree.

When I called, Shana was staring at a blank page with the word "eyes" written at the top. Her ability to create was temporarily blocked, so even an invitation from a linguist, who spoke seven languages but was fluent in none, was enough to lure her out of the house.

Over coffee and pastries, through cigarette and hash smoke, she stared at my eyes, memorizing them for a later time when she would put pen to paper again, and like it or not, the last pair of eyes she would have seen would be mine and so I, humble critic, would wheedle my way into verse.

Her gaze met mine and reduced it to lines and curves and specks of glitter in the iris. Perhaps a furtive glance from time to time.

She turned, nervously looking around the room because she had stared at me for so long. But the question had posed itself. When our eyes met again, she looked openly, intent on absorbing my entire face. And I did my best to grow luminous—making a soft arc of my neck to let her know that my face was also flush because eyes are only part of the body.

She remained distrustful, though, and kept her distance. Hugs and glances seemed to be as close as I would ever get. After the night in the cafe, some hugs were tighter than others, some glances more curious, but the danger had passed for her. Perhaps the editor teased but the chase, alas, was left unseen.

Shana had another poet. I had another critic. In theory, what happens halfway around the world should not disturb either relationship. In practice, we both knew that to give in would be to invalidate those relationships and to promise each other something. More promises were the last thing we wanted to make. We had achieved a perfect love, a dizzying ecstasy of thought and desire, however brief. To test it was to ruin it. I placated myself by thinking that perfect love does not coddle to the crucible of the relationship, and that, in poetry, true love was debased by the mere suggestion of sneaking around. Then again, I inherited none of my grandmother's cabaret frankness, and so never had the guts to confess my feelings.

I saw the dragon but played the Hamlet.

Thankfully, by the time I finished my second year as an undergraduate, I could drink Grandma under the table. And what denial works, gin and dance rip asunder.

The evening began with a group of us meeting for dinner and a couple of drinks. After dinner, we thinned out and a handful of us made our way to a nightclub. Under the insistent tug of alcohol, inhibitions slid to the floor and Shana and I were left in an ever-tightening embrace. My hands began, first keeping time in the air, then at her waist, and circled to clasp each other at the small of her back. They fell with gravity, to rest at the urging of her rear, before finally making their way up again to hold the edge of her shoulderblades and pull her nearer.

Our bodies pressed together, she gathered the skin of my back beneath her fingernails as the clock stretched out its arms to form a line. My knees weakened as I drew my lips away from a soft kiss. We smiled, then kissed again. She traced my lips with her tongue, then pulled away as I opened my mouth to receive it. Her teeth pressed into the flesh of my bottom lip before offering her tongue again as a bashful finger circled her nipple. The song ended and we both knew we had stepped on another ground of no-turning-back.

In the cab, I found my back pressed against the divider as I tried drunkenly to perform oral sex. Her skirt covered my head and her knees locked around my neck. She remained perfectly still, saying only, "will you please stop that," as she pushed my head away.

We turned right, off the main road, onto the red dirt path that led to my house and I was thrown to the side of the car, then raised myself from the floor. In the light from a neighbor's driveway, I met the driver's eyes and did my best to pretend that nothing out of the ordinary happened.

The car pulled to a stop in front of my house and I paid the driver hurriedly as he pursed his lips in disdain. I overtipped him, then fumbled to find the keys to the gate and avoid his stare.

Outside, the moon poured through Shana's skirt to show the shape of her thighs. Inside, my fingers stumbled as they undid the clasp of her bra. But she pulled away.

"Let's talk about this."

No, no, no. Let's not talk. Let's get naked and talk tomorrow. Let's climax just as the sun peaks at the mountains in the north. Please.

I got up and put some music on. When I came back, she had refastened her bra and taken shelter in the far corner of the couch with her feet tucked beneath her. I sat as close as her knees would allow and we unleashed: "What are we doing" and "I don't know but" and "how many people have you slept with" and "seven, eight" and "ever been tested" and "umm" and "what about her; what about him."

As doubt was subdued and ignored, I traced the meeting of her thighs with my fingers and the curve of her ear with my tongue. The buckle of my belt yielded to a firm tug. With one hand on my chest, she climbed on top of me as another hand held me just close enough to feel her warmth. A gentle pull guided me inside of her.

She rose again as I writhed beneath her. She teased again as I clutched her waist, before finally falling slowly to touch my thighs with hers. Long caresses gave way to short thrusts. "I want you to come inside me," she whispered.

I wanted to. But hours of gin and dance and the waning night had taken their toll. Guilt clambered out of the cellar to meet the sun, hoisting itself up on my favorite leg. As it became obvious that I would not survive the onslaught, I tried furiously.

Shana, aware of what was happening, came to rest against my legs, then swept her hair back to kiss me. We cuddled as I tried to apologize.

"Shh." She covered my mouth with open fingers and held her head to my chest until sleep started to overcome us.

We made our way to the bedroom as the sun pushed through the slats of the shutters, and as we curled around each other to fall asleep, there was only the hint of a smile on her face.

But what promises gin and guilt greedily stole away, the subconscious restored with humility.

Sometime that morning I dreamt that we were holding hands, kissing from time to time, as she guided me through the chambers of her insides. Under a vaulted ceiling, she led me to a fountain where I stopped to cool my thirst. And I kept taking longer and longer sips until she came so hard that I didn't want to.

Communion

J Z B

You have sensed her presence in the universe while walking silently
     along the shore at dawn
And have glimpsed her bronze body as it fades
     in the distant skies at sunset.
Her voice beckons for you in the darkness
     as you awaken to the anguish of her tears.
Like oceans and like drums you have felt the thrusting rhythms
     of her hips, the tremors of her thighs, and her passions
     bleeding to explode.

She bids you enter her sanctuary
     Draped with silken walls of diamonds
        Rose, rubies, carnelians, and gold
     Where ancient prayers of thanksgiving and praise
     Swell from her moist lips echoing your name.
Come as she offers her first fruits to you
     in His name.

The Ballad of Sadie LaBabe

TIM SEIBLES

Sadie LaBabe was a magic sister
Lord, even a blind man couldn'a missed'er
Her sultry skin was dark as shade
Her mind cut sharp as a butcher's blade
And the brothers who stared at Sadie's thighs
Would shake their heads and moan and cry

'Cause Sadie moved like water poured
The shapes she shaped had angels floored
She knew her walk turned wind to fire
A wink from Sadie turned brains to mire

The mellow fellas tried to talk that sly
They'd high-sing "Sadie!" when she walked by
But if she stopped to pass some time
Their lines went stale and sank to slime
She yawned she'd heard it all before—
Stuff bad boys write on bathroom doors

'Cause Sadie pours like rivers move
Her black skin rocks men toward the blues
She won't be mine, she won't be yours
She bit Eve's apple down to the core

Now J. T. Kade was Billy-Dee handsome
His humble home they called **Love Mansion**
He was ice cream cool and built like a panther
Whatever the question J.T. was the answer
The sisters crowned him King of the Land
He could make a girl faint just by holding her hand

.   .   .

So one fast day this last July
King Cool J.T. came boppin' by
Now Kade had come from way up in Philly
His eyes were steady, his lines were chilly
He said he'd come down Dallas way
For this heavy-hittin' hammer they called LaBabe

'Cause Sadie loved like honey tasted
She'd groove you till your life was wasted
Her tongue was silk, her touch was satin
She'd soothe you till your hills would flatten

But Sadie heard what the sisters said
About this brother who broke their bread
She made the pledge, "This Saturday night
I'll be home alone by candlelight
And if this Kade is what ch'all say
I won't mind much if he comes my way"

'Cause Sadie's heart could hold an ocean
She moved more ways than there was motion
Let tight be fat and tall be low
You gonna maybe-with-Sadie, she gonna stop your show

Three days went past and kept on goin'
By Saturday night a light breeze was blowin'
With candle-shine flecked in her eyes
Sadie sat lazy while the crickets cried
Her blouse was cotton, her shorts were suede
She had big doubts about this Kade

But from the porch there tapped a noise
And though the screen she caught his voice
"Say, Lady-Sadie, won'tcha let me in
I got some wine and some time to spend
I'm knockin' here 'cause I know you're there
Wanna slide my hands through your thick black hair"

.   .   .

So Sadie smiled and licked her lips
Said "*Grease* and slide under since you're so slick
The pleasure's my treasure, we won't need no wine
I like your style and I've heard you're fine—
Let the body be danced and the soul be dazzled
Let's make love shapes till the stars get frazzled"

They talked awhile then he touched her face
She twined her arm around his waist
The chatting stopped, the kissing started
The routes they used had not been charted
They rocked the sofa, then bumped the door
They bruised the stairs, they warped the floor
The storm they raised blew out the candles
He held her hips like they had handles
A whole day passed and neither seemed tired
If sex is electric this coupe was wired

So Sunday went off when Monday morning came on
Sadie stood up and stretched, but Kade was gone
The grapevine says he's in a home
For those who run where none should roam
They say he sings, he stutters, he raves
About some lady he calls LaBabe
For him the world has come unhinged—
He yells, "Sadie loves like a big fish swims!"
The doctors scratch their heads and frown
They drug his milk to calm him down

While Sadie sips soda by a swimmin' pool
Her mind is clear, her skin is cool
Sometimes she feels a little sadness
For drivin' Kade to that sweet madness
But Sadie holds what most let fall—
"*If you're gonna half-step don't step at all!*"

'Cause Sadie played in the Garden of Eden
She tamed the snake and taught him readin'
She won't be mine, she won't be yours
She ate Eve's apple and asked for more

Malkai's Last Seduction

KIINI IBURA SALAAM

"the most powerful seductions are executed against the silence of few
   words"
Sometimes, I feel

shoulder shrug

like a motherless child.

cheek rub against shoulder

Sometimes, I feel like a motherless child.

body slump

At twilight, when the world is settling down for rest, Malkai is turning over
inside. The colors of dusk pierce him like a rusty pin breaking skin. Yellow
gets him in the gut. Auggghhh. It is the color of his home skies. Orange
knocks him in the temple. Hhhhhhh. It's the color of his soil. Rose pushes
against his heart. It is, like here, the color of love. Malkai's spirit groans with
aching for home. Nothing can soothe him. He spends his hours speaking the
words. He and his people have little use for human languages, but he feels the
moan, he understands the feelings she sings about. The wall in that woman's
voice wraps itself around his loneliness and strokes his painful yearning to be
among his own people. He spends hours speaking the words, but in his own
language: shoulder shrug, cheek rub against shoulder, body slump.

The buzzing that had settled in Cory's ears over the past couple of days was
Malkai coming to get him. When the first "zzzzzz" licked his eardrums,
Cory had swatted at the air around his newly pierced earlobes. A meddle-
some mosquito—he imagined—hovering near his ears. He made repeated
attempts to shoo it away, but his arms soon grew tired. His shoulder ached
from throwing his biceps into repeated attack arcs and his fist grew bored
finding no tender little bug crushed in its grasp. Eventually he shrugged his
shoulders and decided to live and let live.

Like any constant noise will, the buzzing eventually disappeared from
Cory's conscious mind. Seeing Malkai's frame draped in a relaxed stance at

the base of a huge sycamore tree brought the "zzzzzz" back into Cory's awareness. The sound reconstructed itself gradually, like the pieces of a forgotten dream slowly becoming crystal clear. Cory hadn't yet connected Malkai with the buzzing. He peeked at Malkai's body out of the corner of his eye while subconsciously biting his lower lip. What Cory discerned through the thick of his lashes was a mass of pulsating energy. Cory felt it radiating from Malkai in waves. It buzzed around Malkai's form, building a composite of legs, arms, and wings. Wings? Cory flipped his head quickly to face Malkai as though to catch a culprit in the act of thievery. All he saw was Malkai's brown body swaying back and forth in slow motion like a heavy breadfruit ready to drop to the earth. No wings. Cory dismissed his vision as a hallucination induced by the sun's glare. He lifted his hand to his forehead and brought much-needed shade to his eyes.

When Cory walked past Malkai, the buzzing reconnected itself to his eardrums with a zoom. Cory stopped short. The hair on the back of his legs felt like it was on fire. In the pit of his belly a million atoms danced a nervous rumba. His heart threw itself into convulsions, but he couldn't look back. Cory felt if he looked back the "zzzzzz" would take over his brain and push him into insanity. He put his thumb between his lips, gnawed on his skin, and begged for his legs to unlock so he could walk away.

The noise now had a source: Malkai (a mosquito he was not).

Though Malkai's skin might have felt like the brush of a thrush with humming wings, it sheathed a strong solid body that could not be crushed with a smack. Malkai's mouth, too, was used for sucking, but not for bloodsucking. The tongue housed in Malkai's mouth was flat and thick and warm, quite contrary to the mosquito's hollow tube. The swell of a mosquito bite is negligent when compared to the silent soul swelling that pounds against your insides after contact with Malkai's lips.

The soft brush of something against Cory's skin roused him from his frozen stance. It wasn't a mosquito that had been flying around Cory's ears, as he had first imagined, it was a moth. Cory automatically responded to the moth's flirtatious touch with a shoulder jerk and an ear swat. Malkai, who had been lazily passing time under the sycamore's shade, straightened and focused when his eyes registered Cory's motions. Those involuntary movements spoke volumes to Malkai; in Malkai's language, Cory had just whispered come on in.

Cory had no way of imagining a velvet people who spoke through balletic motions and muscle spasms, arched arms and bent necks. A people who thrived on human nectar. A nation that consisted of beings who were physically similar but biologically distinct. And he could not imagine that a simple little shoulder jerk and ear swat could signal to someone who stood watching him from a distance under the shade of a sycamore tree that it was time to close in.

Cory's appearance on the horizon meant that Malkai had found his last seduction. When the meaning of Cory's motions hit Malkai, his hands flew up in the air in a gesture of relief. Malkai's muscles almost popped trying to contain themselves from celebrating. That he had some nectar to collect before he could return seemed a mere formality. Malkai had plans, plans that did not include a lengthy chase. Malkai allowed his homesickness to cloud his judgment. Thus, Malkai made no provisions for elongated discussions that would discern the safety of his assignment. By whatever renegade tactics he had to employ, Malkai was getting the nectar he came for, completing his last assignment, and going home.

Now.

Cory had begun the seduction. Only he had done so in ignorance. Didn't understand he was parading his openness when he turned to face Malkai and offered up a weak, uncertain smile. Didn't realize he was making it easy for his seducer when he sat quietly under the shade of the next tree (an oak), close enough to make pursuit unnecessary. Was too dumb to know it was on when Malkai appeared in front of him with a huge grin plastered across that velvet face. The grin should have told Cory something. It was all teeth. It was without calculation or hesitation.

There was no shame neither.

It was Malkai whose voice rode the wind first. Cory's tongue appeared at the corner of his mouth to wet his lips in nervous preparation. Before even responding to Malkai's approach, Cory looked over his shoulder attempting to scan the area that surrounded the oak tree. His search for intruding eyes revealed his anxiety, but it was an unnecessary revelation. Cory's anxiety was visible, he was suffocating in it and his worried eyes were pounding out an S.O.S. on Malkai's face. Cory's paranoid gestures were like spoken confessions in Malkai's mind. Malkai skimmed his fingers over the back of Cory's, and then held it with the intention of erasing Cory's tension. Cory glanced up in confusion and found himself caught in Malkai's brown eyes.

The buzzing stopped.

Cory could no longer feel the breeze. Malkai's finger began a slow circle over the skin of Cory's palm, and Cory found himself releasing secrets that had never before crossed his lips. It was like acupuncture, and Malkai's fingers were the needles. When Malkai pushed on Cory's palm, Cory felt something wrap around him and squeeze the conversation out. Then somewhere, a little girl screamed, Cory's mother cursed, and Cory blinked. With that blink Cory regained something like consciousness and jerked away. Heart first, then hand flying away from its resting place in Malkai's firm grasp. Cory looked down at his hand, eyes clouded with disbelief. He could almost make out a trial of wildfire where the kiss of Malkai's fingers had seared his flesh. Something inside him cringed. He turned his head away and bit his lip in indecision.

The second his hand was free, Cory's mind started buzzing. His mind buzzing all the way through chatting introductions, appraising glances, and Malkai's smooth descent to a seated position next to him. The buzzing in Cory's mind was nothing like the buzzing that Malkai had sent to sit in his ears. Cory's buzzing was visual. It was composed of images of large square men tottering on tiny angular spiked heels. A television clip of a pedaphilic priest and jagged pages from porno magazines displaying studs in ripped overalls. No, Cory's buzzing was not at all like Malkai's.

The blood vessels in Cory's hands were so strained they were threatening to burst. Cory stared at his shaking palm and his fluttering lifelines gave way to images of his and his cousin's blurred bodies as his cousin chased him though his adult-empty house, of their nude bodies pressed together in his parents' empty bed, of their tingling bodies working together to achieve that sweet sweet release. Malkai's index finger crossed Cory's fluttering lifelines and obliterated Cory's chase-and-catch memories. I did not come to earth to encourage the reminiscing of reluctant assignments, his finger insisted.

Seduction is the stuff that dreams are made of. The tugging of strings you didn't know existed. The answering of questions you didn't ask. An invisible orchid-lined path, heavy with the scent of musk. A feeling of déjà vu propelling the heavy chain of events, yet forcing hesitation with every step for it's a déjà vu never before felt. Seduction is the thing that makes a memory, crushes many dreams, and puts a twinkle in your great-grandmother's eye.

Cory's mind had become a blackboard upon which complex theorems were frantically being worked out. Spurred on by velvet touches, hinging on "what if" and fear, Cory shakily built the type of mathematic sentences he had learned could prove any geometric fact. "If someone sees me, then the whole world will perceive me as abnormal." "If I do this, then everything I have done up until this day will be called into question." "If I enjoy this interaction, then what am I?"

The chalk snapped in Cory's mind and left him solutionless. Math abandoned, Cory offered a shaky-fingered reply to Malkai's velvet-fingered advances. The hands began to dance. First teasing palm-rubbing with fingers, then fingertips rubbing against each other. The hands repeatedly closed and opened. Cory's fingers were no longer shaking. Malkai's fingers were no longer alone in their advances. The palms begin to separate after meeting. The movements of their two brown hands mirrored the intimate dance of lovers. Cory, fascinated, kept his eyes glued to the undulating hands, and sighed in wonder at how good such simple movements could make him feel. He would never approach handshakes the same way again.

Malkai's fingers soon grew tired of palm-rubbing and hand-fucking. They began to wander to Cory's wrist, up his arm, to Cory's shoulder, and to the nape of his neck. They lingered there for a second. Long enough for Malkai to contemplate the next move . . .

. . . and also for Cory to contemplate his. Cory wanted to believe the dancing hands was the climax of his daring adventure. Thought that hand-fucking with a total stranger was risqué enough to merit a lifelong memory. He still didn't realize the film had just started, the theme music was playing, the opening credits were rolling, and he was the leading lady. Anyone peeping from afar, watching the seduction play out as if on the silver screen, knew where Cory would be in scene two.

. . .

Ass naked, fingers in mouth, chest heaving, belly trembling, body spread across bed sheets . . . or grass . . . lips moist from nervous licking, lowered eyes, staccato breath, flared nostrils . . .

Cory kept replaying how he had gotten to this point. How was it that he had landed under an oak tree in the web of a velvety hand-fucker whose motions, intent on turning him out in plain view of the whole entire world, had him pressing through the fly of his new green silk boxers. Cory's eyes closed involuntarily when he felt Malkai's hand on his chest. A muscle he didn't know existed twitched in his groin. His ears were burning with embarrassment. Could anyone see them? Senseless fucking was never part of his agenda.

The seducer stares ahead toward the end of the road and, with his head cocked at a devious angle, calculates how long it will take to get there. The seduced looks behind at the beginning of the road and, with his brow creased with concern, wonders how it slipped so far away. Cory's entire life, it could be argued, was an attempt to avoid such an event as this one. He discreetly avoided eye contact with men who wore their privacy in public like an expensive coat of chinchilla. Didn't want to rub shoulders with those who stood outside their closets for fear of contamination. Purposely refused his hands' desire to linger on the shoulder of an especially intriguing friend. Newspaper clips announcing trysts in the park left a bitter taste in his mouth. That he could be so caught up so as to release control, let down his guard, and act against his morals unnerved him.

This had been a propless seduction. There was no sensual wailing floating in the air, no liquid intoxicant on ice, and no satin sheets beneath Cory's back. In fact there was nothing Cory could blame his transgression on. He was resting against the dirty bark of an old tree atop a hill covered with dying grass. This was no fantasy, yet it was about to come true. Nothing short of a miracle could have brought Cory to this point. At this moment, the miracle was simply a touch so utterly sensual, an understanding so undeniably sexual, that it could not be ignored. Every refusal Cory had forced his body to accept in the past decade, delivered him—a willing participant—in Malkai's lap. Each little impulse he had previously suppressed quietly collected itself into an explosive mass, and now, two clasped palms were coaxing the explosion.

. . .

If there were a movie camera hovering somewhere in the skies, as Cory imagined there must be at this seminal point in his life, it would close in on the oak tree that sheltered the seduction from great distance. It would encompass the green form before swooping through the twisted, leafy branches to reveal Cory and Malkai's heated embrace, then it would pass over Malkai's shoulder to reveal a brown moth resting on the tree bark and close in on the moth's wings as it fluttered by, tickling the kissers and rousing them from their soul-suckling.

The battle within Cory had been won. The mutiny was complete. Now, Cory had forgotten there had been any dissent and was completely concentrated on devouring those lips which devoured his fear, his indecision, his revulsion until Cory couldn't wait. Cory couldn't wait to break down barriers and go where he had never gone before. To bring shame upon his family. To participate in an act he would never verbalize to anyone. To create a memory to file next to his and his cousin's afternoon pleasure trips. Only this time it could not be excused by age. Only this time there would be no aunt to say, "Don't worry, they're just little boys. It's perfectly normal." There would only be condemning eyes and accusing fingers.

And hate.

Arms encircle and crush solitude from lonely bodies. Lips soothe and push tenderness through teeth and down the throat. Fingers feel and leave a trail of shivers along passion-warmed skin. Cory had often found peace— or at least momentary joy—crushing some woman in his embrace. But he had never been crushed. Nor had he been seduced. Cory had never been the one with thoughts of escape up until the last moment. He had never silently questioned his participation in the act. Or even wondered what he was doing there. Cory had always been the one with the head full of plans. The calculations, the formulas, and the theories that would lead to penetration.

Yet here he sat, under the boughs of an oak, ready to agree to anything this thick-fingered stranger suggested. A dog squeezed out a marathon of barks without stopping for breath, compounding the painfully sweet bursting feeling splitting Cory's chest. His cinnamon fingers wanted to know the contours and textures of Malkai's velvet skin. Cory stood with his toes hanging off the brink of discovery and felt the intense desire to shuffle backward to a safer spot. His will faltered, did he really want to uncover the secrets he was coaxing out of hiding? Certainly he could live life without knowing what it's like to be fucked under an oak tree by a velvet stranger. He took one more glance back to that point at the beginning of the road, but it was too late to look back. This is the now.

Mid-seduction.

This is the now, Cory, and those are lips inching up the back of your neck. This is the now and you don't know the owner of those lips. You've just met him under this tree. You can't take him home to meet your family or to your apartment to help you paint your walls. You don't even know if you will see him again. Ignoring his fresh whispers of doubt, Cory bravely turned his face to Malkai's and opened himself under the caress of the breeze and the watchful eyes of the skies. It was all-consuming curiosity that made him think of all women who had ever loved him. It was pride that made him consider how shocked they would be to find him here—half naked, crushed in a strange man's embrace, in plain view of the world.

All philosophy went out of the door when Malkai attacked Cory's lips with a finality that shook Cory straight through his to-hell-with-society resolve. Malkai pressed his body against Cory's. Cory's eyes rolled back in their sockets and his shoulders dropped into relaxation. He boldly began a wind and grind that signaled he had left all questions and doubts behind. Or at least swallowed them, so that they might resurface at a less crucial time.

When Cory opened his eyes he was startled to find himself reclining on one of the wide branches of the oak tree. But that wasn't the cause of his rushing breath. Cory shivered under the breeze's command. He saw what he gathered to be large wings folding down into Malkai's back. Under the intensity of the moment he could not focus on supernatural visions. His eyes felt heavy, like they did when sleep had a powerful hold upon him. His mind was all scrambled up and confused, like when he was abruptly disturbed in the middle of an intense dream. Malkai's lips on Cory's open thighs were too distracting.

The birds must have been shocked: Cory and Malkai's bare backs writhed and undulated as the sensations traveled up and down their spines. The squirrels must have been pissed: Cory and Malkai jerked like epileptics, shaking the branch and disturbing the tree's peace as the sensation took over their nervous systems. The ancestors must have nodded knowingly. Though muscles cramped and body parts twisted, pain was not felt. Not until the dam broke and the waterfall flowed.

One of the last visions that burned in Cory's retina that day was a golden glow radiating from Malkai's body. If he hadn't just had his mind blown, Cory would have noticed that the glow was most intense where Malkai's lips touched his body. If he hadn't been reclining on a branch twelve feet in the air, he might have realized that the glow was coming from him and that Malkai was drawing it out of him. He might have even concluded that the entire love dance had been executed to render him so full and so yielding, so as to make Malkai's nectar collecting possible.

But Cory's feet were not firmly on the ground. And his mind was far from its clearest state. Tracing the path of an after-sex glow was not at the height of Cory's priorities. Cory confused the glow of his own nectar with the setting sun and squinted in its glare. Through the slits of his half-closed eyes, Cory saw Malkai's head thrown back and that moth from the tree softly land on Malkai's lips. Cory slowly reached out a shaking hand to brush it away. Then, as if on cue, tons of moths softly attached themselves to Malkai's body. Sure that his eyes were tricking him Cory rubbed them with a sweat-soaked hand and blinked rapidly. When the moths began to flap their wings with the speed of light, Cory stuttered some phrase of incomprehension. They took off with Malkai's body. Cory drew in a deep breath, rested his throbbing head back and closed his eyes in disbelief and exhaustion.

When Cory woke, it was to the light of night. When he opened his eyes he first saw darkness, then his eyes dilated into focus and he began to discern the cocoa-brown ridges of bark. As Cory's mind raced to orient his body to his surroundings, his eyes flitted around seeking something familiar to grab on to. His body welcomed him back into consciousness with the tingling sensations of a painful resting place, his skin greeted him with the gritty roughness of dirt. Cory sighed. His chest was tender where the bark of the tree had rubbed against it. As he turned his head upward toward the sky, Cory's nose brushed the base of the tree and his ear separated from the earth packed around the tree's roots. Cory sat up and supported his weight with his trembling right arm.

The moon was low that night. Low and heavy. The fingers on Cory's left hand itched to try to touch it. With his hand stretched out and his arm fully extended, Cory felt a memory tug at his gut. He didn't remember Malkai, but he remembered a feeling. He thought of his mother, but the minute she appeared in his mind, she disappeared. He could not hold her there unless he thought of his grandmother, his best friend's mother, and that crazy woman who sat on the corner selling religious papers. They all had to be present simultaneously for Cory's mother to remain in his thoughts. It was as if the singular had been erased from Cory's mind. His thoughts would no longer focus on individuals. He could only focus on groups. He couldn't remember his job, his vendettas, or his debts. He couldn't remember his closet either. Nations of communities had set up camp in Cory's mind and he began to work connections and create links between them. He lowered his head in exhaustion. A night breeze blew past him and his skin rose with goose bumps. Cory realized he was naked except for a pile of moths' wings resting in his lap. Cory cursed softly.

Untitled

WINSTON BENONS, JR.

*T*he whistling sound of the brook skipping across the rocks. The dense foliage emitting a coolness, like a sip of mint tea. The sun's rays massaging John's back as he enjoys the natural pleasure of being at one with a woman. Vines, gripping his wrists preventing his hands from touching . . . feeling . . . caressing. Her body lying underneath him enjoying his rhythm. She wraps herself around him parting his thighs with her feet. He feels a sharp pain, a sharp pain he can't get away from. With all his movement trying to break loose he draws it farther into him. Now enjoying penetration as well as being penetrated he moves with the strength and grace of a tide in motion. With all his nerve endings being stroked he is taken over by physical pleasure. He shrieks, shivers, releases his glory. His lovers cut his arms free from bondage. He turns and lightly caresses Gail's face as she is breathing heavily with a feverish grin and a tool strapped to her waist.

Chastity

JANICE W. HODGES

baritones dance
on tender drums

fumbling fingers
spilling rum

chastity snaps
thighs get weak

breathing harder
nipples leak

Seduction

DE ANN DIAX

When I see you
I will dance with your eyes
kiss your cheek softly
put my hand on my thighs
I will suck on my lip
touch tenderly my breast
trace down my own hip.
I will cross my own leg
lean forth beside you
feel the drop of my egg.
I will touch your skin
feel my heart quicken
as your arousal begins.
I will feel the rise in your pants
take my place beside you
as we begin our sweet dance.
The stroke of your hand
I will slowly undress you
feel the force of your man.
I will taste your sweet softness
and I will wonder
did I really dream this.
Oh when I see you
what ecstasy we'll share
and I will be pleased
when I've done what I dare.

The Writer

ESTELLE FARLEY

He makes love with words
Afraid of silence—
it may break the spell.

His gifts are in words
Unsure of his talents
he talks you into loving.

After, the silence returns
and you ponder how it happened.

Leaving him alone,
slight smile on his face.

Encountering Ecstasy

LINDA WHITE

I had never believed in the power of attraction until the day he entered my life. I was on a bus of all places, immersed in a book that asked me to take a journey to the far reaches of space and believe in incredible luck. He didn't ask to sit down, but the second his arm touched mine proved to be the most intensely sexual moment of my life. I turned to him suddenly, wanting to see the face that had elicited such a response from my body. And he turned to my invitation and smiled. That smile, wrapped up in the bonnet of warm chocolate, pulled me in, sucked me into his mysterious world. I looked away, pretended to return to my book. I felt him look away, finding other interests in the people on the bus. But his arm still brushed occasionally against mine. The touch was fire, burning flames coursing through my body. Did he know that he had that effect on me? Did he do this on purpose?

My body would not cooperate with me. It tingled and quivered at every touch. It longed for him, begged him to indulge it. My mind struggled for supremacy, but in the lure of wild passions, who can win? The only thing that seemed to work well was my mouth, except it required constant moistening in anticipation of wrapping itself around his mouth. I closed the book and decided to focus on the setting outside the window. It helped me move away from him at least. But I found out quickly how truly cruel my body can be. Without his touch, it hungered. The intensity of my beating heart was only a foreshadowing of something more potent. I almost didn't see the signs. Almost let the feeling engulf me. My body wanted him and would have him. My legs were tensing, tingling. My groin was preparing itself without my consent. He will come, it promised. Or you will.

The sudden revelation of my predicament startled me away from the outside scene, forced me to confront the presence beside me. Was he a demon, able to blow his hot breath upon me and will me to submission? Surely, no ordinary man would bring an orgasm by simply sitting beside a woman. Especially me. And it was coming. Every move I made to halt its climation only aided it, made it stronger. Even the thought of getting up and finding another seat was vehemently shot down, for the movement itself almost sent me reeling with pleasure. I would like to know that he didn't sense my discomfort, that he was another of these listless passengers on this bus. But I could feel the warmth rising in him as well. At this point I didn't care if it was illusion or reality. He had to feel this too. He had too. And then I came.

In my room at home, I could scream, relish in its power. But here on this crowded bus, I could only moan. Quietly. The passion locked my legs and I held on to ecstasy as long as I could. I didn't know how I appeared to the other people. To him. I didn't know if they understood what was happening to me. If he understood. I just couldn't let the feeling go. I felt too good. Then it began to ebb, and I began to regain control of my body. He reached toward me, and with my heart threatening to explode from the scent of his body, pushed the button to alert the driver to stop.

As the bus slowed, he glanced at me briefly, smiled brilliantly, and got up to wait. It took all of my remaining willpower to remain in my seat. To let him go. The doors to the bus swished open. Seemed to suck the air from my lungs. Then he was gone. I saw him cross the street, and I watched him walk for as long as I could. As the bus turned the corner, I lost sight of him. I didn't dare look at the others in the bus. Had they seen? Did they know? At last I smiled at the questions. Who cares if they saw? Who cares if they knew? I had had the best bus ride of my life and I planned to finish it.

Butterfly

LANA C. WILLIAMS

Herbie Hancock's Thrust,
flew Butterfly through
the 70s, and
we hung on,

tight keystrokes clawing channels,
sax and sex colliding
through car radios where
backseat virgins got played—
loudly

thighs spread apart,
greasy like fried chicken,
juicy for a lickin,
tender, golden,
succulent
and altogether boned . . .

back when
brothers had wings in midnight blue,
translucent in coming rain,
shooting sparks
deep inside black wholeness.

The Flower

LENARD D. MOORE

One Autumn night
in my father's black '63 Chevy
I crawled on top of her.
Her brown legs opened
like wings going nowhere
or a flower
a bee climbs into.
I pulsed inside the warmth
of an unfamiliar world,
striking her dark petals.
Her tongue liked the light,
as it whitened the air
smelling of sex.

I Long

CAROLE HILL FAULKNER

I long for whispers in the morn
about the splendor we shared
I long to tell you how I am yours
to hear how you are mine
I need to look into your eyes
so I can watch you looking back
I long for the remembering of the time
You came only to fill me and we were still
and I was happy to feel you inside me
and in that moment it was enough
that connection made as we laid still
it was my heart
that pumped and pumped and pumped

I long to hear your voice in my ear
the silent speeches from your eyes
the fullness of your mouth
when holding back a torrent of things
I know you want to say "This is deep"
Daddy it's very grand!

I long to share my emotions with you
although spontaneous
once placed they're unchanging
no matter what
and if I move on in my life
you will always be with me
not like a ball to a chain
but like an arm to a hand
this is getting serious
doesn't look like it's going away

. . .

I long to have a life that allows my love
for you to be protected
and always to express myself
to slide my voice into your heart

I long for you to lick me with your tongue
for you to beat my back with your penis
so that I can feel its weight of want

I long to have your arms about my waist
and to watch your shadows as the sun moves
from the east to the west
to the night of the moon
and airy breath of the stars
my sight of them could never be impaired
by clouds
for I shall always see through them
I am invincible
and so to my darling
is my affinity to life

and it's now inclusive of you
and I share with you
that I long I long
I long . . .

surrogate lovers

EVANGELIST JANNIE JAMES

no more love songs
please no more dreams and myth and the
cooing and oohing
and the babee babee
babee
that always contradicts her responses of
never had a man who could
never had a man who would
once I had a man to leave me crying
at the door with a houseful of
burning memories
and thought it pains her to trade her
smokey robinsons
for a shake-your-ass-tune
or to tell marvin gaye that he will have to
jack-off tonight
she's simply tired of getting turned on
only to get
turned off
cause the record came and went at her
peak
and she's lying there
done lost
it and won't get it again
cause using a longer one
or slowing the speed
rarely helped in these matters any
and you could never tell a record
where to touch
where to satisfy
the prophesy of the beat
in your heart

the one two three of the man for every
woman
the four five six of the love
which by the way
eluded me
at the disco
cause the chicks there were two-steppin
to the love songs
and she was doing the shake
and happy to shed her tears
and accept the music for what it was
but they preferred to two-step
arms wrapped around themselves
blissful pretentions
spilling from their mouth
dancing with dreams and myth in
painted smiles
and frequently crying between records

Cajunto Sabor

BARON JAMES ASHANTI

Two bodies as island
a mystic cross that marks
the spot where the myth
of 69 divided by
male & female=lovers
reclined in the infinite

Aromatic sounds spiraled
from her pussy
as dream-catcher that
summoned me by sense of taste
and there are never enough
notes from that song

When tongues/mouths & sucking noises
swallow time and the smell
of pollination heavily hung about
the room . . .

In the afterward
the pungent urgency
of her succulent sex surrounds
the world like a clinging vine

while she rubs my senses
across her face & bobbed hair
as makeup/good to go
on her way to work . . .

the credibility of lust
is slippery when wet!

A Reminiscence

LEAH JEWEL REYNOLDS

Take the softness
and with it
wash me
cleanse me gentle/
unctuous worship   me
my lips' love's
longing
and spirit me
so I don't forget

Afterword

NEW TALES, NEW BLACKNESS:
CONSTRUCTING THE WHOLE SELF
THROUGH EROTICISM

ark Eros is as enjoyable as any anthology about eroticism could be. Sight and emotions, richly experienced, are tools that enable the reader to witness, explore, or be at one with that which is erotic. As you read the poems, plays/scripts, fiction, letters/reflections, and probe the photographs, you begin to realize that *Dark Eros* is of, in, and part of the African-American literary canon. African-Americans have been writing erotic literature for some time now; however, it took a length of time for that literature to be collected into a single volume.

Yet I can only go back as far as *Erotique Noire* to begin to mention names of writers/artists whose erotic stories and poems have appealed to so many readers. Yes, that is the book that got me interested in erotic literature and led me to Peter Harris's magazine, *The Drumming Between Us,* which features black erotic poetry. The writers who wrote so engagingly tenderly about the erotic in *Erotique Noire* are Ntozake Shange, Kalamu ya Salaam, Audre Lorde, Frank Lamont Phillips, Akua Lezli Hope, Saundra Sharp, Reginald Martin, Gloria Wade-Gayles, E. Ethelbert Miller, and Terry L. McMillan, among others.

I did not realize how little I knew about erotic literature until I was given a copy of *Erotique Noire.* It took some time before I began to read the anthology. I remember when people did not talk openly about anything erotic or even close to it for that matter. Those times were during my childhood years. I did not even overhear such talk in my community, because the adults just did not discuss eroticism around our childhood ears. So that meant we, as children, certainly did not discuss anything erotic either. We boys just explored what we thought was natural to do with girls. That was our knowledge of eroticism, though we did not call it erotic. We did not even know the word at the time.

Anyway, I let those unsayable thoughts settle in the back of my mind; then I began to read *Erotique Noire* day by day. So now I anxiously read *Dark Eros.* How quickly time slips away now, as I read page after page of *Dark Eros* in one sitting. How vividly the words conjure up images of that which is sensual in my head. How easily pleasurable memories

3 8 9

resurface, the experiences of the five senses working eroticism. *Dark Eros* is all that and then some, as the saying goes. There is much blackness revealing itself in the volume; and there are wings of eroticism taking flight at all times.

Yet there is something unexplainable about the sense of the erotic, enabling the reader to experience that which is at once magical and mystical. The finely crafted literature, *Dark Eros,* takes risks that will spellbind readers into thinking they are looking through a lens at a literary peep show. The reader understands what the erotic is, how it works, and how it affects the parties who are engaged in eroticism. This anthology is blackly eloquent, unfolding the erotic to the bone. This volume informs the reader that the black self has an erotic need and longs to fulfill that need at any hour. Moreover, the reader can feel the heat coming on and, most of all, cannot control the temperature. Like rap lyrics, the erotic words in *Dark Eros,* throb in the reader's ears, making him/her aware that the moment is completely uncontrollable. That is the spell the erotic puts on an individual.

When the erotic nature comes on, there is much improvising, like Pamela Fleming in Cecil Brown's story, "The Film Teacher." The erotic nature can also turn an individual inside out, upside down, and all the way around like Sara in Niama Leslie JoAnn Williams's story, "Cutting." Gilda Squire's story, "The Assistant," demonstrates just how the erotic nature might come on at any time. The story also shows how uncontrollable the characters, Damion and Tabitha, are with their erotic selves. The way that these characters cannot stop themselves in the heated moment is the same way that the reader won't be able to stop reading *Dark Eros.*

On the other hand, Rebecca Delbridge's poem, "No Turn on Red," demonstrates that there are certain boundaries that the erotic must not cross. The persona in the poem worried about curfew, though she was involved in the erotic. It is important to note that the persona was not free to groove with the erotic, which is present before her. It is only in certain cases like this when the erotic nature cannot take over. However, nothing can hold back the experience of reading *Dark Eros.*

Thus, with this collection of black Eros, Reginald Martin includes many new voices. One such voice is Lana Williams. Her poem "Butterfly," contributes to the tenderness and sensuality that emerges throughout *Dark Eros.* This poem exposes the true black self, which refuses to be concealed in the passionate moment of eroticism. Williams's poem unfolds with music (jazz in this particular instance) like so many erotic moments of blackness. The beat arouses the erotic and becomes contagious. The merging is a joyous sound. This merging where bodies move like one four-beat body. Another new voice is Jade D. Banks, whose short poems swing full ripeness of the erotic light.

As I sit writing, August afternoon rain drips down the large living room window of my house. The sound of the rain and hum of the fan upstairs conjure up memories within me about the erotic nature—when it came on like slow rain. I begin to wonder how the rain makes one think about the erotic self. There is something in me that says memory brings on the erotic. But, at times, it is amusing what memory brings to an individual. There is great pleasure in the amusing, however, and strange to say, the amusing can easily relax an individual into an erotic self. Yet *Dark Eros* can prepare an individual for the erotic self too. So the reader must watch out for what might come on as true eroticism constantly hovers upon him/her like congregating clouds. Yes, the berries are black and the juice is sweet in this anthology. Then too, the photographs add to the richness of the volume. The photographs speak like the words in *Dark Eros,* but deftly visual as the individuals exhibited in the hot moment of eroticism.

It is no accident that Reginald Martin compiles this volume with the black erotic self in mind. He realizes that the writers/artists are engaged with eroticism in their works, though they create in isolation. It is the responsibility of a writer to take us to higher heights while neologizing age-old topics and ideas. The writers are clear and concise, thoughts are related in brisk and brief language, patterns of comparison keep steady beats of direction and flow, and most important, each writer states without hesitation and with a '90s kind of forwardness—eroticism is hot and a way out of the madness because eroticism is love. The achievement in *Dark Eros* is in raw emotions within the heart, blending the magical and the mystical. This book is for the ceaseless eroticism in you, the reader. Witness the emergence of a literature long overlooked that can no longer be ignored. The heat is on now; and the sweat is dripping like the summer sky through my window.

Lenard D. Moore, Raleigh, North Carolina,
sitting in the love seat in my front room, 4:09 P.M.

About the Authors

Ibu Abu is a native of Chicago, Illinois, now living in Milwaukee, Wisconsin. He is an accountant and has been published in *Tri-Quarterly*.

Baron James Ashanti is a prominent New York City writer.

Reece Auguiste is an internationally known script writer and film maker from London, England. He currently resides in Memphis, Tennessee, and his latest project is a documentary on the life and civil rights contributions of Reverend Benjamin Hooks.

Calvin Baker is a New York–based writer whose first novel is *Naming the New World*.

Jade D. Banks, a Harrisburg, Pennsylvania, native, was liberated in a recent encounter at a local bookstore signing. She truly appreciates the fact that this form of erotica shows that black people are not homogenous.

Anthony Barboza is an internationally known erotic photographer based in New York City.

Danita Beck is an erotic painter from Memphis, Tennessee, and is currently completing her sixth one-woman show in only one year.

Playthell Benjamin is a well-known writer and radio personality in New York City.

Winston Benons, Jr. "Rendered in the human image—Framed in ebony. My eye's prism is the gateway to home. Spectral thoughts, from severe adoration to peaceful discontent, translate to ardent words that make up the conscious and unconscious volumes of life. What is—the writer?"

Victor E. Blue is a graduate student in history at North Carolina Central University. A native and resident of Raleigh, N.C., he received his bachelor's degree in journalism from the University of North Carolina at Chapel Hill. He has worked for several newspapers and wire services. His poems, essays, and reviews have appeared in publications in North Carolina, Indiana, and Illinois.

Mawiyah Kai El-Jamah Bonami is a twenty-four-year-old wife/mother/writer whose words have appeared in *FreeForm* magazine, a magazine based in Atlanta which focuses on pure art expressed through self; and also in *Fertile Ground*, a literary journal featuring African writings from across the diaspora, edited by Kalammu ya Salaam and Kysha N. Brown.

Nadir Lasana Bonami was born in New Orleans, Louisiana, in 1972 and is a 1995 graduate of Southern University at New Orleans. Mr. Bonami's work has appeared in the 1996 issue of *FreeForm* magazine and has also been featured in *Fertile Ground*. He won second place in 1994 and Honorable Mention in 1995 for his poetry in Suno's Literary Contest. Mr. Bonami is a member of Nommo Literary Society, a writer's workshop headed by Kalammu ya Salaam.

Cecil Brown is the author of *The Life and Times of Mr. Jive Ass Nigger* and *Click Song*. Brown in currently a professor at the University of California, Berkeley.

Kysha N. Brown writes with NOMMO Literary Society, a writing workshop based in New Orleans. She performs with Kalammu ya Salaam's Word Band and is co-publisher and co-editor of *Fertile Ground*, an annual journal of Black literature.

Valinda Johnson Brown writes on the sensuality and seduction of food. She works as a freelance food writer for the *Atlanta Journal-Constitution*. With her culinary training, from the New York Cooking School of Peter Kump, and the inspiration she receives from husband Ed's remarkable cooking, she is propelled to prepare for family and friends and catering clients only those foods that tingle the senses and warm the heart.

Chezia Thompson Cager's works here are inspired by Jean Toomer's *Cane*. She has just won the Artscape 1996 award for the book *Power Objects*. Cager's new book is *The Presence of Things Unseen: Giantalk* from Maisonneure Press.

Lesslie W. Clark is a native Memphian. She is currently a full-time student at the University of Memphis majoring in journalism/magazine editorial with a minor in African-American literature. She is also the devoted and womb-weary mother of a five-year-old son.

Cheri Daughtery is a Memphis businesswoman who thrives on the eroticism of color in daily life.

Rebecca Delbridge, a talented emerging young poet, is the youngest member of the Carolina African-American Writers Collective. She recently relocated with her mother, Oktavi, to Durham, North Carolina and attends Hillside High School.

De Ann Diax is a Bronx, New York–based writer testing the boundaries of eroticism.

Joy Doss is an experienced erotic writer currently working as a personal trainer in Memphis.

Elle is the pen name of a hip-hop promoter in Detroit, Michigan. Her claim to fame is that she reads at least four hundred pages of something every day.

Estelle Farley is a member of the Carolina African-American Writers Collective; she graduated from Fisk University with a degree in chemistry. Her work is featured in *Fertile Ground* and the forthcoming *Beyond the Frontier*. Most recently, Farley has shared her work at the International Black Arts Festival in Atlanta and is working on her first novel.

Carole Hill Faulkner is an established erotic writer from New York City.

Lurlynn Franklin is an award-winning painter, set designer, and writer who received an M.F.A. from the Memphis College of Art.

Jennifer Gibson is the owner of her own lingerie shop in New Orleans, Louisiana. She plans to begin a free 1-800 erotic phone service for blacks only.

Cassie Granberry currently resides in Miami, Florida, and is the author of *Black Breeze*, an erotic novel at the manuscript stage.

Jeul A. Harris is a recent graduate of the University of Tennessee at Martin. He began writing poetry at the age of fifteen. He believes that inside the mind lay the most beautiful and erotic thoughts and that unlocking the soul through paper and pen clears the temple of one's despair.

Helvettika, a pseudonym for a Jackson, Mississippi, reporter, is currently on assignment on the streets of Tunica, Mississippi, where she works as a part-time developer and full-time student of the art of Delta living.

Jennifer Holley is a paralegal for a major law firm in Atlanta, Georgia. She is both a rap lyricist and a rap music promoter. She writes: "CARPE DIEM, my child! If I told you all the secrets it might turn your blood to spit."

Perry Holmes, a native of Seattle, Washington, currently resides in Louisville, Kentucky, and prides himself on being the head of the only black grunge band in America.

Scott Jackson is a New York–based writer living in Hamden, Connecticut.

Evangelist **Jannie James** is a Pentecostal minister and a prominent speaker of the word of eroticism on various soapboxes in midtown in Atlanta, Georgia. She is childless, but has personal beliefs she feels will lead to wonderful child-rearing years in the future.

Honoree F. Jeffers is a graduate of Talladega College and received an M.F.A. in Creative Writing from the University of Alabama. Her poetry has been published in *Caze Canem I*, *African-American Review*, and *Crab Orchard Review*.

Hughes Jones is from Scottsdale, Arizona, and owns one of the largest minority-owned landscaping businesses there.

Glenn Joshua, whose work has been published in the black southern anthology, *Fertile Ground*, is a member of both NOMMO Literary Society and The Word Band. Joshua is also the 1992, 1993, and 1994 first-prize winner of the Southern University at New Orleans National Library Week Poetry Contest. A professional firefighter, he currently lives in New Orleans with his wife Rhonda and son Jamaal.

Ajuba Joy is a certified substance abuse prevention health educator, and is presently employed at North Carolina State University. She received her B.A. degree from Shaw University in Raleigh, and a masters in public administration from North Carolina Central University. Joy has self-published two collections of poetry, *Timeless Motions* and *Rhythms*. Joy has just returned from a trip to Ghana and her realization of the impact that the idea of ancestry has on all our writings will be evident in all her new works.

Kazedge is a resident of Louisville, Kentucky, where she teaches the philosophy of art at a local community college.

Saddi Khali, "I only feel erotic when I'm breathing," is an extensively experienced, but as of yet, largely under-published, twenty-three-year-old New Orleans writer/rapper. He is also a member of The Word Band, NOMMO Literary Society, and the hip-hop group Intellectually Speaking. His work has appeared in *Exquisite Corpse*, *Fertile Ground*, on his own line of T-shirts and greeting cards, and will appear in his first collection of poetry: *Guerilla Wordfare & Other Ammo for Automatic Assault Writers*.

Willie James King thrives on safe-sex eroticism and works as a teacher in Montgomery, Alabama. He has been published in *Obsidian II* and *Confrontation*.

Sharon A. Lewis is from Lawton, Oklahoma. This is her first entry into the erotic realm.

Lovechild is a published author handled by the Menza Literary Agency of New York.

Lenard D. Moore, the most acclaimed African-American haiku writer of the twentieth century, was born in Jacksonville, North Carolina, and graduated Magna Cum Laude with a B.A. degree from Shaw University. Moore is a poet, playwright, essayist, book reviewer, and fiction writer. While he is best known for his book *Forever Home*, he is also the author of *Desert Storm: A Brief History*. He is the founder and executive director of the Carolina African-American Writer's Collective and is the founding publishing editor of *Earlobe*.

Randall Moore is a bisexual writer from Los Angeles, California, who plays the organ for a gospel choir.

Nightingale is a part-time social worker and full-time high priestess of love in a prominent underground nightclub in Pittsburgh, Pennsylvania. She states, "I want to be a full-time writer, but I spend too much time making love to my husband. When he can't satisfy me, I take out my pencil and satisfy myself." Her fondest wish is to write about an erotic experience in Graceland.

Kenneth Norfleet is an established medical professional in the Washington, D.C. area. His excerpt, "Binghamton Bad Boy Blues," is from the forthcoming novel of the same name from Pyramid Valley Books.

Oktavi, a New York native who resides with her daughter Rebecca in Durham, North Carolina, has performed as a featured reader in the Greater Los Angeles area. She has participated in the California Arts Council, Artist-in-Communities Residency program.

Frank Lamont Phillips is one of the most published black writers in America. Currently, he labors as a graduate student in the M.F.A. program of the University of Memphis and teaches in the Memphis City Schools. Frank's next book will be a series of erotic vignettes on ebonics.

Leah Jewel Reynolds of St. Louis, Missouri, hosts a cable talk show called *Spotlight* and is editor of the journal *Quest*. She also writes a column for *Intermission* magazine. She just completed her M.A. in communications and is currently working toward an M.A. in business-human resources. Reynolds is a blissful newlywed.

Rae-Ree Richards is the head of the international division of one of the largest international shippers in the world.

Enuf Sed is a Photo Systems Analyst in Kansas City, Missouri. This is her first foray into eroticism.

Kalammu ya Salaam is a New Orleans writer, and is founder of the NOMMO Literary Society. His most recent books are *The Magic of JuJu, An Appreciation of the Sixties Black Arts Movement*, and a travel book, *Tarzan Cannot Return to Africa, But I Can.*

Kiini Ibura Salaam is a native of New Orleans, founding member of the Red Clay Collective, and author of the forthcoming *Rebellious Energy*. She is presently working on a book-length project and searching for happiness.

Herr Reverend Schmidt is the pseudonym for a black Pentecostal minister from Berlin, Germany. He is currently struggling with his faith coalescing with his homosexuality.

Tim Seibles is the author of three books of poetry, *Body Moves, Hurdy Gurdy*, and *Kerosene*. An NEA fellow in 1990, he received the Open Voice Award from the National Writers Voice Project in 1993. Currently, he is a member of the creative writing faculty at Old Dominion University in Norfolk, Virginia.

Faithful Senghor is a Miami Beach native and now a member of the Key West Writing Colony.

Shangé is currently a lecturer and freelance writer living in New York City. A short story, essay, and poetry writer, she has been published in various mediums including *Testimony: Young African-Americans on Self Discovery and Black Identity* and *Mandala*. She is currently working on a collection of short stories and poems under the working title *Grandma Stories*.

Tina South-X is the pseudonym for a senior legal counsel for a major corporation headquartered in Boston; South-X recently converted to Islam and lives in Holyoke, Massachusetts.

Gilda N. Squire is an erotic writer from the Bronx, New York.

Christopher Stanard is a former Assistant National Publications Chair for the National Society of Black Engineers and former section editor of *NSBE* Magazine. He has had poetry published in *Catalyst, Drumvoices Revue*, and *The Christian Way*, among numerous other publications.

StarrStarr is an erotic dancer from Indianapolis, Indiana, currently completing her M.B.A. in Bloomington, Indiana.

Jerry W. Ward, Jr. is the Lawrence W. Durgin Professor of Literature at Tougaloo College in Ridgeland, Mississippi. He is one of the best known black literary critics in America and his most recent book is *An Anthology of Southern Literature*.

Dryervonn Washington (Vonn "Dickie" Dawg), is a twenty-one-year-old native of Detroit. He is now completing his senior year at Western Michigan University. Vonn "Dickie" Dawg has written over one hundred fifty erotic poems.

Linda White is a Ph.D. candidate in English at Howard University in Washington, D.C.

Lana C. Williams is a producer/editor/writer/artist, and is executive producer of La Jan Productions, Inc., a writers' consortium. La Jan was formed in 1995 to address the needs of African-American poets and writers in North Carolina to find venues for performances. She is also associate editor for *New Visions Literary Review*—a multicultural on-line, electronic literary review available on the World Wide Web. Her works have appeared in *Women's Words*, Volumes I & II, and *Our Voices: How Our Ancestors Speak*, among other publications. She also has several performances under her fertile wings.

Niama Leslie JoAnn Williams is a writer, scholar, and adjunct professor who is particularly concerned with the emotional survival of her people; thus, she teaches African-American literature, her primary interest, with an emphasis on spirituality. She is also a doctoral student in African-American Studies at Temple University, located in Philadelphia, Pennsylvania. Ms. Williams was born and raised in Los Angeles, California.

Liv Wright is a freelance writer who lives in New York City, the host and producer of "Reading Between the Lines," a news commentary and call-in program that airs on Time Warner Cable of Manhattan. She is a native of Harlem.

Xavier is the pseudonym for a male model and writer who dwells in the foothills of the beaches in St. Thomas, where he and all his alter egos work as freelance writers on the joys of celibate-eroticism. Xavier has often appeared in *Vibe* and *Sears* brochures.

Brother Yao currently resides in Capital Hills, Maryland, where he is an M.F.A. student at the University of Maryland. He has been recently published in *Soul Fires*, and is continuously studying the craft of poetry.

JZB, Chiké Carter, Shannon Cook, Janice W. Hodges, Andre Mollet, Nina Leonette Small, Amanda Townsend, and **Eunice Townsend** have made invaluable erotic contributions to this volume.